RISING CHINA:
POWER AND REASSURANCE

RISING CHINA:
POWER AND REASSURANCE

EDITED BY RON HUISKEN

ANU
THE AUSTRALIAN NATIONAL UNIVERSITY

E PRESS

ANU

E PRESS

Published by ANU E Press
The Australian National University
Canberra ACT 0200, Australia
Email: anuepress@anu.edu.au
This title is also available online at: http://epress.anu.edu.au/rising_china_citation.html

National Library of Australia
Cataloguing-in-Publication entry

Title:	Rising China : power and reassurance / editor: Ron Huisken.
ISBN	9781921536588 (pbk.) 9781921536595 (pdf)
Notes:	Bibliography.
Subjects:	National interest--China.
	Confidence and security building measures (International relations)--China.
	Security, International.
	International relations.
	China--Foreign relations.
	China--Politics and government--21st century
Other Authors/Contributors:	
	Huisken, R. H. (Ronald Herman), 1946-
Dewey Number:	327.51

Cover design by ANU E Press

Table of Contents

Multilateral processes: countering or reflecting regional cleavages?

Acknowledgements

The conference on which this book is based was made possible by an Australian Research Council (ARC) Linkage Grant (with the Department of Defence as 'industry partner'), awarded to the Strategic and Defence Studies Centre in 2005. The editor is indebted to the ARC and the Department of Defence for this support.

In addition to the authors represented in this volume, a number of people made an invaluable contribution as panellists or discussants to the broader dialogue that took place during the course of the conference. The editor would like to express his gratitude to the following people in this regard: Dr Doug Kean from the Office of National Assessments; Dr Rod Lyon and Dr Mark Thomson from the Australian Strategic Policy Institute; Dr Malcolm Cook from the Lowy Foundation; and Professor Robin Jeffrey, Professor Hugh White, Professor Paul Dibb, Professor Geremie Barme, Professor Anthony Milner, Admiral (Rtd) Chris Barrie and Dr Richard Brabin-Smith, all from The Australian National University.

Contributors

See Seng Tan

See Seng Tan is an Associate Professor at the S. Rajaratnam School of International Studies (RSIS), Nanyang Technological University, Singapore. He directs the school's research program on multilateralism and regionalism as well as its executive education department. He previously served as the Deputy Head of Graduate Studies. His most recent publication is *Bandung Revisited: The legacy of the 1955 Asian–African Conference for International Order* (co-edited with Amitav Acharya, 2008, National University of Singapore Press). He recently completed a stint as Visiting Research Associate at the International Institute for Strategic Studies, Asia (IISS-Asia).

Koji Watanabe

Koji Watanabe is Senior Fellow at the Japan Center for International Exchange. Joining the Foreign Ministry in 1956, Koji served as Japanese Ambassador to Saudi Arabia (1988–89), Italy (1992–93) and Russia (1993–96), and Minister in Beijing (1981–84), Deputy Foreign Minister, Sherpa for the G7 Houston and London summits and Japanese co-chairman of the US–Japan Structural Impediments Initiative Talks. Now President of The Japan Forum, he was on the Board of Governors of the Asia–Europe Foundation (ASEF) and the National Public Safety Commission, and former Executive Advisor to the Japan Business Federation (Keidanren).

Richard A. Bitzinger

Richard A. Bitzinger is a Senior Fellow with the S. Rajaratnam School of International Studies (RSIS), Nanyang Technological University, Singapore, where his work focuses on military and defence issues relating to the Asia-Pacific region, including the challenges of defence transformation in the Asia-Pacific, regional military modernisation activities and local defence industries, arms production and weapons proliferation. Richard was previously an Associate Professor with the Asia-Pacific Center for Security Studies (APCSS), Honolulu, Hawai'i, and also worked for the RAND Corporation, the Center for Strategic and Budgetary Affairs and the US Government.

Fan Gaoyue

Fan Gaoyue, born in 1952, joined the People's Liberation Army (PLA) in 1970 and has worked in the PLA Academy of Military Science since 1989. Now a Senior Colonel and Research Fellow in the academy, Fan's research and writing has focused on American affairs, including joint operations, military training, military strategy and military transformation.

Li Mingjiang

Li Mingjiang is Assistant Professor at the S. Rajaratnam School of International Studies (RSIS), Nanyang Technological University, Singapore. His main research interests include the rise of China in the context of East Asian regional relations and Sino–American relations, China's diplomatic history and domestic sources of China's international strategies. He teaches two courses: the History and International Politics of the Cold War and Chinese Security and Foreign Policy. He received his PhD in Political Science from Boston University. He has also studied at the Foreign Affairs University (Beijing) and the Hopkins-Nanjing Center. He was a diplomatic correspondent for *Xinhua News Agency* from 1999 to 2001. Li has previously taught political science and Chinese politics at Boston University, Tufts University and Suffolk University. He has published and presented papers on China's domestic politics and foreign policy.

Qingguo Jia

Qingguo Jia is Professor and Associate Dean of the School of International Studies of Peking University. He received his PhD from Cornell University in 1988. He was a Research Fellow at the Brookings Institution between 1985 and 1986. He has taught at the University of Vermont, Cornell University, the University of California at San Diego, the University of Sydney in Australia and Peking University. He has published extensively on US–China relations, relations between the Chinese mainland and Taiwan, Chinese foreign policy and Chinese politics.

Zhang Tuosheng

Zhang Tuosheng is a Senior Fellow, Chairman of the Academic Assessments Committee and Director of Research with the China Foundation for International Strategic Studies. Formerly an officer in the PLA, he was posted to the United Kingdom in the early 1990s as the Deputy Defence Attaché. His main research interests are Sino–American relations, Sino–Japanese relations, Asia-Pacific security and Chinese foreign policy.

Yu Bin

Yu Bin is Professor of Political Science at Wittenberg University (Ohio, United States) and Senior Research Fellow at the Shanghai Association of American Studies. Yu earned his PhD from Stanford University (1991) and his MA from the Chinese Academy of Social Sciences (1982). Yu's professional activities have included attachments to Fudan University, Stanford University and the East West Center in Hawai'i. Yu is the author and co-author of several books and more than 60 scholarly articles. His current research focus includes China–Russia relations.

Ron Huisken

Ron Huisken is Senior Fellow at the Strategic and Defence Studies Centre, The Australian National University. He spent a number of years at the Stockholm International Peace Research Institute and the UN Centre for Disarmament Affairs before joining government (1981–2001), predominantly the Departments of Foreign Affairs and Trade and of Defence. He returned to academia in 2001 with research interests in US security policies, East Asian security processes and non-proliferation.

Robert Ayson

Robert Ayson directs The Australian National University's Graduate Studies in Strategy and Defence Program and is a Senior Fellow in the Strategic and Defence Studies Centre, The Australian National University. He has taught in New Zealand universities and served as an adviser to the New Zealand Parliamentary Select Committee on Foreign Affairs, Defence and Trade. The author of *Thomas Schelling and the Nuclear Age* (2004, Frank Cass, London and New York), his research interests include strategic concepts, Asia-Pacific stability and Australia–New Zealand defence issues.

Brendan Taylor

Brendan Taylor is a lecturer in the Graduate Studies in Strategy and Defence Program at the Strategic and Defence Studies Centre, The Australian National University. His teaching and research interests are focused on North-East Asian security, US foreign policy, economic statecraft and alliance politics. He graduated from the University of Waikato (New Zealand) and earned his MA and PhD from The Australian National University.

Zhao Gancheng

Zhao Gancheng has been with the Shanghai Institute for International Studies (SIIS) since 1985 and is now a Senior Fellow and Director of the South Asia Studies Program. He is the author of one book and the co-author of another and has written numerous articles on Indian politics and diplomacy, China–India relations and South Asian regional security developments. He has a new book under way that looks at the international politics of rising powers from a development perspective. Before his focus on South Asian studies, he worked in the SIIS on European studies as a research assistant, and also in research management and international exchanges as Research Fellow, Deputy Director and Director.

Introduction

Ron Huisken

Asia looks and feels very different now compared with the Cold War period. Back then, American pre-eminence was a given even though the US presence in the region was far from ubiquitous or overwhelming. Washington shaped events in Asia with comparatively loose reins. America's unremitting focus was the contest with the Soviet Union and the pre-eminent prize in that contest was always Europe. Certainly from the late 1970s, after the United States withdrew from Vietnam, the primary front in the Cold War moved decisively back to Europe.

In Asia, the United States had a huge geopolitical asset in Japan, the world's second-largest economy with first-order industrial and technological capacities. Japan, however, was also a state with a very modest political and security profile so it did little to create an impression of a comprehensively powerful 'Western' partnership at the helm of Asian affairs.

The sense that Asia now works differently and is marching to a different drum can be traced to a single source: the re-emergence of China. During the past 30 years, China has set new benchmarks for fast and, above all, sustained economic growth. From at least the mid 1990s, China's economic numbers—trade, investment, raw material demands—have assumed proportions that have made it a player of consequence in the global economy and a decisive force, naturally, in East Asia. It is now commonplace to observe that there is nothing new about this: China has been the dominant economic power in Asia for most of recorded history. This historical norm, however, was interrupted early in the nineteenth century—too far into the past to be recognisable and readily accommodated by the actors in today's international arena. A powerful China therefore feels new and unfamiliar.

The United States burst onto the global stage in a comparably dramatic fashion a century before China—that is, in the three to four decades before World War I. Washington was hesitant and reactive about employing its power and influence. In Asia, as Aaron Friedberg (2003:17) has observed, America's involvement developed through reactions to a series of events 'followed by a major, largely unplanned, expansion in the tangible manifestations of US power in Asia, and somewhat more gradually and subtly, by an eventual broadening in the conception of American interests and responsibilities in the region'.

China offers a complete contrast. The dominant impression gained from a study of China's behaviour during the past three decades is that of a country engaged in the deliberate, determined, thoughtful and patient construction of what it calls 'comprehensive national power'. China is taking no chances. In particular, it has endeavoured—with considerable success—to be highly disciplined and avoid any premature muscle flexing. It is fiercely insistent that it is still in the early stages of overcoming extreme poverty and weakness, interested only in contributing to a harmonious regional and global environment to facilitate this huge internal task and neither capable of nor inclined to engage in 'strategic' calculation. China's leaders have, in fact, declared that they are determined to prove the realists wrong and to play their full part in ensuring that China's rise does not also give rise to the instabilities and, eventually, conflict that accompanied the attempts by Germany and Japan in the past to carve out prominent positions for themselves in the Anglo-American world order.

This could be a somewhat forlorn hope. As set out in the following chapters, China has elaborated an extensive and reassuring narrative on its foreign, security and defence policies and has become increasingly confident and assertive in its bilateral and multilateral diplomatic practices. Inescapably, perhaps, questions and unease linger. For one thing, China is intimidatingly large. The capacities that it could possess by 2050 are daunting. The following chapters remind us that, even if China (or India for that matter) does not currently have the capacity to disturb the basic equilibrium of the international system, the behaviour of others can be shaped importantly by the prospect that it will have the capacity and, possibly, the inclination to do so in the future. It is important in this regard that China's system of governance remains stubbornly devoid of visible and reliable internal checks and balances. Further, Deng Xiaoping's famous 24-character maxim about 'keeping a low profile, hiding our strengths and biding our time' retained its iconic status for many years despite reinforcing the message of calculation and manipulation that emanated, inadvertently but all too clearly, from China's public diplomacy.

The net affect of these factors is a considerable dissonance in the international arena in respect of China's rise. China's burgeoning power threatens to outrun its strenuous efforts at reassurance. China's government evidently feels that it should be taken at face value while many of the states that it impinges on are disposed to be cautious, watchful and attracted to hedging strategies if they are available. Among other things, the chapters in this volume make particularly clear that China has demanding relationships with all four of the larger powers that it attaches primary importance to: the United States, Japan, Russia and India.

All of these strands of thought are reflected in the presentations that follow in this volume and in the discussions provoked by these presentations. Whether it is in the management of China's key bilateral relationships, the conduct of multilateral diplomacy or the elaborate endeavours to disguise the filling out of its military capabilities, one encounters the incongruity of a China striving to appear harmless and inconspicuous while literally bursting at every seam.

The point was made in the discussions among contributors to this volume that although intentions were notoriously difficult to divine, China's long and uniquely well-documented history could be invoked to confirm a deep-seated reluctance to use power, even when it was indisputably predominant, for purposes of aggression or expansion. This seems on the surface to be a heroic assertion even on factual grounds, let alone serving as a dependable basis for responding to the China of the foreseeable future.

Equally, however, there was an illuminating discussion that stressed the extent to which a more powerful and influential China was the natural and inevitable consequence of its economic success. One did not have to ascribe a hidden agenda to China or to fault other major powers for failing to counter China's waxing influence. China had to accept that a moving elephant affected the behaviour of those close by no matter how docile the elephant appeared or professed to be. Others, for their part, had to make room for this new elephant and to be cognisant of its interests and idiosyncrasies.

The reality, of course, is that in recent decades China's leaders have had to jettison existential threats from rogue superpowers and propagating revolutionary ideology as foundations for the authority and legitimacy of their rule. They must now lean rather heavily on delivering stability, prosperity, international respect and regional and global influence to shape events in China's interests. They bring to this enterprise a distinctive set of assets and attitudes, including: an authoritarian, one-party government; an unusually high degree of concern about the natural cohesion of the State (Tibet, Xinjiang, Taiwan); impressions of China's 'rightful' place framed at least in part by circumstances that prevailed centuries ago; and a conviction reinforced by millennia of experience that good governance requires that diversity of opinion be vigorously contested through the relentless articulation of the thinking that supports the leadership's view of harmony, stability and prosperity.

There are other aspects of the prevailing 'reality' that are important to the challenge of coming to terms with China's rise and trying to envisage how this entity will behave as its relative power and influence continue to grow in the coming decades. Perhaps the most important of these was Deng Xiaoping's far-sighted conviction in 1978 that China's future would remain bleak unless it enmeshed itself with the global economy, and his supporting contention that fundamental geopolitical trends made an existential threat to China improbable into the indefinite future. This policy setting overturned an ancient and enduring preference for autonomy. Deng and his supporters gambled that China could reap the economic harvest and manage any social and political consequences considered unacceptable. The basic premises of this grand strategy have been questioned from time to time as seemingly transformational events unfolded—the domestic unrest that culminated in the Tiananmen Square incident in June 1989, the demise of the Soviet Union in December 1991, the stubborn durability of unipolarity during the 1990s and its virtual codification when the Bush Administration came into office in the United States in January 2001—but on each occasion China's leaders reaffirmed the core elements of Deng's policy settings.

China's openness to the global economy lies at the heart of the optimism that social and political change within China will be inexorable, that these changes will give rise to dependable internal checks and balances and allow greater confidence that a powerful China will be a self-disciplined and responsible international actor, and that external actors can endeavour to engage China to encourage and intensify this process.

A second important source of reassurance in the medium to longer term is the likelihood that there will be a relatively large number of states that could legitimately be characterised as major powers. In the next half-century, China could well become statistically the largest state in the world, but there will be a bunch of states and blocs in addition to the United States that even a mature China will have to take very seriously—the likes of Japan, India, Russia, the European Union and perhaps others.

The outlook that emerges from these observations is that there is little to be gained from characterising the China question in epochal terms: that it will become irresistibly powerful and disposed to view regional 'harmony' as compliant behaviour by all in its extended neighbourhood; that it will break down internally and descend into chaos; or that everything depends on engineering a transition to a recognisable form of democracy. The more sensible outlook is to view China as a certain member of the select group of the world's leading states, that its leadership is fundamentally realist and inclined and more capable than its counterparts in democratic countries to frame policy options with a long-term perspective. This is a China with whom other states, including Australia, will have compatible, competing and clashing interests that can be exploited to mutual benefit or that have to be managed to minimise costs and risks as the case may be. There are already indications that China's confidence in its future is beginning to outgrow Deng's counsel that China needed, in effect, to be deceptive to avoid premature challenges to its aspirations. There was nothing modest about the message China endeavoured to send via the Olympic Games in 2008. Beyond this very conspicuous gesture, however, if growing Chinese confidence translates into a more honest and transparent articulation of interests and aspirations, the prospects for healthy and focused engagement with other states can only increase.

At the level of the forces that will shape the strategic parameters of the Asia-Pacific region—that is, the basic image that each of the major powers forms of the others—perhaps the most ominous possibility is that the less confidence other states have in China's internal checks and balances the stronger will be the propensity to entertain external variants that China, in turn, will view as antagonistic, leading, very probably, to an intensified militarisation of regional affairs. China, hopefully, will appreciate sooner rather than later that its visible capacities are beginning to speak more loudly than its strenuous rhetoric on 'peaceful development' and a 'harmonious world'. Harmony, it should be remembered, is very much in the eyes of the beholder. It is of some interest to imagine asking some leading American observers if there were periods in the twentieth century that they would characterise as harmonious—that is, when the international system seemed to be running particularly smoothly from Washington's perspective—and then inviting comment from their counterparts in other states.

While it could not be said that there was consensus on this core question, the strong sense that emerged from much of the discussion at the conference was that it was certainly imaginable that the United States and China, in particular, could build and sustain a constructive and resilient relationship and keep at bay the forces that could lead to a slide into antagonism. 'Imaginable', of course, does not mean straightforward. Arriving at a mutually acceptable relationship of power and influence that is very different from the one that has prevailed in the past half-century and that also leaves other major players content will demand statesmanship of a consistently high order.

It is hoped that the following chapters illuminate these and other themes on the broad question of living with a powerful China. On the earlier occasions when China was the pre-eminent power in Asia it was almost continuously engaged in military campaigns near and beyond the boundaries of its empire. That is something worth thinking about given, as they say, that while history may not repeat itself, it is prone to echo into the future.

Reference

Friedberg, Aaron 2003, 'United States', in Richard Ellings and Aaron Friedberg (eds), *Strategic Asia 2002–03: Asian aftershocks*, National Bureau of Asian Research, Seattle.

China's key bilateral relationships: partners or just peers?

Chapter 1

The outlook for US–China relations

Ron Huisken

At some point in the past 60 years, US–China relations have occupied nearly every imaginable niche on the spectrum: allies against Japan, bitter adversaries in Korea and de facto allies against the Soviet Union (after a period in which China could not decide which of the superpowers it feared the most so it elected to view them as conspiring to harm China). Since the end of the Cold War, the relationship has been more stable but only relative to the gyrations during the Cold War. It has still been an inherently turbulent relationship.

It is instructive to note that there is one niche on the spectrum that the relationship has never appeared to occupy: relations that could reasonably be labelled as easy or comfortable.

It is of some interest to ask when the United States first 'saw' China as a player of consequence.

In 1991–92, then Secretary of Defence, Dick Cheney, was casting about for a new road-map, some coherent guidance for how the United States, and the Pentagon in particular, should approach a world without the Soviet Union. He was attracted to a 'post-containment' grand strategy put together by a small group of senior officials who subscribed to a school of thought called neo-conservatism: Paul Wolfowitz, Lewis Libby and Zalmay Khalilzad in particular. A core postulate of this grand strategy was that the United States should 'endeavour to prevent any hostile power from dominating a region whose resources would, under consolidated control, be sufficient to generate global power'. The central corollary to this proposition was that the United States had to remain sufficiently strong to make any resort (or relapse) to collective global leadership not only unnecessary but unfeasible. The neo-cons cited the period up to 1945 as evidence that collective leadership, or leadership by a 'balance' of major powers, was inherently unstable and prone to yield large-scale hegemonic war.

While this Pentagon construct characterised Asia as 'home to the greatest concentration of traditional communist states', it was the residual risk of a revival of Russian power together with Japan and Germany that seemed to be singled out as the key challenges. China, it seems, was not yet visible—at least not to the Pentagon. [1]

Just four years later, in November 1996, speaking to a joint sitting of the Australian Parliament after securing a second term (and after the confrontation with China over Taiwan in March 1996), President Bill Clinton conveyed a far more portentous assessment of China:

> The direction China takes in the years to come, the way it defines its greatness for the future, will help decide whether the next century is one of conflict or co-operation.

> The emergence of a stable, an open, a prosperous China, a strong China confident of its place in the world and willing to assume its responsibilities as a great nation, is in our deepest interests.

This posture—one of anticipating a powerful China while characterising the kind of powerful China that the United States would be comfortable with—has broadly endured during the ensuing decade or more.

In 1999, at the outset of his campaign for the presidency, George W. Bush's one-liner for the media on foreign and security policy was: 'I believe the big issues are going to be China and Russia.' This position hardened later in the campaign, when Condoleezza Rice, Bush's principal foreign policy adviser, wrote in the January–February 2000 issue of *Foreign Affairs* that 'China is not a status quo power but one that would like to alter Asia's balance of power in its own favour. That alone makes it a strategic competitor, not the "strategic partner" the Clinton administration once called it.'

This mind-set shaped the administration's thinking in office. The 2001 Quadrennial Defence Review (QDR), perhaps the only major policy statement prepared before the dreadful events of 11 September, for the first time in decades put Asia ahead of Europe and the Middle East as Washington's arena of primary interest and concern. In a discrete but unmistakable reference to China, the QDR 2001 observed that 'Asia is gradually emerging as a region susceptible to large-scale military competition…The possibility exists that a military competitor with a formidable resource base will emerge in the region'.

This resolve to give priority attention to China's challenge to America's position in Asia evaporated in the aftermath of 11 September. The Bush Administration greatly simplified the test for being regarded as a friend of the United States: 'You are either with us or you are with the terrorists.' China did enough to be ranked a friend. President Jiang Zemin promptly conveyed China's sympathy and support; China supported US pressure on Pakistan to get behind the campaign to crush al Qaeda and the Taliban, it did not resist US penetration of Central Asia for additional bases to support operations in Afghanistan and it agreed to share intelligence with the United States on the terrorist threat. As a quid pro quo, China sought (and received) only the listing of an Islamic separatist movement in Xinjiang as a terrorist organisation.

Taking a broader perspective, the unintended and certainly unanticipated consequences of 11 September included a strategic windfall for China of incalculable proportions. Rather than having an America focused on its position in East Asia, China secured for the better part of another decade an America almost totally distracted and, for good measure, squandering its hard and soft power in Iraq. At the same time, it had the US Secretary of State, Colin Powell, characterising US–China relations as better than they had been since the Nixon era.

As the 1990s progressed, the 'unipolar moment' that Charles Krauthammer detected in 1989 looked as though it could become a more enduring phenomenon. That prospect probably evaporated about 2003–05, not least because, in terms of international standing, the trajectories of the United States and China were so strikingly opposed. Mainstream thinking, at least in the academic arena, reverted to where it had been when the Soviet Union collapsed—that is, regarding unipolarity as probably transient and anticipating the emergence of a condition of multipolarity.

In its second term, the Bush Administration did what it could to counter the image of having little capacity to think of issues other than Iraq. On China, it used a sharp acceleration in Chinese military expenditure as a metaphor for a worrying lack of transparency about strategic intent. Other major policy statements and assessments concerning China (the 2005 QDR and the annual statement on the military power of the People's Republic of China mandated by Congress) began to use noticeably stronger and more direct language on the scale and imminence of the effects that China could have on the established order in East Asia.

In a major policy development in September 2005, the administration's Deputy Secretary of State, Bob Zoellick, invited China to reflect on how profoundly it had leveraged the established economic and security order to accomplish its spectacular rise, invited it to become a 'responsible stakeholder' in this order, including its future adaptation, and spelt out the sort of policy settings in key areas that Washington would regard as evidence of China's determination to play such a role.

The Zoellick speech, although clearly vetted by the White House, reportedly received a frosty reception in Donald Rumsfeld's Pentagon and other conservative circles. One presumes that it was seen as the White House losing its nerve and taking a first step away from the central neo-conservative thesis that the United States could and should protect and strengthen unipolarity.

The Zoellick proposal was a belated reversion to Clinton's 1996 formula: to emphasise that Washington still strongly preferred engagement over containment but that China had to respond in a number of areas to protect this American preference. The preferred language from the State Department these days is that 'rather than trying to contain China, we are trying to help *shape its choices* as it rises to influence so that China plays a responsible and stabilizing role in the international system'. [2]

The imminent end of the Bush Administration naturally induced massive interest in taking stock of America's circumstances and a deluge of advice on what the new administration should see as its options and priorities. Equally typically, this interest is not confined to the United States and the presidential candidates. Observers everywhere, but especially those in East Asia (that is, close to China), also sought to shape the choices America made.

There is an astonishingly wide gulf between respected observers on what has happened to America's position in the world, and especially in Asia, in the past decade. Kishore Mahbubani, in a 2007 essay entitled 'Wake up, Washington', contended that in Asia, the most important geopolitical theatre of the current century, Washington continued to believe that the cards were stacked in its favour while ignoring a crucial emerging reality—namely, that the best geopolitical card players were in Beijing, not in Washington. Indeed, Mahbubani (2007), anxious to see the United States continue its uniquely positive role in the region, lamented that 'while Washington has been distracted and incompetent, Beijing has been focused and competent'.

Fareed Zakaria (2008) has a broader but not dissimilar thesis, contending that the 'rise of the rest' will mean that the United States has to step down and cope with a less central role in global affairs, developing new, more collegiate stratagems and techniques to bring its influence to bear. For Kurt Campbell and Michelle Flourney (2007), in an essay for the noisy but rich American debate about what the next American president should do, the first in a daunting list of challenges was to 'reverse the decline in America's global standing'. They go on to assert that the 'next president must seek to restore US moral authority and credibility, redefine US leadership in the post-Cold War, post-9/11 era, and signal to the American people and the world that a fundamental course correction is taking place'.

Specifically on Asia, two former members of the Bush Administration, Victor Cha (2007) and Michael Green (2008), have contested the thesis that the administration's preoccupation with Iraq has been so complete that China, in particular, has had what amounts to a free ride in inserting itself into the spaces that the United States left unattended. Cha contends that 'President George W. Bush's Asia policy has worked'. These rebuttals usefully qualify the more extreme assessments of how much ground the United States might have lost in East Asia, but they hardly begin to outweigh the flood of observations to the contrary.

(It seems safe to conclude that a significant slice of elite opinion in the United States has accepted that America's standing in the world has undergone a worrying erosion in the past eight years, and that it has become harder for

Washington to translate its continuing pre-eminence in the economic and military spheres into influence over events. US opinion polls suggest that the majority of ordinary Americans vaguely share this perception. One manifestation of this view has been the flurry of inquiries into 'smart' power, or how the United States might learn to do what it has done unconsciously for so long—namely, to much more often than not bring its power and influence to bear in favour of policy settings that most other states want to support or at least be seen as not opposing. Barack Obama explicitly made this erosion of American standing a major indictment of the Bush Administration and Republican management of American foreign policy, and the arrest and reversal of this erosion a prominent element in his own platform.)

Where might the Americans come out on this core issue of their standing in this rapidly evolving world of ours, and how could it shape the approach they take towards China? We can start with the safest presumptions.

- The next administration can hardly fail to conclude (as the Bush Administration has done as discreetly as possible since about 2006) that the embrace and implementation of the neo-conservative prescription for capitalising on unipolarity has cost the United States dearly on the international front, and is unpopular domestically.
- The next administration will certainly share the view that East Asia is the central geopolitical theatre of this century and that China is and will remain the most immediate and the most consequential manifestation of the transforming order with which the United States must deal.
- The next administration is unlikely to succumb to any sense of pressing urgency to alter the US posture in a particular arena, least of all with respect to China. That would be seen as unbecoming, but it would also stem from confidence that the United States still had assets that were unmatched in weight and diversity, and that Washington needed, above all, to be seen to be recovering its poise.

Quite clearly, one is speaking here of changes of emphasis. Iraq will continue to be a significant drain on the time and political energies of the new administration, at least in its first term. Moreover, the United States has been relatively inattentive to, rather than absent from, Asia. It has engaged in a variety of significant activities that could be characterised broadly as 'hedging' against China's rise. Indeed, one could probably make a case that these hedges were in part compensation for the inability to press alternative ways of shaping events in Asia. Moreover, as a number of American and Asian observers continue to point out, Washington is likely to find that, on balance, Asian states would still like to see more America, not less, in their region—provided, of course, that it is the right kind of America.

An important ingredient in America's palatability as the regional hegemony for the past 60 years has been the fact that it is a distant power. That distance has helpfully diluted US power and influence and softened perceptions of dominance. China does not have that advantage (although proximity certainly has offsetting benefits). Beijing has worked very hard indeed, and with considerable success, to attenuate the inescapable misgivings that its proximity and immense weight generate in neighbouring states, but one suspects that it will be a very long time before states in Asia, if they have the choice, will prefer to push the Americans away.

Washington's hedging or countervailing strategies include sweeping geo-strategic initiatives such as undertaking to facilitate ending India's detachment from the international mainstream by leading the campaign to accept it as a legitimate nuclear weapon state (that is, stepping over the fact that it is not a party to the nuclear Non-Proliferation Treaty (NPT) and that it demonstrated its nuclear weapon status as recently as May 1998). In a similar vein, Washington has intensified and transformed its security relationship with Japan, both encouraging and responding to strengthening Japanese instincts to loosen the historical constraints on its security and defence role. An important element in this regard has been the establishment of a trilateral (United States, Japan, Australia) forum for security discussions, recently elevated to the (foreign) minister level. Washington has also worked patiently with governments in South Korea to protect the alliance from the stresses of North Korea's nuclear and missile programs, the lure of a rising China and generational change within South Korea.

At a more prosaic level, the reconstitution of Guam as a strategic hub in the Western Pacific has been a conspicuous development involving the continuous deployment of bomber and fighter aircraft along with the home-porting of nuclear submarines equipped with land-attack cruise missiles. More generally, the dominant shares of American SSBN and SSN assets are now deployed in the Pacific rather than the Atlantic.

Further, questions from the US Congress about the implications of prospective developments in China's military capacities for the adequacy of projected US capabilities have produced assessments that the United States might want to reconsider its plans in a number of areas, including:

- the number of aircraft carriers home-ported in the North Pacific and available to respond quickly to East Asian contingencies (the Pentagon thinks that five to six would be better than the current two to three)
- the adequacy of the projected US force of frontline combat aircraft (F/A-18E/J-35/F-22)
- the adequacy of the projected force of Aegis-class naval platforms (23) and the number of SM-3 ballistic missile interceptors (147) that these platforms will carry.

Equally, there is overwhelming evidence that US military capacities drive the capability priorities and aspirations of China's People's Liberation Army (PLA).

There is more than enough here, in my view, to support the proposition that the United States and China have a real job ahead of them to ensure that the instincts to engage (which carry the presumption of success in building a constructive and resilient relationship) remain compelling relative to the instincts to hedge (which carry the presumption of failure).

The likelihood that the United States and China could define their interests in a manner that the other finds unduly constricting is probably rather high. That said, both powers will find that pressing too hard to secure the upper hand will produce countervailing postures by third parties in the region who are loathe to make an enduring choice between the two.

The United States and China will be genuinely responsive to international opinion and attitudes. In the US case, this sensitivity will stem from perceptions of real damage done to US interests by the recent experiment with assertive unilateralism (or offensive realism). In the case of China, it is an instance of wanting the 'full monty'. China is a keen student of the phenomenon of power: in all probability, the Chinese secretly regard themselves as the world's leading authority on this elusive but crucial phenomenon, with a superb intellectual tradition and a history rich in practical experience. China's own historical experience as well as observations of the United States in recent decades will have persuaded it of the reality of 'soft power'—the qualities of respect and admiration that so decisively boost a state's 'hard power'. As former President Clinton put it rather memorably at the Democrat National Convention on 27 August 2008, 'the world has always been more impressed by the power of our example than the example of our power'.

Now that China can presumably sense that great power status is securely within reach, it is determined also to not jeopardise this accomplishment by being impatient or cutting corners and putting at risk international perceptions of its legitimacy as one of the world's leading states.

China's 'security community', it seems to me, is profoundly realist. China seems determined to patiently and methodically construct the most invulnerable portfolio of power available to it. It will not repeat what it judges to have been its own mistakes in the past, including the very distant past, and it is determined to learn from what it judges to have been the mistakes and successes of others.

The continuing attraction of the concept of 'comprehensive national power' (CNP) within official, think-tank and academic circles in China is one indicator of the deliberate, methodical manner in which China is endeavouring to construct its rise. CNP is a tricky concept to measure and to manipulate analytically. Estimates by various agencies in China of its relative CNP—now and projected into the future—are all over the place. China can rank first, third or eighth and the names of those ahead or behind can vary. What this analytical technique reinforces, however, is the crucial importance of balance in the portfolio of power. It is also an analytical technique that encourages long-term thinking, and one that gives exposure and prominence to strategies that would be seen in the West, and especially in the United States, as so indirect as to be unworthy of the label 'strategy'.

For example, a student of the United States might hypothesise that as America's voice in Asia's political and economic evolution becomes less dominant, it will become harder to persuade Congress to bankroll an undiminished effort to do the heavy lifting on regional security and stability. The United States has been a generous provider of these 'public goods' but there will be limits to its selflessness. China's security community and political leadership, on the other hand, could well assess this possibility as sufficiently probable and adequately timely to form the foundation of a national security strategy.

The United States, rather characteristically, will be less patient and less methodical, but one can be confident that it will gravitate towards a consensus on why and how it took the course it did and settle on some broadly sensible course corrections to do better in the future.

As mentioned, there is an avalanche of advice and counsel on how the next administration should posture itself to better protect and advance US interests. Here are two examples to convey the flavour of American thinking on foreign and security policy.

The first comes from a group of scholars from the Brookings Institution and the Center for a New American Security (Kurt Campbell again), the members of which have combined to form the Phoenix Initiative (Brookings Institution 2008). The starting point of this Democrat-leaning group is that, as American power is not unlimited and as the United States cannot presume that it has an entitlement to lead, the most consequential judgments that the new political leadership will face will be to decide wisely how, when and with whom to lead. The report goes on to suggest that the new administration should initially focus its energies on and aspire to strategic leadership in five areas: counter-terrorism; nuclear non-proliferation; climate change and oil dependence; the Middle East; and East Asia. The summary version of the last priority reads as follows:

The United States must renew its commitments to comprehensive engagement in Asia. We must maximize the prospects that China and India will rise as open, vibrant markets and stable rights-regarding governments, while also reassuring long-standing friends and allies of US security commitments and willingness to cooperate on issues of concern throughout the region.

From the other side of the political fence we have Douglas Paal, who in recent years has served on the National Security Council and as Director of the American Institute in Taiwan. Paal (2008) contends that America is in reasonably good shape in East Asia but he attributes this largely to the instinct in Asian capitals to adopt balance-of-power strategies intended to keep the Americans close as China's influence grows. Paal argues that Washington has essentially paid lip-service to its own rhetoric about the 'Pacific century' and the world's economic centre of gravity shifting to Asia and has lost touch with the pace and extent of change in the region. His prescriptions for a more proactive US posture include the following.

- Ensuring that key appointments reflect Asia's emerging pre-eminence, particularly a clearly designated cabinet-level Asia advocate.
- Taking the lead in making some hard choices about the instruments and processes intended to manage regional affairs. Specifically, to scrap the Group of Eight (G8) unless it formally includes China and India and to critically review the Asia-Pacific Economic Cooperation (APEC) group because it is too broad and only incidentally capable of addressing issues other than trade. Paal considers that there is a palpable appetite in the region for some rationalisation of the existing multilateral processes but also suggests that the United States should revisit the question of subscribing to the Association of South-East Asian Nation's (ASEAN) Treaty of Amity and Cooperation to improve its bargaining position.
- On regional security, Paal argues that the United States should anticipate a future in which it has to share the military stage with China and India and seek multilateral security arrangements that will allow it to divest itself of sole responsibility to provide the public goods of security, stability and predictability.
- With regard specifically to China, Paal urges a prompt intensification of engagement through the 'responsible stakeholder' agenda: no reviews, no reflections on engagement versus alternative strategies, just an upgrading of the senior dialogue to secretary of state/foreign minister level.

A plausible outlook for US–China relations in the next decade or so might read as follows. The relationship will be an energetic one, exemplifying the widespread assessment that it is and will remain the single most important bilateral relationship in the world. It will be a turbulent relationship given the fundamental differences in the maturity of power in the two states, the stark differences in values, culture and systems of governance, and given that the United States will walk away from the simplicity of the post-11 September test that it set to determine whether others were 'on side' or not. All that being said, the prospects for protecting and expanding a core of constructive engagement seem to be reasonably good, certainly not trivial.

On the US side, one could anticipate an intensified engagement with China across the range of political, economic, military and global/transnational issues, a more creative and challenging US posture on institutions and processes designed to shape the regional order and more energetic diplomacy across the Asian region generally.

I would expect China, for its part, to continue to prefer doing what has worked so well to this point: to keep a low profile and as far as possible disguise its growing hard-power assets, and try to be elusive when others want to come to grand, binding understandings or agreements. China's continuing priority into the foreseeable future will be to protect a relationship with the United States that supports unfettered trade, investment and technology transfer. All of this makes perfect sense if you consider yourself to be a thoroughly incomplete power and still in a comparatively weak bargaining position. That said, China in 2009 will be far more ready to do strategic business with the United States than it was in 2001 when the United States first resolved to put China at or near the top of its agenda.

None of this, of course, amounts to a reliable prescription for a 'harmonious world'. States can make mistakes, events can be mismanaged, poor judgments can be made about the opportunities and constraints in play at any given moment. Nor can we rule out the possibility that American and Chinese conceptions of their core interests, arrived at in full awareness of the other's power and interests, could still lead to instincts to dispute, contain or contest the other's aspirations.

Sources of friction, or worse, are not difficult to identify:

- if US–Russia relations continue to worsen, how China positions itself between the two could have far-reaching consequences
- China could contest any US effort to establish authoritative regional mechanisms that include it as a member
- the continuing urgency of China's military development plus resistance to transparency and US 'hedging' strategies offer fertile ground for friction
- US perceptions that China is seeking a Sino-centric trading regime in Asia
- China placing its immediate economic and political interests ahead of 'responsible stakeholder' obligations in respect of onerous regimes
- US perceptions that it is being blocked out of Central Asia
- an effort to consolidate or strengthen China's extensive claims in the South China Sea could press one of the United States' traditional hot buttons: freedom of the high seas.

To hazard a net assessment: there are grounds for cautious optimism that the US–China relationship will not trend towards becoming the most dangerous alongside being the most important in the world. It seems all too clear, however, that leaving the future of US–China relations to the natural forces at work within and between the two countries would be verging on the heroic. Some determined statesmanship on both sides would be not only reassuring but probably closer to a precondition for a satisfactory outcome.

References

Brookings Institution 2008, *Strategic Leadership: Framework for a 21ˢᵗ century national security strategy*, July 2008, Brookings Institution, Washington, DC.

Campbell, Kurt M. and Flourney, Michelle 2007, *The Inheritance and the Way Forward*, June 2007, Center for a New American Security, Washington, DC.

Cha, Victor D. 2007, 'Winning Asia: Washington's untold success story', *Foreign Affairs*, November–December.

Green, Michael J. 2008, 'The Iraq war and Asia: assessing the legacy', *Washington Quarterly*, Spring, pp. 181–99.

Libby, L. 1990–91, 'Remarks on shaping US defence strategy: persistent challenges and enduring strengths', *America's role in a changing world. Part 2*, Adelphi Papers no. 257.

Mahbubani, Kishore 2007, 'Wake up, Washington: the US risks losing Asia', *Global Asia*, Fall.

Paal, Douglas H. 2008, *Asia—Shaping the Future*, June 2008, Carnegie Foundation for International Peace.

Tyler, Patrick E. 1992, 'US strategy plan calls for insuring no rivals develop: a one-superpower world', *New York Times*, 8 March 1992.

Zakaria, Fareed 2008, *The Post-American World*, W. W. Norton and Company, New York.

ENDNOTES

[1] For additional information on this Pentagon strategy see, Libby (1990–91) and Tyler (1992).

[2] Thomas J. Christensen, Deputy Assistant Secretary for East Asian and Pacific Affairs, Statement before the House Committee on Foreign Affairs, Subcommittee on Asia, the Pacific, and the Global Environment, 27 March 2007.

Chapter 2

Closer and more balanced: China–US relations in transition

Jia Qingguo

Since US President Richard Nixon's historic visit to China in 1972, China–US relations have gone through some fundamental changes. For a long time, the relationship was characterised by limited contact, restricted areas of cooperation and asymmetrical interactions, with the United States taking initiatives and China reacting to them. More recently, however, this mode of relationship has been changing, with far-reaching implications for both countries and the rest of the world. It is important for policymakers as well as academics to appreciate the direction and nature of such changes. This chapter is intended to represent and analyse such changes and their implications for future development of the relationship.

Trends of change

A review of the development of Sino–American relations suggests that some broad trends of change in the relationship are under way: 1) from limited contact to comprehensive engagement; 2) from cooperation in restricted areas to cooperation in most aspects of the relationship; and 3) from asymmetrical to more balanced interactions.

From limited contact to comprehensive relations

To begin with, the relationship has been changing from limited contact to comprehensive engagement. When President Nixon visited China in 1972, the two countries had almost no contact with each other—largely a result of a 20-year US policy of isolation and containment against China after the Korean War. Their economies were completely independent of each other and there were few people-to-people contacts between the two countries. Since then, especially since China's adoption of its policy of openness and reform in 1979, the two countries have developed comprehensive relations with a high and still increasing degree of economic interdependence.

Trade and economic relations between the two countries have grown dramatically in breath and depth. According to the US Commerce Department, China–US trade in 2007 amounted to US$386.7 billion, representing 12.7 per cent growth from 2006 (<http://www.uschina.org/statistics/tradetable.html>).

Table 2.1 China's trade with the United States ($ billion)

	1998	1999	2000	2001	2002	2003	2004	2005	2006	2007
US exports	14.3	13.1	16.3	19.2	22.1	28.4	34.7	41.8	55.2	65.2
% change	10.9	−8.0	24.4	18.3	15.1	28.5	22.2	20.6	32.1	18.1
US imports	71.2	81.8	100.0	102.3	125.2	152.4	196.7	243.5	287.8	321.5
% change	13.8	14.9	22.3	2.2	22.4	21.7	29.1	23.8	18.2	11.7
Total	85.5	94.9	116.3	121.5	147.3	180.8	231.4	285.3	343.0	386.7
% change	13.4	11.0	22.6	21.4	21.2	22.8	28.0	23.3	20.2	12.7
US balance	−56.9	−68.7	−83.7	−83.0	−103.1	−124.0	−162.0	−201.6	−232.5	−256.3

Note: US exports reported on FOB basis; imports on a general customs value, CIF basis.
Sources: US International Trade Commission, US Department of Commerce and US Census Bureau.

Because of the different methods of compiling statistics, Chinese figures are quite different. According to the Chinese Ministry of Commerce, the trade volume between the two countries in 2007 stood at US$302.08 billion, representing 15 per cent growth from the previous year (<http://zhs.mofcom.gov.cn/tongji.shtml>). By any standards, however, the trade volume between the two countries is huge. As a result, the United States is China's second-largest trading partner and China is the United States' third-largest trading partner.

In terms of investment, by the end of July 2007, US companies had invested in 53 754 projects in China with an actualised value of US$55.42 billion. By the end of June 2007, Chinese companies had invested close to US$3 billion in the United States (<http://finance.people.com.cn/GB/71364/6316169.html>). According to the US Department of Treasury, China was holding US$652.9 billion in US Government Treasury bonds by October 2008 (<http://www.treas.gov/tic/mfh.txt>). Meanwhile, increasing numbers of Chinese companies are listed on US stock exchanges and increasing numbers of US retirement funds are investing in China's stock markets (Carrel 2007). Consequently, the two countries' economies are more closely tied up with each other than at any time in history.

Besides increasing economic relations, the two countries have developed close political contacts. Top leaders of the two countries regularly meet and talk on the phone. Lower-level officials are meeting and talking with each other all the time. Various mechanisms have been set up to facilitate such contacts, most prominent of which are the strategic dialogues between the officials of the two countries at the ministerial level. Numerous Chinese and American official delegations travel across the Pacific. As a result, no longer is there any significant communication problem between the two countries.

A military relationship has also been forged, although still in a limited and hesitant way. After the traumatic Hainan air collision, the two militaries gradually resumed a relationship. Among the exchanges, in January 2004, General Richard Myers, Chairman of the US Joint Chiefs of Staff, visited Beijing. In October 2004, Cao Gangchuan, Chinese Defence Minister, paid a visit to Washington, DC. The then US Secretary of Defence, Donald Rumsfeld, visited China in the autumn of 2005. In November 2006, General Gary Roughhead, Commander-In-Chief of the Pacific Fleet, visited China. In March 2007, General Peter Pace, Chairman of the US Joint Chiefs of Staff, visited China. In May 2007, Roughhead's successor, General Timothy J. Keating, visited China. In addition, the two countries have engaged in military or defence dialogues such as defence consultative talks between senior officials of the two defence departments and the Consultation Mechanism to Strengthen Military Maritime Safety. They have also exchanged naval vessel port calls ('US Navy vessel pays port call to Qingdao', *China Military Online*, 23 May 2007, < http://english.pladaily.com.cn/site2/news-channels/ 2007-05/23/content_824047.htm >; 'China takes positive attitude towards military co-op with US', *Xinhua*, 14 September 2006, <http://english.cri.cn/2946/2006/09/14/167@139430.htm>). More recently, the two militaries even conducted a military exercise together (<http://jczs.sina.com.cn/2006-09-21/2032399999.html>). There are also press reports to the effect that the two militaries are talking about conducting anti-terrorist and disaster relief joint military exercises in the near future ('China and US navies may conduct anti-terrorist joint exercises', < http://mil.chinaiiss.org/content/2008-5-4/4155326.shtml >; 'Commander-In-Chief of the US Pacific Fleet: China and the US militaries may hold disaster relief joint military exercises next year', *Global Times*, 18 July 2008, <http://war.news.163.com/08/0718/09/4H4GS42100011MTO.html>).

At the societal level, exchanges have been intensive. In addition to the hundreds of thousands of students crossing the Pacific to study in the other country, tens of millions of people travel between the two countries for business, family visits, cultural exchanges and holidays. According to a news report (< http://news.xinhuanet.com/fortune/2005-05/12/content_2947950.htm >), the number of flights between China and the United States was already 54 a week in 2005 and was projected to reach 249 a week in six years.

From restricted cooperation to extensive cooperation

For many years after President Nixon visited China, cooperation between the two countries was restricted to the strategic realm—that is, to containing perceived Soviet expansion. Gradually, cooperation between the two countries extended to trade, education and cultural realms, especially after China adopted its policy of openness and reform in 1979. The end of the Cold War removed the anti-Soviet rationale for strategic cooperation; however, economic, cultural and societal interests in the relationship were strong enough to sustain the relationship. Even the Tiananmen Square incident in 1989 did not break the trend of development. As China's domestic politics stabilised, especially as its economy resumed rapid growth and its international influence increased, the two countries found more reasons to expand and deepen cooperation between them. Over time, such cooperation had covered not only most areas in relations between the two countries, but issues at the regional and global levels.

At the bilateral level, the two countries saw cooperation increasing in areas including the environment, immigration, cross-border crime, rule of law, intellectual property rights, the war against terror as well as economic relations and educational and cultural exchanges. Before Ma Ying-Jieu came to office in Taiwan in March 2008, as separatists pushed for Taiwanese independence more aggressively, the two countries even found it necessary to cooperate on the Taiwan issue. Both were determined not to let Taiwanese separatists drag them into an unnecessary military confrontation ('Chinese, US presidents meet over bilateral ties, issues of common concern', <http://news.xinhuanet.com/english/2003-10/20/content_1131209.htm>).

At the regional level, the two countries have been engaged in cooperation in maintaining peace and stability as well as economic prosperity in the region. The Chinese Government has welcomed a constructive US presence in the region. [1] The US Government has encouraged China to play a positive role in regional cooperation such as its participation in the Association of South-East Asian Nations (ASEAN) Regional Forum (ARF) and Asia-Pacific Economic Cooperation (APEC) as well as other official and unofficial regional dialogue mechanisms. One often cited example of this cooperation is the two countries' joint efforts to manage the North Korean nuclear crisis.

At the global level, the two countries are cooperating on an increasing number of issues including environmental protection, UN peacekeeping, humanitarian disaster relief, maritime safety, free trade, smuggling, cross-border crime, non-proliferation of weapons of mass destruction (WMD) and the war against terrorism.

From asymmetrical to more balanced interactions

For a long time after Nixon's visit to China, interactions between the two countries were largely asymmetrical—that is, more often than not, the United States set the agenda and took the initiative while China responded, although China tried to adhere to its own principles and to defend its perceived core national interests in doing so. During the late 1960s and early 1970s, it was the Nixon Administration's decision to play the China card in its efforts to achieve détente with the Soviet Union and to seek a face-saving exit from the Vietnam War that provided an opportunity for China to improve its relations with the

United States in an effort to alleviate its security predicament. During the early 1980s, it was in part Ronald Reagan's Administration's pro-Taiwan rhetoric and gestures that led to the Chinese Government's decision to reorient its foreign policy from one that sought a strategic alliance with the United States against perceived Soviet expansionism to one that emphasised independence.

During the early 1990s, it was Bill Clinton's Administration's policy of forcing political changes in China that led to China's stiff resistance, resulting in rounds of conflict between the two countries. In the late 1990s, it was the Clinton Administration's decision to abandon its policy of linking China's human rights issues with trade and adopting an engagement policy on China that made it possible for the two countries to conclude an agreement vowing to work towards a constructive strategic partnership (Qingguo 2004). At the turn of the century, it was the George W. Bush Administration's hardline approach towards China that pushed relations between the two countries to the verge of confrontation and its subsequent shift of attention to the war on terror and solicitation of China's help in this that made it possible for the two countries to develop a positive relationship, which former Secretary of State Colin Powell described as the best of all times (Qingguo 2003:3).

This situation, however, has been undergoing some subtle but fundamental changes in recent years. Increasingly, China does not just respond to US initiatives, it takes some actions on its own to which the United States finds it necessary to respond. For instance, China's efforts to bring about a peaceful resolution of the North Korean nuclear crisis led to US agreement to the three-party and subsequent six-party talks in Beijing in recent years (Park 2005:76). Also, China's effective diplomatic efforts to cultivate good relations with its South-East Asian neighbours provided the rationale for the Bush Administration to pay more attention to the region (Economy 2005). At the moment, China is still largely on the receiving end of China–US interactions, however, a change of direction is becoming more and more discernable.

In essence, after more than three decades of contact and interactions, the two countries are finding themselves in a state of comprehensive engagement, more extensive cooperation and more balanced interactions.

Growing stakes, China's rise and converging values

Explaining these developments, one can identify the following major factors in operation: 1) growing stakes; 2) China's rise; and 3) convergence of values.

Growing stakes

Over time, China and the United States have developed important stakes in their relations. As demonstrated in the previous section, their economic welfare is increasingly dependent on the other's economic performance and both hope the other's economy maintains healthy growth. For instance, in the current global economic crisis, China hopes that the United States will be successful in getting itself out of recession soon and the United States hopes that China will try to boost its domestic demand so that healthy growth in the Chinese economy will contribute to an early end to the US economic recession. Both countries also share interests in promoting market reform, the rule of law, human rights protection and environmental preservation in each other's country. Their interests even overlap on the Taiwan issue: both sides wish to maintain peace and stability in the Taiwan Strait and, for that purpose, oppose Taiwanese separatism.

At the regional level, China and the United States have acquired increasing stakes in promoting stability and prosperity in Asia. Both have important economic relations with the region. Both have deep concerns about the nuclearisation of the Korean Peninsula. Both have a vested interest in maintaining stability across the Taiwan Strait. Both see their interests more or less congruent with various existing regional security mechanisms and dialogues such as the six-party talks on the North Korean nuclear issue, the ARF, the Council for Security Cooperation in the Asia Pacific (CSCAP) and, more recently, the Shangri-La Dialogue. [2]

At the global level, China and the United States have shared interests in maintaining the international political and economic system. The bottom line is that both are important beneficiaries of current international arrangements. Both support multilateral institutions including the United Nations, the World Bank and the International Monetary Fund (IMF). Both wish to uphold international law [3] and both want to promote free trade. Both want to strengthen international efforts to fight terrorism, the proliferation of WMD, drug smuggling and illegal migration. Both desire international cooperation to meet other global challenges, ranging from environmental protection to dealing with infectious diseases such as severe acute respiratory syndrome (SARS) and avian influenza.

These and other shared interests have provided an expanding material basis for Sino–American cooperation.

China's rise

China's sustained and rapid economic growth during more than three decades has increased its weight in regional and world affairs. According to the World Bank, China became the fourth-largest economy in the world in 2005 (<http://finance.sina.com.cn/g/20060704/02402701910.shtml>). China surpassed Japan and became the third-largest trading partner in the world in 2003 (<http://news.xinhuanet.com/fortune/2005-04/16/content_2837060.htm>); and some economists believed that China would become the third-largest economy in 2007 (<http://business.sohu.com/20070717/n251099606.shtml>). China is not only a large economy and a big trading partner, it is the most dynamic of the large economies in the world. Its contribution to regional and global economic growth is increasingly being felt. According to a World Bank estimate, China has contributed an average of 13 per cent to global economic growth every year since its entry into the World Trade Organisation (WTO) in 2001 (<http://www.sjzmbc.gov.cn/public/show.jsp?id=20060907158578>). More recently, the World Bank predicted that China's contribution to global economic growth would exceed that of the United States (<http://business.sohu.com/20070913/n252117130.shtml>). Rapid economic growth has enabled China to improve its people's living standards, modernise its backward defence facilities and enhance its diplomatic capacity. It has also made China more relevant in world affairs and the world more relevant to Chinese affairs.

Unlike some previous rising powers, China has deliberately chosen the path of peaceful development. It has sought to settle its border problems through negotiations and compromise rather than through coercion and war (<http://news.sina.com.cn/c/2005-01-06/17165448971.shtml>). It has tried to seek mutually beneficial economic relations with other countries through supporting a freer international trading system rather than through practising a beggar-thy-neighbour policy. It has increased participation in international cooperation on a whole range of issues, from the environment to non-proliferation of WMD. It has also made greater contributions to international efforts to maintain peace and stability. It is against such a background that the outside world, especially the United States, finds that it is in its interests to welcome and accommodate China's rise so far. It is also against such a background that China–US interactions are becoming more balanced.

Convergence of values

After more than three decades of practising its policy of openness and reform, China has changed in many ways. Among other things, it has replaced its centrally planned economy with a market one. It has attached increasing importance to the rule of law as one of the most important means by which to govern and advance social justice. It has publicly advocated the protection of human rights and has adopted many measures to improve its own human rights situation. Among other things, the National People's Congress, China's legislature, passed an amendment to the constitution in March 2004 stipulating that the State respected and protected human rights (<http://www.wutnews.net/news/news.aspx?id=6634>). It has also tried to introduce democratic reforms such as nationwide village-level elections and measures to broaden participation in the selection of leaders at various levels of the Chinese Government and in the policymaking process. More recently, Chinese Premier, Wen Jiabao, said that China believed it wanted democracy and would make more efforts towards achieving this (<http://www.ce.cn/xwzx/gnsz/szyw/200703/16/t20070316_10718768.shtml>). As a result of this, Chinese have already embraced such values as free trade, the rule of law, freedom and democracy. It is true that vast differences remain in practice; however, at the conceptual level, the value difference has been narrowing. Such changes have provided an expanding value basis for Sino–American cooperation.

Challenges and constraints

Despite the positive developments discussed in the previous sections, China and the United States are also facing some serious challenges in their relationship. These include: 1) zero-sum perceptions of interest on the part of some people in both countries; 2) differences in values and political priorities; and 3) structural uncertainties brought about by the rise of China.

Zero-sum perceptions of interest

Some Americans subscribe to the view of 'offensive realism' [4] and believe that the interests of the established powers and those of the rising ones will inevitably collide. They believe that the United States is the established power and China a rising one; and, given the current trend of development in China, China presents the most serious potential threat to the United States. Thus writes offensive realist scholar John Mearsheimer (2001), 'Over time…China could become the most powerful rival the United States has ever faced.' The sentiment also resonates in the Pentagon's *Quadrennial Defense Review Report* released in September 2001: 'Although the United States will not face a peer competitor in the near future, the potential exists for regional powers to develop sufficient capabilities to threaten stability in regions critical to US interests' (US Department of Defence 2001:4).

According to this perspective, the relationship between China and the United States is a zero-sum game: what is good for China is bad for the United States and vice versa. Thus, those who hold this view see China's economic growth as a threat to the United States rather than in terms of improved living conditions for the Chinese people and new opportunities to boost US economic welfare; they regard China's efforts to improve its relations with its neighbours as China's attempt to expand its influence at the expense of the United States (Tkacik and Dillon 2005–06); they consider Chinese hopes to improve military-to-military relations with the United States a conspiracy to steal US military secrets rather than an effort to build confidence and trust between the two countries. In other words, they believe the rise of China is not a benign development but a dangerous challenge to US supremacy (<http://www.intelligencesquaredus.org/TranscriptContainer/China.pdf>). They therefore advocate a policy of containing and restraining China.

Some in China hold similar views about the United States. To them, the United States, as the established power, is not going to allow China to rise, even peacefully. US efforts, such as enhancing its military alliance with Japan, developing military ties with China's neighbours, especially India, prolonging its military operations in Central Asian states, selling weapons to Taiwan and strengthening its military presence on Guam are various aspects of a grand strategy aimed at containing China. Even US initiatives to promote international cooperation to deal with climate change are viewed as a way to undermine China's competitiveness. In response, they believe that China should and must be prepared to meet such a challenge militarily (see, for example, <http://yulimin.javaeye.com/blog/27457>).

Such views on both sides reinforce one another and at times generate much suspicion in both countries, which threatens to undermine the basis of their cooperation.

Differences in values and political orientation

Differences in values and political priorities between the two countries also generate suspicion and hostility. Despite significant changes in values in China in the past decades, as discussed in previous sections, China remains different to the United States in terms of certain values and political priorities. As a socialist country led by a communist party, China's official ideology is still Marxist, although with Chinese characteristics, according to the Chinese Government. As an Asian country attaching relatively greater weight to communal than to individual interests, China is less willing than the West wishes to protect individual rights and interests. And, as a developing country undergoing rapid economic and social transformations, China gives priority to economic development and political stability over political liberalisation and democratisation.

In the eyes of most Americans, China's political system is not democratic: there is no multiparty competition, no free and competitive elections, no rule of law, no free press and no free association. Since most Americans subscribe to the theory of democratic peace—that is, democratic countries do not fight each other—they are worried that if China remains undemocratic as it rises, it will pose a threat to the security interests of the United States (Twining 2007). They therefore push their government to put pressure on China to democratise in a way they want to see. This in turn restrains the US Government from taking a more consistent and constructive approach towards China, complicating interactions between the two countries.

Structural uncertainties brought about by the rise of China

Although most Americans do not share the offensive realists' views on China, they do feel uncertain about the implications of China's rise. After all, the sheer size of China means that its rise will inevitably bring about substantial changes in the world. No-one can fully foresee what this means in terms of security, economics, energy, the environment and other areas of international concern, let alone people's job security and lifestyles. Therefore, their feelings of uncertainty are only natural. Uncertainty breeds caution, however, and caution makes it easier for people to subscribe to arguments in terms of worst-case scenarios. If not handled well, this situation could lead to popular support for efforts to hedge against China. Such efforts would in turn lead to Chinese feelings of insecurity and efforts by them to boost their defence, resulting in additional uncertainties on the part of others.

Prospects for development

Given the rise of China and the weight of the United States in world affairs, how these two countries manage their relations will be of paramount importance for the two countries and for the world as a whole.

After more than three and half decades of renewed contacts, China and the United States are closer, their cooperation is more extensive and their relations more balanced than before. With greater stakes in their relationship and in the current international order, with China determined to pursue a peaceful rise and with their values converging, the two countries have a better chance and a greater need than ever before to develop a cooperative partnership. After all, in the age of globalisation, when effective outsourcing is the key to success, there is no better place for the two countries to outsource than to each other in their efforts to attain their respective national ambitions and welfare, and those of the world as a whole. Imagine a world in which China and the United States take the lead on climate change! Imagine a world in which China and the United States join efforts with other countries on energy security!

As discussed in previous sections, challenges and restraints will, however, continue to hamper the development of the relationship. Some people in both countries will continue to hold a zero-sum approach to the relationship. The rise of China will continue to generate uncertainty and fear on the part of many in both countries, making them easy targets for anti-Chinese or anti-American political rhetoric. The remaining differences in values and national priorities will also continue to hinder genuine understanding and effective cooperation between the two countries.

Therefore, while the two countries have a better chance to develop a cooperative partnership than ever before, there are still many uncertainties. Leaders of the two countries will have to exercise vision and wisdom if they wish to chart the relationship to a positive future.

References

Carrel, Lawrence 2007, 'These China mutual funds keep soaring', 1 October 2007,
      <http://www.thestreet.com/funds/mutualfundmonday/10382025.html>

Economy, Elizabeth 2005, 'China's rise in Southeast Asia: implications for Japan and the United States', *Journal of Contemporary China*, August, pp. 409–25, <http://www.google.cn/search?complete=1&hl=zh-CN&inlang= zh-CN&newwindow=1&q=elizabeth+economy%2C+China%27s+Rise+in+Southeast+ Asia%3A+Implications+for&meta=&aq=null>

Mearsheimer, John J. 2001, 'The future of the American pacifier', *Foreign Affairs*, September–October 2001.

Park, John S. 2005, 'Inside multilateralism: the six party talks', *The Washington Quarterly*, Autumn 2005.

Qingguo, Jia 2003, 'The impact of 9-11 on Sino–US relations: a preliminary assessment', *International Relations of the Asia-Pacific*.

Qingguo, Jia 2004, 'Narrowing differences but diverging priorities: Sino–American Relations, 1992–2000', in Ezra Vogel, Yuan Ming and Tanaka Akihiko (eds), *The Age of Uncertainty: US–China–Japan triangle from Tiananmen (1989) to 9/11 (2001)*, Harvard University Press, Cambridge.

Tkacik, John J. jr and Dillon, Dana 2005–06, 'China's quest for Asia: Beijing fills a vacuum', *Policy Review*, no. 134, December–January, <http://www.hoover.org/publications/policyreview/2920211.html>

Twining, Daniel 2007, 'Asia's challenge to China', *Financial Times*, 25 September 2007, <http://209.200.80.89/publications/article.cfm?id=343>

US Department of Defence 2001, *Quadrennial Defense Review Report*, 30 September 2001.

ENDNOTES

[1] For example, Ambassador Zhou Wenzhong's speech to the Asia Society, 22 September 2005, <http://www.china-embassy.org/chn/zmgx/t213523.htm>

[2] In 2006, '[f]or the first time since the Dialogue began six years ago, China sent its first high-level' delegation (<http://www.iiss.org.uk/whats-new/iiss-in-the-press/june-2007/the-shangri-la-dialogue-beyond-talk>).

[3] This also applies to the United States despite its stronger unilateral inclination in recent years.

[4] The term is borrowed from the title of a study group meeting of the Council on Foreign Relations held in December 1998 in New York (<http://www.cfr.org/public/resource.cgi?meet!1646#>).

Chapter 3

China–Japan relations at a new juncture

Zhang Tuosheng

China–Japan relations now stand at a new juncture after more than a decade of turbulence and nearly two years of recovery since the end of the Cold War. Whether China and Japan—two major powers in East Asia—will be able to establish a comprehensive strategic relationship of mutual benefit and realise long-term friendship and cooperation in the new conditions will affect not only the destinies of the two countries but the future of the region and the world at large.

I

China and Japan resumed diplomatic relations in 1972. Remarkable progress was made in the next two decades. Despite some friction from time to time, friendship and cooperation were the mainstream of bilateral relations.

Due to profound changes in the international situation and in the domestic circumstances in the two countries, China–Japan relations entered a long period of turbulence after the mid 1990s. During this period, differences and frictions increased and intensified. After 2004 in particular, disputes between China and Japan broke out on a host of issues, including history, Taiwan, territorial and maritime rights and interests, energy, the growth of Japanese military power, the US–Japan military alliance, Chinese military development, the entry into Japanese waters of a Chinese submarine and Japan's pursuit of permanent membership of the UN Security Council. Strategic misgivings [1] became more apparent. With the complete interruption of high-level exchanges at the end of 2005, [2] China–Japan relations reached their nadir since the establishment of diplomatic ties. [3]

There are many factors behind the sustained deterioration in bilateral relations. The most serious frictions occur on the questions of history, Taiwan and territorial and maritime rights and interests. When diplomatic relations were established, however, these problems had existed for a fairly long time and had not prevented the two sides from forging diplomatic ties nor had they obstructed growth of bilateral relations. Why, then, did they stand out in the late 1990s?

In the author's opinion, the reason lies in profound changes in domestic and international circumstances, including: the end of the Cold War and the disintegration of the Soviet Union and changes in US policy towards China; the rising comprehensive national strength of China and long-term recession and stagnation of the Japanese economy; the withdrawal of old-generation leaders from centre stage in both countries and Japan's entry into a period of national transformation; [4] China and Japan becoming the two big powers in East Asia [5] and rising nationalism in both countries; the expansion of pro-independence forces in Taiwan and the rise of the Taiwan question; and the impact of the modern media.

The most significant factors are the end of the Cold War and the need to recalibrate the relationship not only in the absence of a common threat (the Soviet Union) but in circumstances in which, for the first time in history, China and Japan are major powers. Neither country was adequately prepared for these major changes and their deep influences, and both lacked effective ways to resolve their differences in this new situation. As a result, the friendly atmosphere between the two countries deteriorated, frictions increased and strategic misgivings deepened. The bilateral relationship developed from one dominated by friendly cooperation with occasional friction or competition in the early 1990s, to the coexistence of cooperation and competition and then to a situation in the new century in which friction and competition exceeded cooperation—as represented by the comprehensive deterioration of bilateral political and security relations.

The deterioration of China–Japan relations not only harmed the strategic interests of the two countries, it had an adverse effect on the stability and development of East Asia, thereby causing serious concern in other countries, including the United States.

II

With joint efforts by both countries, a long-expected turn in China–Japan relations was marked by the ice-breaking journey of Japanese Prime Minister Shinzo Abe in October 2006 and the return visit by Chinese Premier Wen Jiabao in April 2007.

After accepting the Chinese invitation, Prime Minister Abe visited China on 8 and 9 October 2006. The two sides reached important common understandings, such as: working together to overcome political barriers and comprehensively promote bilateral relations, resuming exchanges and dialogue between leaders, correctly appraising each other's path to development, accelerating consultation concerning the East China Sea in pursuit of joint development, and constructing a mutually beneficial relationship based on common strategic interests (*China–Japan Joint Press Communiqué*, 8 October 2006). The visit, dubbed an 'ice-breaking journey', served to break the political stalemate between the two countries, thus opening the door to further improvement and development of bilateral relations.

Premier Wen paid a reciprocal visit to Japan in April 2007, the first visit by a Chinese premier in seven years. The two leaders agreed on ways to properly handle their countries' differences and on the basic meaning of measures to be taken for strategic, mutually beneficial relations. [6] Premier Wen's speech in the Japanese Diet was widely welcomed. The visit also marked the thirty-fifth anniversary celebration of the normalisation of relations and the China–Japan Culture and Sports Exchange Year. The successful visit by Premier Wen consolidated the improvements in bilateral relations begun in October 2006.

The major turn in Sino–Japanese relations was manifest in three areas.

First, the two sides agreed to remove political barriers to the development of bilateral relations, thereby breaking the political stalemate that had formed because of former Japanese Prime Minister Junichiro Koizumi's visits to the contentious Yasukuni war shrine for six consecutive years. Japan decided to adopt a policy of ambiguity on the question of the Yasukuni Shrine [7] and China dropped its insistence on Japanese leaders' public commitment to not pay tribute at the shrine. In the joint press communiqué issued on 8 October 2006, the countries vowed to 'properly handle issues that affect development of bilateral relations and enable strong movement of both political and economic wheels'. It was a decision made after careful thought by leaders of both countries. Given that differences over history are hard to resolve fundamentally in a short time, this serves to prevent these outstanding issues from damaging bilateral relations. Some people in both countries found the agreement rather fragile and predicted an early reversal of the situation. The sceptics have been proven wrong. In 2007, neither Abe himself nor the majority of his cabinet members visited the Yasukuni Shrine. The pragmatic and forward-looking attitude of China towards the question of history also greatly decreased the influence of wrong opinions in Japan. [8]

Second, the two sides agreed to resume and strengthen high-level exchanges. Remarkable progress has since been made in this regard. In today's international relations, in particular between major countries, high-level exchange is a basic condition for the development of normal state-to-state relations. On this basis, mutual trust between leaders can play a uniquely positive role in facilitating the improvement and development of relations between their countries. For some time, however, the steady worsening of China–Japan relations seriously obstructed high-level contact, which became the weakest link in bilateral ties. Starting with Prime Minister Abe's visit to China in 2006, high-level exchanges resumed rapidly. Leaders of the two countries met not only at international gatherings, they soon engaged in reciprocal direct visits. The resumption and strengthening of high-level contact are substantive parts of the major turn in the relationship and will play a substantial role in consolidating improvement and preventing reversal.

Third, the two sides reached common understanding on establishing a strategic, mutually beneficial relationship, which reset the baseline of bilateral relations on common interests. In 1998, China and Japan made it very clear in their joint statement that the two countries would commit themselves to establishing a friendly and cooperative partnership for peace and development towards the twenty-first century. Unfortunately, under the circumstances at the time, such a vision did not become the reality of a common understanding between the two governments and peoples and efforts made to that end were soon overwhelmed by increasingly acute differences and confrontation. The idea of jointly establishing a strategic, mutually beneficial relationship represented a redefinition of China–Japan relations and marked a major change in mind-set. It indicates the determination of both countries to abandon the old idea of 'no two rival tigers on the same mountain' and to start to work together for mutual benefit. A strategic relationship of mutual benefit goes beyond differences and puts expanded common interests in a primary position. It also goes beyond bilateral cooperation and extends the basis of China–Japan relations to broader areas of regional and global cooperation.

With overall relations changing for the better, China–Japan exchanges and cooperation are warming, growing and strengthening in many fields. The two sides have strengthened cooperation on resolving the North Korean nuclear issue and maintaining stability on the Korean Peninsula. Negotiations on the East China Sea have gained pace. A joint research program on history, guided by both governments, has been formally launched. Momentum has been created for the resumption and development of military relations. The two sides have also agreed, in addition to a strategic dialogue, to establish high-level economic and energy policy dialogue mechanisms. There has also been an upsurge in non-governmental exchanges.

This major turning point in China–Japan relations was calculated and deliberate rather than accidental.

First, continued worsening of relations had seriously damaged the strategic interests of both countries. In the five years in which various disputes had surfaced, public sentiment had become increasingly confrontational and mutual strategic suspicions had escalated. With the outbreak of large-scale anti-Japan demonstrations in some Chinese cities in 2005, people began to worry that the situation of 'cold politics and a warm economy' [9] between China and Japan could move towards 'cold politics and a cold economy'. Meanwhile, the danger of an accidental military clash in the East China Sea was increasing. All of the above-mentioned risks, if realised, had the potential to bring unthinkable damage to Sino–Japanese relations. The worsening relationship constituted a huge barrier to China's peaceful rise and Japan's pursuit of the status of a normal state. Breaking the political stalemate, effectively controlling differences and guiding bilateral relations towards stability and improvement gradually became the desire of both countries.

Furthermore, the worsening of China–Japan relations had caused much concern in the international community. It not only slowed efforts to establish an East Asian economic community, it led to a serious imbalance in the China–US–Japan triangle. [10] No country in East Asia wishes to be forced to make a choice between China and Japan; and the United States' policy desire of expanding security cooperation with China while strengthening the alliance with Japan has been seriously challenged. Moreover, although the US Government has long been reluctant to comment on wrong historical views in Japan, the growing salience of the Yasukuni Shrine problem and consequent rising criticism from the US Congress and strategic studies circles put the Bush Administration in an embarrassing position. The international community, including the United States, wished to see the stability of China–Japan relations restored as soon as possible.

Additionally, ever since 2005, the two governments—and China in particular—had been attempting to break the political stalemate and improve bilateral relations. A meeting between President Hu Jintao and Prime Minister Koizumi in Indonesia in April 2005, [11] which saw the start of strategic dialogue at the vice-ministerial level and the resumption of consultations over the East China Sea the next month, raised hope for an improvement in bilateral relations. Even after the two sides' efforts were again stalled by Koizumi's visit to the Yasukuni Shrine, [12] contacts continued in 2006, with exchanges between the two ruling parties, a foreign ministers' meeting, strategic dialogue [13] and consultation on the East China Sea. During that process, with changes in Japanese public opinion [14] on the question of the Yasukuni Shrine, China began to release positive signals [15] and subtle changes began to appear in the attitude of some important politicians in Japan. [16] Finally, the two sides seized the opportunity provided by a change in Japanese leadership and agreed, after arduous negotiation, to develop and improve friendly and cooperative relations—the result of which was the long-awaited turn in bilateral relations.

III

Marked by Prime Minister Yasuo Fukuda's and President Hu's trips, China–Japan relations have again come to a new historical juncture and are facing important opportunities.

In September 2007, Prime Minister Abe resigned unexpectedly and was succeeded by Fukuda against the backdrop of a Liberal Democratic Party (LDP) electoral defeat in the House of Councilors. On taking office, Fukuda stressed that relations with China constituted one of the most important sets of external relationships for Japan and he expressed determination to press ahead with the strategic relationship of mutual benefit. He soon made it clear that he would not visit the Yasukuni Shrine and indicated that Japan's Asian diplomacy should resonate alongside the growth of its alliance with the United States, while giving up the diplomacy of values pursued by Abe's Cabinet. The Fukuda Government has continued the general policy of developing and improving relations with China and has pursued a more positive policy towards China, which has won high praise and a positive response from Chinese leaders.

From 27 to 30 December 2007, despite a very busy schedule at home, Prime Minister Fukuda broke with convention and visited China just before the New Year, fulfilling his promise to 'visit China as soon as possible'. In a series of meetings, leaders expressed the political will to strengthen the strategic relationship of mutual benefit and jointly open good-neighbourly, friendly and mutually beneficial cooperation between China and Japan. [17] They discussed and reached a number of new common understandings on maintaining high-level exchanges, properly handling major and sensitive issues between the two countries, developing cooperation in priority areas such as energy, environmental protection and finance, expanding personnel exchanges, exploring joint development of the East China Sea and strengthening defence exchanges and political and security dialogue (*Xinhuanet*, Jinan, 30 December 2007). After the meetings, the two countries published a joint press communiqué on promoting cooperation in the areas of the environment and energy. Prime Minister Fukuda's speech at Peking University was well received by the university faculty and students. Similarly, his visit to Qufu, Shandong, the hometown of Confucius, was significant in highlighting the common historical source of Chinese and Japanese cultures.

Prime Minister Fukuda's visit to China was a complete success and was considered a trip that heralded the arrival of spring. Compared with the previous, first round of reciprocal visits between Chinese and Japanese leaders, this particular trip was characterised by a warm and friendly atmosphere, which gave the two sides greater expectations for the future.

After meticulous preparations, President Hu paid a state visit to Japan from 6–10 May 2008. The ultimate purpose was to 'enhance mutual trust, strengthen friendship, deepen cooperation, and plan for the future so as to push ahead with [a] strategic and mutually beneficial relationship between China and Japan in an all-round way'. [18] During the five-day visit, President Hu engaged in some 50 events. He met with Emperor Akihito, held talks with Prime Minister Fukuda, met various Japanese leaders and old friends, gave a speech at the Waseda University and had extensive contact with the Japanese people.

The visit produced three important outcomes. The first was the signing of a joint statement between China and Japan on fully promoting a strategic relationship of mutual benefit. This statement built on three political documents between China and Japan [19] that enshrined the latest developments in bilateral relations and provided principles to guide the long-term growth and development of the relationship. The second was the publishing of a joint press communiqué between the Chinese and Japanese Governments on strengthening exchanges and which identified 70 items of cooperation. Third, the sight of the top Chinese leader interacting in a friendly and pragmatic way with a cross-section of Japanese people was well received by the Japanese public and was very positive for improving the two sides' perceptions of each other.

The hugely successful visit by President Hu was dubbed a trip in the 'warm spring'. [20] After ice breaking, ice melting and heralding spring, China–Japan relations have finally moved into a new spring.

Since September 2007, remarkable progress has been made in developing the strategic relationship of mutual benefit. The various dialogue mechanisms have all been resumed and developed. Various people's exchanges, particularly among youths, have been given a huge push. [21] The two sides continue to strengthen regional security and economic cooperation. Even the military-to-military relationship has achieved significant momentum. [22] After the earthquake in Wenchuan, Sichuan Province, Japan extended assistance without delay and disaster relief cooperation is still proceeding on an unprecedented scale. The two countries have reached principled consensus on joint development of oil and gas fields in the East China Sea, marking an important step towards joint development there (see reports on *Xinhuanet*, Beijing, 18 June 2008). Cooperation between the two countries in areas of non-traditional security, such as finance, energy, the environment and climate change, has also been comprehensively strengthened.

IV

Looking into the future, the general trend for the long-term development of China–Japan relations has been set. The path ahead will sometimes be tortuous but, on the whole, the outlook appears relatively bright. This judgment is based on the following considerations.

First, after years of intense friction, China–Japan relations have moved out of the long period in which both countries failed to adapt to post-Cold War circumstances [23] and into a new stage of development. Both sides have drawn on the lessons of the past decade or more and reached an important conclusion that long-term peace, friendship and cooperation are the only choices for them. A logical extension of this is reflected in the joint declarations that China and Japan are 'cooperation partners rather than [a] threat to each other', [24] that they 'support each other's peaceful development' and that they will 'work together for the creation of a world of lasting peace and common prosperity'. [25] Strengthened bilateral, regional and global cooperation between China and Japan will forcefully contain their differences and link their interests more closely.

Second, the three major differences between China and Japan have been brought under relatively good control and frictions are decreasing. Although their differences on the question of history are unlikely to disappear soon, they are far less likely to become dominant factors again in bilateral relations since China is determined to adopt a pragmatic and forward-looking attitude and the domestic and external environments of Japan have changed. The two countries still differ on the question of Taiwan; however, since Japan will not easily change its one-China principle and the policy of not supporting Taiwanese independence, and with the clear relaxation of the situation across the Taiwan Strait since the spring of 2008, the likelihood of serious friction between China and Japan over this issue has been greatly reduced. On the question of territorial and maritime disputes in the East China Sea, China and Japan have reached agreement to 'make the East China Sea a sea of peace, stability and cooperation' and have made initial progress on the steps towards joint development. Although there is still a gap between the desire for joint development and real accomplishments, the shadow of a military conflict has disappeared.

Third, apart from highly mutually complementary economic cooperation and trade, non-traditional security issues including finance, energy, the environment, climate change, infectious diseases and terrorism are rapidly expanding areas of cooperation. The two sides clearly have more common interests than differences in the non-traditional security arena. In the future, strengthened cooperation in these areas will become fuel for the two sides to consolidate and develop their relations.

Fourth, the developments and improvements in the past two years have laid an important foundation for major progress in China–Japan relations. Apart from the abovementioned achievements, sound momentum has been achieved for the resumption and promotion of the various dialogue mechanisms that are conducive to strengthening bilateral, regional and global cooperation between China and Japan. Furthermore, the pragmatic measures taken by both sides to improve their relations and the positive progress made have won extensive support from the two peoples and the world community.

Additionally, the expected stable growth in China–US relations and the rise of 'neo-conservatism' and 'neo-realism' [26] in Japanese political thinking will also benefit sound development of China–Japan relations in the future.

As President Hu pointed out, China–Japan relations now have a solid foundation for growth to a higher level and stand at a new starting point. Against the backdrop of deepening economic globalisation and regional integration, China–Japan relations are all the more strategic and important globally. The two sides must work together and waste no opportunity to push their relations to a new high. [27]

We must, however, be sober-minded and acknowledge that there are still multiple difficulties and uncertainties in China–Japan relations and it will not be all smooth sailing. The two sides should be fully prepared for this.

First, although the three major points of sensitivity and friction have been fairly well controlled, they will continue to exist for a long time. On these questions, there is still a large gap between the two sides in terms of perception, policy, desired solutions and expectations. The possibility of any of the above issues regaining prominence cannot be excluded although the likelihood of all three intensifying at the same time is not high. Moreover, differences about the Japan–US military alliance, modernisation of the Chinese military force, Japan's pursuit of permanent membership of the UN Security Council [28] and China's full market economy status will remain difficult to manage. If handled carelessly, these issues could also have major negative impacts on the future of bilateral relations.

Second, the seriously confrontational popular sentiments that formed during the period of deteriorating relations will take time to change. With bilateral relations warming up, the sentiments of the two peoples towards each other are undergoing positive changes. On the whole, however, these changes lag behind the improvement and development of state-to-state relations and have constituted restraint on bilateral relations. Examples include the radical reaction of Japanese public opinion to the poisoned-dumpling incident, [29] the playing up by some Japanese media of the Tibetan incident and incidents during the Olympic torch relay [30] and the negative reactions of some Chinese citizens to the initial shipment of earthquake relief materials by Japanese military aircraft and to the agreement on principles guiding joint development of oil and gas fields in the East China Sea. This reflects the fragility that still exists in bilateral relations and indicates that some important differences will still take time to resolve.

Furthermore, considering the above two points plus the two countries' different social systems and ideology, the deeper strategic misgivings between the two countries will not simply disappear because of the new definition of bilateral relations in formal documents. Such strategic misgivings can be expected to persist and to stand out from time to time among the general public, the strategic research community and government departments in both countries, exerting negative influences on the development of bilateral relations in all fields. It can, however, be said with certainty that if the strategic relationship of mutual benefit continues to progress, mutual political trust will also grow while strategic misgivings will decrease.

Finally, the unstable Japanese political situation is still a fairly big uncertainty. On 1 September 2008, Prime Minister Fukuda, who was in favour of actively developing relations with China, followed the example of his predecessor, Abe, and resigned, [31] leading to chaos in the Japanese political situation once again. On 24 September, Taro Aso, who had long been considered a hawk, was elected as the new Prime Minister of Japan. On taking office, Aso was confronted with the various challenges that had defeated his predecessor and had to focus on economic problems and domestic affairs. The anticipated election is unlikely to resolve the underlying sources of instability in Japan's political situation. [32] If the Japanese political situation remains unstable, it could delay the process of China and Japan strengthening their cooperation and resolving differences, or even introduce new variables in Japan's foreign policy and policy towards China. This is, frankly, quite worrisome.

To sum up, it might appear that the prospects for relative stability in China–Japan relations in the future are quite bright. This does not, however, mean that the relationship will be tranquil. Future China–Japan relations will be rather like China–US relations since the end of 2001. In other words, dialogue and cooperation will accumulate and strengthen; differences will continue to exist or even rise one after another but remain controllable; misunderstandings will gradually decrease and political trust will gradually increase. If China–Japan relations can develop as such, the platform for their cooperation will become broader, mutual sentiments between the two peoples will turn again towards respect and friendship and the most difficult issues between the two countries could gradually be resolved. In the end, the two big countries will be able to find a path to strategic mutual benefit and become friendly partners in cooperation with major influence in a multipolar world.

Such a prospect will benefit China and Japan, East Asia and the Asia-Pacific region and be conducive to world peace, stability and prosperity.

Reference

Xinsheng, Wang et al. 2008, 'Changes in Japanese political thoughts and China–Japan relations in recent years', *Research on History of China–Japan Relations*, vol. 2.

ENDNOTES

[1] China worries about Japan 'reviving militarism' or 'pursuing a path to military power'. Japan, on the other hand, worries about the 'China threat'.

[2] In 2002, after Prime Minister Koizumi visited the Yasukuni Shrine again, in disregard of strong Chinese opposition, national leaders of the two countries stopped visiting each other but maintained meetings on international occasions. After Koizumi's fifth visit to the shrine in October 2005, even bilateral meetings on international occasions were interrupted.

[3] China–Japan relations experienced a down turn in 1995–96. At the time, however, frictions did not appear all at once, nor did bilateral disputes intensify to such an extent.

[4] The transformation was made manifest as follows: the old system of conservative and progressive forces, each holding one-half of the power, disintegrated, with conservatism becoming dominant in politics and society and new state-ism on the rise; major adjustments were made to domestic and foreign policies in pursuit of shaking off the shadow of a defeated state and acquiring the status of a political or even military power commensurate with an economic power as a 'normal state'.

[5] In this situation, neither side wishes to see the rise of the other's influence in East Asia and both worry about competition from the other. Japan is particularly worried about China's rise. In reality, the rejuvenation of China cannot be stopped and it is also natural for Japan to develop from an economic power to a political power, although its development potential cannot be compared with that of China given its geographic, population and resource restrictions.

[6] The basic meaning of a strategic relationship of mutual trust between China and Japan is that China and Japan will jointly make constructive contributions to peace, stability and development in Asia and the world through cooperation at bilateral, regional and international levels and, in that process, both will obtain benefits and expand their common interests and promote their bilateral relations to a new high. See *China–Japan Joint Press Communiqué*, 9 April 2007.

[7] That is, refraining from explicit statements about whether the shrine will be visited—a sharp contrast with Koizumi's public statement of intention to visit every year.

[8] In Japan, some people have long claimed that China will always play the history card with Japan and that even when the Yasukuni Shrine problem is resolved China will take on other historical issues to dwarf Japan.

[9] Since 2001, even with continued tension in the political and security fields, economic relations between China and Japan have maintained fairly good growth; this has been called 'cold politics and a warm economy'.

[10] Post-World War II history suggests that a stable and relatively balanced development of China–US–Japan relations is the real cornerstone of peace and stability in East Asia.

[11] During the meeting, President Hu put forward a five-point proposal for developing and improving China–Japan relations. Koizumi expressed the view that the Japanese side stood ready to follow the spirit contained in the five-point proposal and actively push forward friendly relations between Japan and China. See *Xinhuanet*, Jakarta report, 23 April 2005.

[12] On 17 October 2005, one year and nine months after his previous visit, Koizumi visited the Yasukuni Shrine for the fifth time. This was the last day of the third round of China–Japan strategic dialogue.

[13] The three rounds of strategic dialogue that took place from February to September 2006 played an important role in the two sides' efforts to finally break the political stalemate.

[14] In the summer of 2006, *Nikkei Business Daily* reported a record made by late IHA Chief Minister Tomita Asahiko of remarks by Emperor Showa revealing the latter's strong dissatisfaction in his late years with the Yasukuni Shrine housing level-A war criminals. At the same time, opinion polls in Japan showed that more than 50 per cent of respondents opposed or were not in favour of Japanese leaders paying tribute at the Yasukuni Shrine.

[15] In February 2006, while meeting seven friendly organisations from Japan, President Hu made it clear that as 'long as Japanese leaders clearly make a decision not to visit again the Yasukuni Shrine hosting Class A War Criminals, I would like to have dialogue and meeting[s] with Japanese leaders on improving and developing China–Japan relations'. In August, he made a similar statement to the new Japanese Ambassador, Yuji Miyamoto, on the occasion of the presentation of the latter's credentials.

[16] It was rather eye-catching that, in the summer of 2006, then Chief Cabinet Minister Abe, who was regarded as most likely to succeed as Japanese Prime Minister, moved away from full and open support for paying tribute at the Yasukuni Shrine and adopted an attitude of neither confirming nor denying media reports about his visit to the shrine in the previous spring.

[17] The Prime Minister explicitly hoped that 2008 would be 'recorded in history as a year of rapid development of Japan–China relations' and 'the first year of [a] leap forward in Japan–China relations'.

[18] Speech by Hu Jintao during a joint interview by resident Japanese media in Beijing (*Xinhuanet*, Beijing, 4 May 2008).

[19] Referring to the 1972 Joint Statement, 1978 Treaty of Peace and Friendship and the 1998 Joint Declaration.

[20] Before the visit, with the incidents of poisoned dumplings, Tibet and lack of concrete progress in the consultations concerning joint development of the East China Sea, some Japanese media worried about a possibly unsuccessful visit by Hu.

[21] The year 2008 is the Year of Exchanges Between Young People in China and Japan.

[22] Another symbolic event, besides the first visit by the Chinese Minister of Defence to Japan in August 2007 after nine years, was the first exchange of naval ships, with the Chinese Navy visiting Japan in November 2007 and Japanese ships visiting China in June 2008.

[23] With the end of the Cold War, China's relations with the United States and Japan entered into periods of turbulence. China–US relations moved out of such a situation after 12 years (from 1989 to 2001) and began to achieve relatively stable development. The period of turbulent China–Japan relations also lasted 12 years—from 1994 to 2006.

[24] In the joint statement between China and Japan on comprehensively promoting strategic relations of mutual benefit, China's support for Japan's peaceful development was expressed in the following way: 'In the past 60 years since the end of the 2nd World War, Japan has pursued a path of…peace…and made [a] contribution to world peace and stability by peaceful means, [of] which the Chinese side has a positive appraisal.' Such a statement represents China's full confirmation of the path Japan has followed since the end of World War II and its expectation for the future of Japan.

[25] Joint Statement Between China and Japan on Comprehensively Promoting Strategic Relations of Mutual Benefit, *Xinhua News Agency*, Tokyo, 7 May 2008.

[26] The former is represented by Ichiro Ozawa, the head of the Democratic Party; the latter is represented by Fukuda Yasuo (Xinsheng et al. 2008).

[27] Yang Jiechi on President Hu Jintao's Visit to Japan (*Xinhuanet*, Beijing, 10 May 2008).

[28] The two sides have agreed to strengthen dialogue and communication on UN reform and strive for increased consensus. The Chinese side also expressed the view that it attached importance to Japan's status and role in the United Nations and wished to see Japan playing an even greater constructive role in international affairs.

[29] In January 2008, some Japanese consumers were poisoned after eating dumplings imported from China. Preliminary investigations suggested that the case was isolated poisoning rather than one of food safety caused by pesticide residue. After the incident, the two governments and police departments undertook very good cooperation. The investigation is still under way.

[30] On 4 August 2008, *Daily Yomiuri* reported that, according to an opinion poll it conducted jointly with a Chinese journal, although the image of Japan among Chinese had largely improved, the Japanese perception of China had worsened again because of the above-mentioned incident.

[31] It is reported that Fukuda resigned under pressure over various touchy issues. Besides the many negative legacies from the Koizumi era and the difficulties brought about by oil and food price rises and the financial crisis, one fundamental reason for Fukuda's resignation was the 'twisted Diet'—that is, the House of Representatives and the House of Councilors were controlled by the ruling party and the opposition respectively, leading to the inability of the ruling party to push for implementation of administrative proposals due to obstacles in the Diet.

[32] Furthermore, if confronted with the risk of losing its ruling position, will the LDP support Koizumi or politicians of the same type to return to the political arena? This possibility cannot be excluded.

Chapter 4

Japanese perspectives on the rise of China

Koji Watanabe

Having followed Chinese affairs on and off for the past 40 years, I have personally been struck by the truly dramatic achievements of the Chinese people during the 30 years since the 'reform and opening-up' policy was adopted. In particular, I have been impressed with changes during the past seven years since the International Olympic Committee decided in 2001 that Beijing would host the 2008 Summer Olympics. This was, incidentally, the same year that China acceded to the World Trade Organisation (WTO). The Olympics were a manifestation of everything that the Chinese people had worked for.

Watching the truly spectacular pageants involving tens of thousand performers at the opening and closing ceremonies and noting that the Chinese obtained 51 gold medals, surpassing the Americans, I thought that this could very well be the moment of glory that the Chinese people had been dreaming about for the past 100 years.

The Beijing Olympics were carried out smoothly after the government spent US$40 billion on new infrastructure, including one of the largest new airport terminals in the world, five new subway lines, 34 new bus routes and hundreds of kilometres of new highways (surprisingly, with clean air and no traffic jams), recruited 1.5 million volunteers (including 100 000 at the games themselves), dispatched 100 000 anti-terrorist squad officers and installed one million security cameras.

All in all, the Beijing Olympics were a spectacular success at demonstrating Chinese 'soft power'. It left the Chinese people feeling delighted and proud and the rest of the world amazed, awed and a bit worried.

Worried? Not much, but a little. Where is this emerging, powerful and increasingly nationalistic nation heading?

China's remarkable ability to mobilise vast financial resources and its seemingly limitless human resources, combined with an impressive harnessing of state-of-the-art information technology—as demonstrated in those human pageants in the Bird's Nest Stadium—inevitably invites admiration tinged with some anxiety about the future.

In the shadow of the dramatic success of this sports festival lie a few instances of fakery, suppression of individual human rights and what appear to be excessive security precautions. These are the sorts of things that raise critical questions about post-Olympics China's future direction. Will the Olympics lead to a further opening up of the political system or a further tightening of authoritarian control over society?

These are rather lengthy introductory remarks for my presentation on a Japanese perspective on the rise of China. I have cited the Beijing Olympics because Japanese media reports and commentaries of the Olympics were more sobering than I had expected.

I would emphasise first and foremost that Japan–China relations have improved dramatically since October 2006, when former Prime Minister Shinzo Abe, on assuming the premiership from Junichiro Koizumi, made his first official overseas trip to Beijing to meet with President Hu Jintao and Premier Wen Jiabao. This was the first bilateral meeting between the two countries since 2001.

Premier Wen then visited Japan in April 2007 and Prime Minister Yasuo Fukuda, who succeeded Abe, made a visit to Beijing in December 2007. Most recently, President Hu made an official visit as a state guest of Japan in May 2008.

It is said of Sino–Japanese relations over these two years that first the ice was broken, then it thawed and now spring has come.

Since the dramatic meeting of Abe and Hu in October 2006, Japan–China relations have come to be defined as 'a mutually beneficial relationship based on common strategic interests'. The summit meetings that have taken place since then, in particular President Hu's state visit in May 2008, have addressed issues crucial to the future of Japan–China relations. Those elements are:

- a mechanism for the periodic exchange of visits by the leaders of the two countries, with the leader of one country visiting the other country once a year in principle
- an exchange of high-level visits to discuss issues related to security
- systematic youth exchanges to strengthen friendship and cooperation in the mass media, through sister cities and sports
- joint research on history by Japanese and Chinese scholars
- joint work on making the East China Sea a 'sea of peace, cooperation and friendship'
- bilateral cooperation, with a particular priority on energy and the environment, as well as enhancing cooperation in fields such as trade, investment, information and communications technology, finance, food and product safety, protection of intellectual property rights, improving business environments, agriculture, forestry and fishery industries, transport and tourism, water and health care.

Having cited evidence of the improvement in Sino–Japanese relations in the past two years, I believe one could assume relations are all positive and the future is bright. While public sentiment has improved, it has, however, fallen far short of the dramatic improvements at the governmental level.

For example, according to a joint survey conducted in July 2008—before the Olympics—by *Yomiuri Shimbun*, the largest paper in Japan, and a weekly magazine published by Xinhua News Agency in China, 36 per cent of Japanese respondents said the Japan–China relationship was good while 57 per cent said it was bad. In China, 67 per cent said it was good and 29 per cent said it was bad.

Yomiuri Shimbun explains this sober view on the part of the Japanese public as being due to increasing wariness of China because of its increasing military power and suspicions about food safety as a result of the poisoning incidents involving Chinese-made dumplings. I would add to the list of reasons the Tibetan insurgency and its suppression as reported by the media and, more broadly, continuing concerns about the two countries' different political systems, involving issues of the rule of law, transparency, freedom of the press and accountability.

I believe there are five issues that affect Japanese perspectives on the rise of China—and all contain different degrees of uncertainty. How these uncertainties are assessed plays a critical role in determining Japanese perceptions of China.

The first issue is whether the Chinese economy can live up to the goals stipulated during the Seventeenth Party Congress to sustain more than 8 per cent annual growth and quadruple per capita gross domestic product (GDP) by 2020.

I believe China can achieve this, but whether it can cope effectively with the accompanying social, political and environmental challenges remains an open question. Income gaps between the rich and poor, urban and rural areas and coastal and inland areas are widening. Environmental degradation is serious, particularly with regard to air pollution and water shortages. Finally, there is reportedly rampant corruption at all levels of government, including widespread nepotism. Failure to effectively address these challenges could lead to social unrest and upheaval and prevent the Chinese Communist Party (CCP) from achieving its social and economic goals.

The second issue is the prospect of political reform, itself related to the issue of democracy. Some experts, including a prominent Singaporean politician, claim that the Chinese DNA is not fit for democracy—that Chinese do not believe, with their view of the universe, that democracy is a way to produce good government. Others assert that political reform is inevitable and that the issue is only a matter of order—that is, which reform comes first: economic, social or political.

In an article published in the *People's Daily* on 27 February 2007, Prime Minister Wen said, 'Democracy, the rule of law, freedom, human rights, equality, and mutual respect are not exclusively capitalist values. They have come about as the result of the gradual advance of history. They are common human values' (quote from Li Datong).

I am optimistic, but many others are not.

The third issue concerns China's military build-up. The Chinese defence budget has been increasing at an average annual rate of 10 per cent for the past 29 years. For the current fiscal year, the budget is US$45.6 billion, representing a 17.8 per cent increase on the previous year. In fact, the Chinese defence budget now surpasses that of Japan, which has remained about $41 billion for the past several years.

Concern is exacerbated by the lack of transparency about military expenditure and the planned capacities of the armed forces.

The effectiveness of civilian control is also increasingly coming into question, particularly after the anti-satellite missile test China conducted in January 2007.

The fourth issue is related to the concept of China as the 'Middle Kingdom', an issue that has manifested itself recently in an upsurge of Chinese nationalism. The Chinese characters that combine to form the word 'China' literally mean 'centre' and 'kingdom'. China has historically cherished its centrality in the world and has had a tendency to value what the Chinese themselves call 'great power-ism'.

As China continues to develop rapidly economically and militarily, there are concerns that this notion of China as the Middle Kingdom might resurface and China will aim to become the dominant player—that is, hegemony—in Asia, if not the world. Watching the Beijing Olympics and its impressive, massive pageants, I could not help but be reminded of this Middle Kingdom mentality.

The fifth issue relates to concerns about whether the international community or international system can sustain and accommodate the thrust of Chinese growth. There is little doubt that Chinese development has been peaceful and that the international community has, on the whole, benefited enormously from Chinese economic development.

It is a fact that China, together with the United States, is currently the engine of global economic growth. There is, however, uncertainty about what lies ahead. For example, can massive Chinese foreign currency reserves, which are primarily in the form of US Treasury bonds, keep increasing under the present international monetary system?

In terms of the environment, including issues relating to climate change and energy consumption, China is considered a major actor. It does play a critical role, for better or worse.

These are five issues of uncertainty related to China's future. How these sets of issues are assessed will have a direct bearing on Japanese views of China and will affect whether policies are to be characterised by engagement or hedging. A mixture of the two is also possible, which some have described as 'hedged engagement'.

Those who emphasise China's military build-up tend to advocate a hedging policy. While the Japanese military establishment understandably emphasises the importance of hedging, the danger of falling into a security dilemma should always be kept in mind. The security dilemma, in its simplest form, states that the 'ways and means by which a state tries to increase its security decrease the security of others'.

Let me conclude my observations by re-emphasising that I am basically optimistic about the future of Japan–China relations. Both countries will gain by being friendly and cooperative and both will lose by being antagonistic. In this regard, let me cite a short passage from the joint statement between the Japanese Government and the Government of the People's Republic China on 10 May 2008. Both sides 'recognized that the two countries' sole option was to cooperate to enhance peace and friendship over the long term. The two sides resolved to comprehensively promote a 'mutually beneficial relationship based upon common strategic interests'.

Chapter 5

Sino–Indian relations and the rise of China

Sandy Gordon

Introduction

India and China are the two rising giants of Asia. How they relate once they become powerful will have a significant impact on Asian security. At present, their relationship is ambivalent, with growing people-to-people contacts and rapidly expanding trade, but also abiding strategic suspicion, especially on the part of India.

This chapter seeks to assess the future of the relationship. To do so, it needs to answer three questions. First, will China and India rise equally enough so that they will balance each other's rise? Second, if they do not rise equally and China continues to pull ahead economically and militarily, will this mean that they can remain on relatively benign terms, or will India perforce seek to balance China's rise, and if so, what will this balance look like and how will it shape Asian security? And third, what role, if any, will the United States play in that balance and how might India–US relations evolve in light of a rising China?

In order to fully understand the world in which China and India are likely to rise to power we will also need to gain an insight into the likely evolution of Sino–US relations. Should there be a benign evolution of relations between the United States and China capable of absorbing China's rise into a stable global system, this would likely trump any developments between China and India in terms of the wider Asian order. It would do so because it would go at least some way towards shaping the basic relationship between China and India in positive directions. And, in any case, Sino–Indian tension would not necessarily be powerful enough in itself to dictate the nature of Asian security.

Be that as it may, the Sino–US relationship is a matter others are better equipped than this author to deal with. It is also an issue dealt with elsewhere in this volume. So we will set it aside for the purposes of this chapter. It means, however, that there is an assumption in what we say that China and the United States will remain wary competitors and that China will not necessarily bed down easily as a positive player in Asian security, independently of any bilateral developments with India.

Will India and China rise relatively equally?

China began to engage in economic reform and entry into world markets roughly a decade before India. We see from Figure 1 that before China's entry into world markets, India was, in fact, growing more rapidly. After it liberalised its economy, however, China started to draw away and, significantly for the argument of this chapter, continued to grow more robustly.

Figure 5.1 China and India: average decadal growth

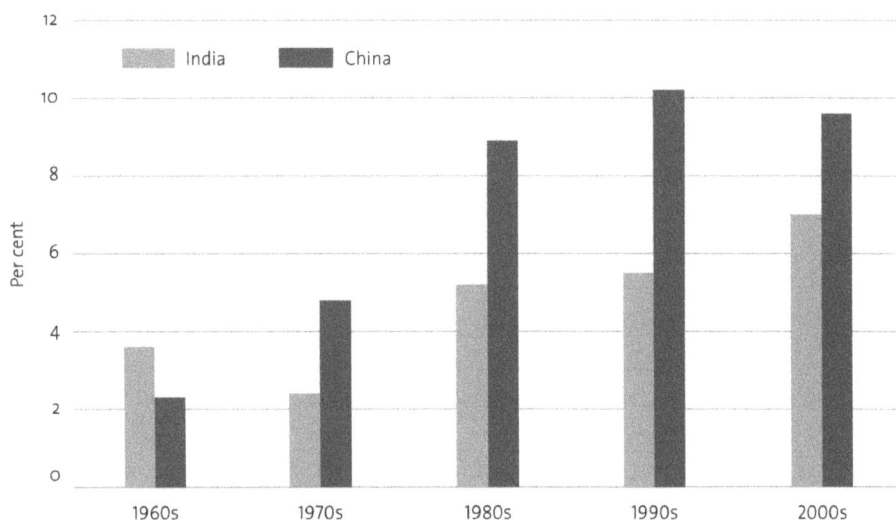

Source: World Bank as reported in Williamson and Zagha (2002) to 1990s, then World Bank.

Source: Gordon, Sandy 2006, *Widening Horizons: Australia's new relationship with India*, ASPI, Canberra.

We see from Figure 1 that after economic reform in 1991, Indian economic growth gathered pace from the so-called 'Hindu' growth rate of 2–5 per cent to an underlying rate of about 7 per cent in the 2000s. Moreover, this pace of growth quickened as the decade drew on and provided India with four successive years of about 9 per cent growth (growth is, however, expected to slip back to 7.3 per cent in the 2009 fiscal year).

We also see from the Economic Intelligence Unit projection (Figure 2) that in market exchange rate measurements and purchasing power parity (PPP), China will continue to draw away from India. According to this projection, India's economy will be roughly half that of China's at PPP rates and about only one-third at market rates in 2030. World Bank projections (Table 1) paint an even more negative picture for India by the earlier date of 2020, with India's share of the world economy at market rates being less than one-third that of China's. These World Bank data are, however, dependent on a significant projected slowdown in China's growth and a somewhat lesser slowdown in India's.

Figure 5.2 Projected growth rates of India, China and the United States in market exchange rates and purchasing power parity

GDP at market exchange rates

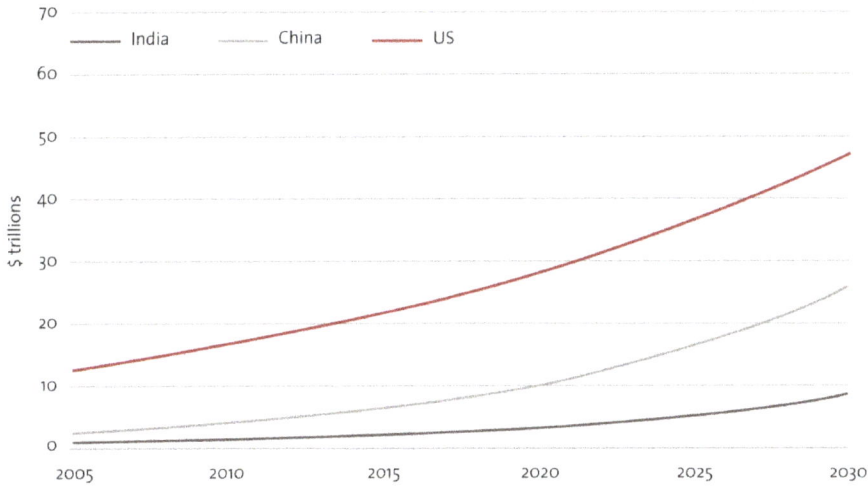

GDP adjusted for purchasing power

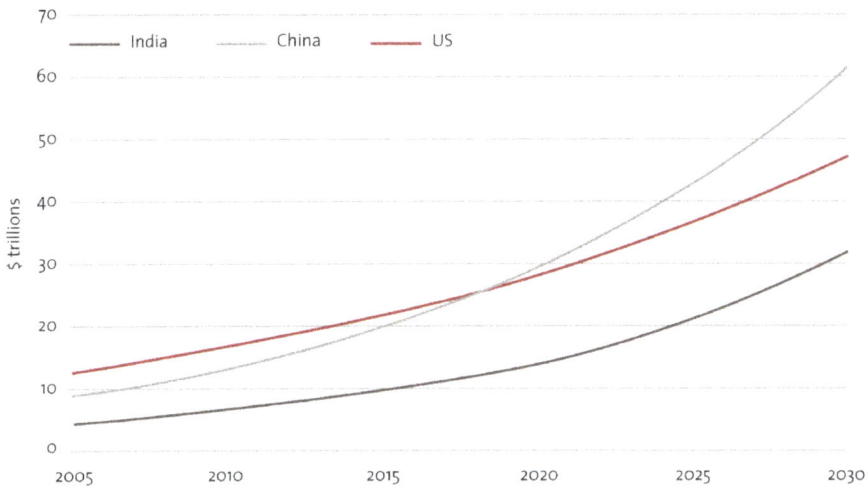

Source: The Economist Intelligence Unit © EIU

As in Winters, L. Alan and Yusuf, Shahid (eds) 2007, *'Dancing with Giants': China, India and the global economy*, World Bank and Institute for Policy Studies (Singapore), Washington, DC, p. 6.

Table 5.1 GDP as a percentage of world GDP in six large economies, 2020 (per cent)

Economy	Share of world GDP (2004 $ and exchange rates)		Average annual real growth rates		Average contribution to world growth		
	2004	2020	1995–2004	2005–20	1995–2004	2005–20
China	4.7	7.9	9.1	6.6	12.8	15.8
India	1.7	2.4	6.1	5.5	3.2	4.1
United States	28.4	28.5	3.3	3.2	33.1	28.6
Japan	11.2	8.8	1.2	1.6	5.3	4.6
Germany	6.6	5.4	1.5	1.9[a]	3.0	3.3
Brazil	1.5	1.5	2.4	3.6	1.5	1.7
World	100.0	100.0	3.0	3.2	100.0	100.0

[a] The World Bank projects an annual growth rate of 2.3 per cent for the 25 countries of the European Union plus the European Free Trade Association, from which we derive the figure for Germany.
Note: Average growth rates are calculated as the average of annual real growth rates (US$ constant 2000) for the period. Similarly, average contributions are calculated as the average of annual contributions. The calculation for the period 2005–20 is based on GDP in 2004 and the projected growth rates.
Source: World Bank 2005b, *World Development Indicators*

Figure 5.3 China and India defence spending, 1997–2007 (US$ billion)

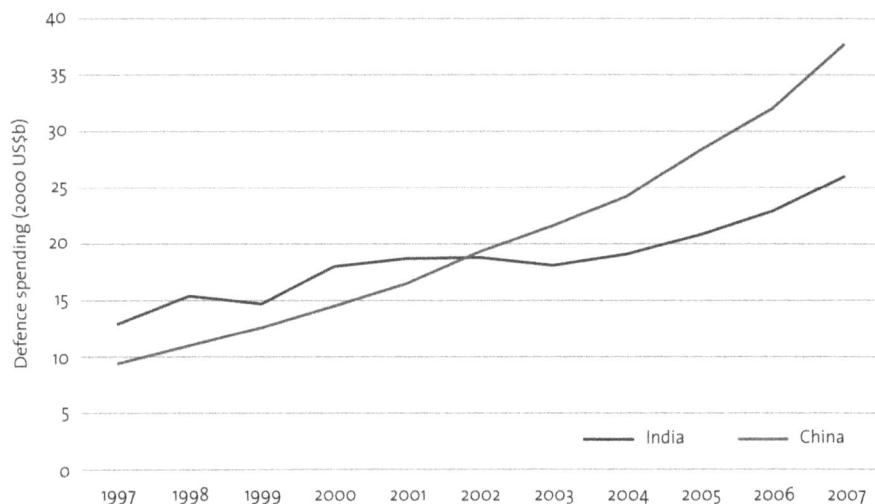

Source: Defence Intelligence Organisation (Australia)

Source: Davies, Andrew 2008, *Asian Military Trends and Their Implications for Australia*, Australian Strategic Policy Institute, Canberra, p. 6.

Moreover, we see from Figure 3 that this economic situation, reflecting more rapid economic growth in China, is reflected in respective defence spending data. These data are drawn from the Australian Defence Intelligence Organisation (as in Davies 2008) and seem somewhat conservative in the case of China, with the latest *Jane's* estimate putting China's expenditure at about $58 billion (*The*

Canadian Press, viewed 26 September 2008, <http:/www. canadianpress.google.com/article/ALeqM5h7mb64TOSdOPW7wvgMNhgC5Bthg>).

Obviously, such economic and defence spending projections depend on assumptions that 'all things will remain equal'. There are several important unknowns in the category 'all things'.

First, there is the issue of political stability in both countries. Commentators have argued persistently that India is both penalised and advantaged by the fact that it has remained a vibrant democracy. It is penalised in the sense that its consensual decision-making processes mean that it has not been able to act forthrightly to develop its economy in the way that China has, enabling the latter to maintain spectacular growth rates in the past three decades. Then again, India might in future be advantaged by the fact that it has already crossed the Rubicon of democratisation, while China has not. That process, should it occur, could also be highly destabilising for China, with concomitant economic effects—or so the argument runs. [1]

This view of the future of China is, however, increasingly subject to challenge. For example, recent research by the respected Pew Research Center (viewed 28 August 2008, <http://pewglobal.org/reports/display.php?Report ID=261>) shows that 86 per cent of Chinese people 'are satisfied with the country's overall direction'. The Pew Center research was conducted after the riots in Tibet but before the May earthquake. The same question asked in 2002 elicited a favourable response on the part of only 48 per cent of respondents. It is also noteworthy that respondents reported far less satisfaction with their own lives than with the general direction of the country. Moreover, the recent global downturn appears to have resulted in a significant decline in factory employment in China. Obviously, the data need to be treated with caution. They do, however, give us pause to consider whether China is, indeed, inevitably bound to liberalise its polity in the foreseeable future.

Aside from the Pew Center's research, there are other views being brought forward to challenge the belief that China must inevitably confront a damaging call for more democracy. According to Ma (2007), 'The links between economic liberalization and political reform...have turned out to be much more complicated and tenuous in the case of China.'

At the same time as doubts are gathering about the inevitability of democracy in China, there is every indication that India's politics will continue to be shaped by unstable coalitions and will be subject to considerable volatility, especially given current energy shortages and inflationary pressures. India's national election, scheduled for May 2009, is likely to result in yet another weak coalition, one that this time might not last the full five-year term.

Are there other factors that could cause economic catch-up on the part of India? Certainly, there are in the longer term, and the most prominent of them is demographics. In Figure 4, we can compare the population 'trees' for India and China.

Figure 5.4 Population 'trees' for India and China, for 2000 and projected for 2050

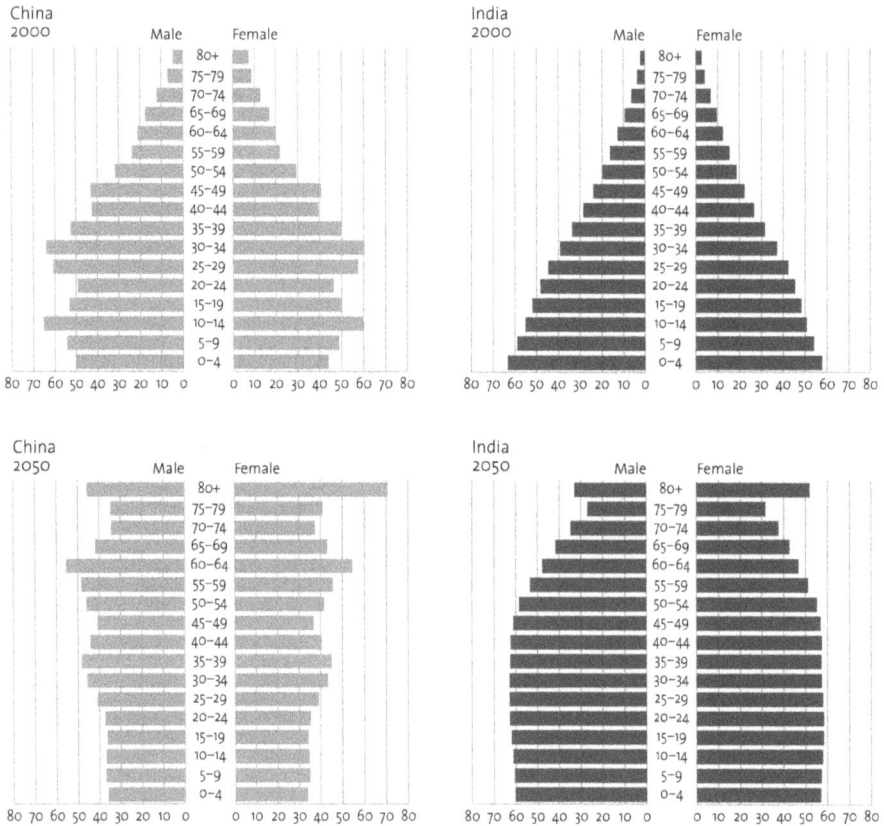

Source: US Census Bureau, as reported in BBC News

Source: Gordon, Sandy 2006, *Widening Horizons: Australia's new relationship with India*, ASPI, Canberra, p. 24.

What is immediately apparent is that India—which will be the most-populous country in the world by about 2030—has a far higher proportion of young people in its population than China. This should in theory erode China's comparative advantage in labour-intensive manufactures by about 2030; but will India pick up the challenge and become the new labour-intensive powerhouse of the world economy?

In the initial stages of India's economic liberalisation, this did not appear at all likely. Indeed, some commentators were even claiming that India had a leapfrog economy that would bypass the labour-intensive phase altogether (Das 2006). Until quite recently, India's labour-intensive push into world markets was restrained not so much by tariff policy as by foreign direct investment (FDI) restrictions, labour laws, lack of infrastructure and state-imposed restrictions on the large-scale manufacturing sector, which had the effect of reserving labour-intensive manufacturing for the small-scale sector (see Arvind 2008).

On the other hand, the enormous capitalisation of the Chinese economy also promises to enable it to substitute capital for labour on an immense scale as its labour force ages, ensuring that it retains a formidable competitive edge and a substantial share of the world economy. The models here would be first Japan and, more recently, Korea and Taiwan.

Of course, the analytical picture is far more complicated than the one we have been able to present above. At the very least, however, we have been able to provide sufficient information to show that it is a big call to assume that India will catch up with China. Indeed, it is quite possible that the World Bank projections provided above will prove fairly accurate.

So what might this mean for Sino–Indian relations?

The effect on Sino–Indian relations

The Sino–Indian relationship is worryingly ambivalent. On one side of the equation we see a flourishing people-to-people relationship underwritten by what is projected to be the world's largest bilateral trading partnership sometime between 2010 and 2020. In the past four years, trade has grown at a phenomenal average of 52 per cent to a total of US$25.76 billion in 2006/07; trade is on track to being worth US$40 billion by 2010 (Acharya 2008:10).

China and India have also made a mutual decision to set aside fighting about their disputed border while the two giants develop their economies and enter world markets—known in the case of China as the 'peaceful development' doctrine. In 2005, the two agreed on a set of 'guiding principles' to govern border negotiations. There is a flourishing process of two-way visits, even at the senior military level, culminating in the visit of president Hu Jintao to India in late 2006 and the reciprocal visit of Prime Minister Manmohan Singh to Beijing in January 2008. In recent years, China's image of India has evolved from that of a weak country of no real consequence to what the Chinese call a 'comprehensive national power'. [2]

This is not, however, a simple relationship from India's perspective. India's trade deficit with China has been growing and now stands at more than US$9 billion. [3] As Chinese imports increase into what should be a labour-intensive manufacturing country, the vaunted trading 'revolution' could look less promising from the Indian perspective. India asserts that China is dumping large quantities of manufactures onto the Indian market. New Delhi has refused vital Chinese investment in key areas that it considers to be security risks, such as telecommunications and port development. It continues to deny China market economy status and resists China's offer of a free trade agreement. Clearly, this is a country that lacks confidence that it can meet the economic challenge posed by its giant neighbour.

The issue of the contested border can also be presented in negative as well as positive terms. China's ambassador to New Delhi shocked India two days before Hu's visit by asserting that Arunachal Pradesh—a populated part of India—was still disputed territory. The Indians were of the view that China had previously conceded that it belonged to India. The Chinese reversal could simply have been viewed as tough negotiating tactics in Beijing, or it could have reflected Chinese concerns about Tawang, in populated Arunachal Pradesh—the birthplace of the sixth Dalai Lama. It was, however, perceived in New Delhi as 'disingenuous yo-yoing designed to keep India second-guessing and on its back foot' (Aiyar 2008). According to the Indian version of the 2005 guiding principles, China also breached those principles in laying claim to a portion of land containing a substantial, settled population. It caused India to question seriously China's veracity as a negotiating partner and possibly to wonder how China might behave once truly powerful.

Closely associated with border issues is the issue of water. According to Ramachandran (2008), China's plans to divert 40 billion gallons of water annually from rivers in Tibet—especially the massive Yalong Tsangpo, which becomes the Brahmaputra in India and subsequently the Megnad in Bangladesh—to the parched Yellow River Basin are causing considerable concern in India and Bangladesh. The situation is exacerbated by the melting of the Himalayan glaciers that feed the great rivers of Asia, on which 47 per cent of the world's population depends. Ramachandran concludes that China's plans mean it will 'acquire great power leverage over India, worsening tensions between these two countries'.

China's growing footprint in the Indian Ocean, and especially in South Asia, is also deeply worrying to a country such as India, surrounded as it is by vulnerable borders and volatile countries with which it is often at loggerheads. China is selling weapons to all India's immediate neighbours except Bhutan and constructing deep-water ports in Myanmar, Bangladesh, Sri Lanka and Pakistan. Although claims of Chinese military bases in Myanmar are exaggerated, India feels surrounded in its own backyard. [4]

India's discomfort with China's growing Indian Ocean footprint is expressed most clearly at the official level in the Indian Maritime Doctrine, issued to the public in 2005. Having declared that the Indian Ocean is India's 'backyard' and outlining an ambitious schedule for Indian naval expansion in the Indian Ocean, the document cites China as a major reason for this expansion in the following terms: 'China has embarked on an ambitious military modernization programme…the [People's Liberation Army] Navy, which is the only Asian navy with an SLBM capability, is aspiring to operate much further from its coast than hitherto.' [5]

India and China have also become locked in urgent competition for energy in the Middle East, Africa, Central Asia and Myanmar. This sense of competition has become all the more urgent for India because of the poverty of its domestic supplies of liquid hydrocarbons and its energy-intensive requirements for maintaining economic growth from a low base.

Some observers assert that India and China have adjusted their competition for energy such that they do not unduly compete in the same markets and inflate prices (Khanna 2008). India was nevertheless shocked to find that natural gas from two leases it had helped to develop in the Shwe field off Myanmar was sold by Myanmar's nationalised oil company not to India, as expected, but to China. This unexpected loss was likely due to pressure on the Myanmar junta from China (see Clarke and Dalliwall 2008; Lees 2006). Moreover, in seeking compensation, India was apparently given sole controlling rights to Sittwe port, which it is developing—but this too was later overturned, again apparently after pressure from China (Lees 2006).

Although the *official* Indian position on China is positive, if one scratches the surface, Indian commentary often quickly descends to visceral suspicion of China. Such commentary ranges from the prominent Indian academic Brahma Chellaney (2008), who asserts that in 'order to avert the rise of a peer rival in Asia, China has sought to strategically tie down India south of the Himalayas', and the commentary of officials such as Admiral Prakash, who said India would keep a 'close eye' on China's naval intentions in the Indian Ocean (OPRF 2005:9), to India's Maritime Doctrine, cited above.

Given this ambivalent relationship, it is not difficult to imagine that if China continues to surpass and draw away from India economically and strategically—as we assess to be the case on present indications—such ambivalence will soon give way to wariness, concern and, ultimately, the more overt desire to balance China's rise.

Balancing China and India–US relations

From India's perspective, there is already a hedging quality in India–US relations, notwithstanding that New Delhi has made it clear to the United States that it does not wish to be a pawn in any balancing game against China, or any other country.

This hedging quality is evident in the evolving strategic relationship, which, significantly, was initiated in 1991 by the then Commander-In-Chief, Pacific Command (CINCPAC), and which has since developed powerful military–strategic overtones, with the apparent agreement of India.

While there are many voices and motives in Washington directing the nature of the Indo–US rapprochement, at the heart of the relationship is the United States' desire to create of India a major Asian military power capable eventually of helping to balance China's rise. It is important to recognise that this ambition does not necessarily imply that Washington believes it can win and maintain India as an ally, but rather that it will unsettle the power equation for China to have another Asian power—and one that is already in competition—rising rapidly in military capability.

The supposition here is twofold: first, a powerful India will be a more benign and pro-United States presence in the region than a powerful China; and second, if the United States refuses to give India what it wants—strategic parity with the P5 nuclear states—then others, such as Russia, will.

This desire on the part of the United States is a major factor behind the Indo–US nuclear agreement, which is not to say that other motives are not also present. The reason why the nuclear agreement is important is that it will be difficult for the United States to support and build Indian power in some key technologies—for example, ballistic missile technology, anti-ballistic missiles and space—without first bringing India into 'the nuclear tent'.

This, then, is the deal—and where it cannot be done directly with US support, it can be done through the surrogacy of Israel, which has drawn increasingly close to India on high-tech military exchanges.

That this interpretation is correct is suggested by statements by the Bush Administration of unambiguous support for India's rise as a *major* Asian military power made at the time when the nuclear deal was first mooted. According to Secretary of State Condoleezza Rice's policy adviser, this shift in US policy is motivated by the fact that the United States' 'goal is to help India become a major world power in the 21st century'. He added, 'We understand fully the implications, including military implications, of that statement' (Rajghatta 2005). [6]

It is also explicit in the type of technologies being transferred to India—through the United States directly and through Israel. These include an ABM system probably based on the Israeli Arrow 2, in turn developed jointly with Boeing with US technology. While Arrow 2 is an anti-tactical ballistic missile, Arrow 3 will have an anti-MRBM capability. India is also to launch Israel's new spy satellite in early 2009; a quid pro quo could be assistance with India's own military satellite program, which will be especially important for its naval targeting in the Indian Ocean and, eventually, a more sophisticated ABM capability. Israel has also sold to India, with US permission (previously denied to China), the Phalcon AWAC system. The United States has also directly sold sophisticated targeting radars and large naval vessels. The United States is also in the market for India's new strike-fighter project.

While the transfer of military technology is important, the deepening military-to-military relationship also brings with it the exchange of military doctrine, inter-operability and intelligence. This is very much an evolving, multifaceted relationship, albeit one focusing on maritime warfare. At its heart is a 10-year defence agreement signed in 2005 and a program of ever more sophisticated exercises, especially in the maritime sphere.

None of this indicates, however, that India will enter any US 'sphere' or abandon its important relationships with other powers, especially Russia. While there have been recent hiccups in the arms sale relationship between India and Russia to do with late delivery, escalating costs and poor supply of spare parts, the relationship is still of considerable importance to India and will not be easily discarded.

Indeed, from India's point of view, it can continue to conduct its strategy of 'playing both ends against the middle', as it has attempted to do, with varying levels of success, as a central plank of its foreign policy over many years. Within this pattern, however, it will likely 'tilt' somewhat towards the United States—the exact reversal of the situation during the Cold War.

As time goes on, and given the hypothesis of a China that rises more rapidly than India, this 'tilt' could increasingly take on an element of power balancing, whether New Delhi feels comfortable with that role or not. Nor is this label likely be used in New Delhi.

Of course, it needn't happen that way, but the drivers of a more successful outcome will have far less to do with Sino–Indian relations and far more to do with Sino–US relations and US–Russian relations. Should competition between China and the United States intensify, China's rise in Asia is unlikely to be an easy one.

As a 'swing' state in Asia—to use the term of the US Central Intelligence Agency (CIA)—India is therefore likely to be courted by a number of other rising powers. It will make the best it can of this situation in order to acquire the means to military and economic power itself—whether it be Russian energy and platforms or US/Israeli high technology.

Conclusion

It is not at all clear whether China and India will rise equally. Indeed, it is somewhat more likely than not that China will continue to draw away from India economically and militarily. Should this occur, India could seek implicitly (or even explicitly) to balance China's rise, either through an intensifying relationship with the United States or, less likely, with Russia. India is, however, unlikely to enter into any formal alliances during this process; and the ultimate nature and extent of this power-balancing arrangement will depend more on Sino–US, Sino–Russian and Russia–US relations than it will on the relationship between those three countries and India.

While the best outcome would be something akin to Coral Bell's (2005) 'concert of powers', such an outcome is not at all certain. Indeed, it is a 'slippery slope' around the edges of a concert of powers arrangement that leads quickly to classic power balancing. A concert of powers implies, among other things, that India and China will be able to control and channel their emerging competition in productive ways. While this too is a distinct possibility, I have tried to show in this chapter that it is by no means a certainty. Indeed, there are some deep-seated concerns in India about a rising China and what this means for India's position in its sub-Himalayan backyard.

References

Acharya, Alka 2008, 'India–China relations: towards a shared vision', *Economic and Political Weekly*, 26 January – 1 February 2008, p. 10.

Aiyar, Pallavi 2006, 'Beijing's growing respect for India', *Asia Times Online*, 14 November 2006, viewed 29 August 2008, <http://www.atimes.com/atimes/China/HK14Ad01.html>

Aiyar, Pallavi 2008, 'China, India resume Himalayan dance', *Asian Times Online*, 19 September 2008, viewed 30 September 2008, <http://www.atimes.com/atimes/China/JI19Ad03.html>

Arvind, Panagariya 2008, 'What India must do to modernise', *Vox*, viewed 30 September 2008, <http://www.voxeu.org/index.php?q=node/868>

Bell, Coral 2005, *Living With Giants: Finding Australia's place in a more complex world*, Australian Strategic Policy Institute, Canberra.

Chellaney, Brahma 2008, 'Assessing India's reactions to China's "peaceful development" doctrine', *NBR Analysis*, vol. 18, no. 5, April 2008, viewed 28 August 2008, <http://chellaney.spaces.live.com/blog/cns!4913C7C8A2EA4A30!596.entry>

Clarke, Ryan and Dalliwall, Sangeet 2008, 'Sino–Indian competition for Burmese oil and natural gas', *Harvard International Review*, 4 September 2008, viewed 1 October 2008, <http://www.harvardir.org/articles/1751>

Das, G. 2006, 'The Indian model (economic development)', *Foreign Affairs*, vol. 85, no. 4, July–August 2006.

Davies, Andrew 2008, *Asian Military Trends and Their Implications for Australia*, Australian Strategic Policy Institute, Canberra.

Desai, Meghnad 2003, India and China: an essay in comparative political economy, IMF Conference on India and China, New Delhi, viewed 30 September 2008,
<http://www.imf.org/external/np/apd/seminars/2003/newdelhi/desai/pdg>

Gordon, Sandy 1995, *India's Rise to Power in the Twentieth Century and Beyond*, The Macmillan Press, Houndmills.

Gordon, Sandy 2006, *Widening Horizons: Australia's new relationship with India*, Australian Strategic Policy Institute, Canberra.

Khanna, Tarun 2008, *Khanna: India–China trade*, Podcast, Council on Foreign Relations, viewed 28 August 2008,
<http://www.cfr.org/publications/15323/>

Lees, Graham 2006, 'India and China compete for Burma's resources', *World Politics Review*, 21 August 2006, viewed 1 October 2008,
<http://www.worldpoliticsreview.com/article.aspx?it=129>

Ma, Ying 2007, 'China's stubborn anti-democracy: hoping for change isn't enough', *Policy Review*, February–March 2007, viewed 30 September 2008,
<http://www.hoover.org/publications/policyreview/5513661.html>

Ocean Policy Research Foundation (OPRF) 2005, *OPRF MARINT Monthly Report*, December 2005, viewed 29 August 2008,
<http://www.sof.org.jp/en/monthly/pdf/200512.pdf>

Rajghatta, Chidanand 2005, 'Arms Americana: US opens military barn door for India', *Times of India*, 9 May 2005, viewed 1 September 2008,
<http://www.timesofindia.com/articleshow/1522939.cms>

Ramachandran, Sudha 2008, 'India quakes of China's water plan', *Asia Times Online*, 9 December 2008, viewed 9 December 2008,
<http://www.atimes.com/atimes/China/JL09Ad01.html>

Selth, Andrew 2007, *Chinese military bases in Burma: the explosion of a myth*, Regional Outlook Paper no. 10, Griffith Asia Institute, viewed 20 August 2008, <http://www.griffith.edu.au/__data/assets/pdf_file/0018/18225/regional-outlook-andrew-selth.pdf>

ENDNOTES

[1] For an expression of this view, albeit a highly nuanced one, see Desai (2003), especially pp. 17–18. See also Gordon (1995:2).

[2] Aiyar (2006), quoting Professor Ma Jiali of CICIR.

[3] All trade data are from the Indian Ministry of Commerce web site, viewed 28 August 2008, < http://commerce.nic.in/eidb/iecn.asp>

[4] On the exaggerated claims of Chinese bases, see Selth (2007).

[5] Copy in possession of the author (no publication details) entitled *Indian Maritime Doctrine INBR [Indian Naval Book of Reference]* 8, with a foreword by the Chief of Naval Staff, Admiral Singh, dated April 2004. The document appears to have been released to the public in 2005. For the quoted passage, see page 69.

[6] Originally in Gordon (2006:40).

Chapter 6

The rise of Chindia and its impact on the world system

Zhao Gancheng

'Chindia' is a newly created term that is being debated in China and India. When Indian politician Jairam Ramesh coined the term a few years ago, the Congress Party was still in opposition. [1] Anyone engaged in China studies for any length of time would perceive the potential for India and China if the two nations could address their existing problems. The term therefore points to a future in which the two Asian giants can produce a new force in the international system. That force would presumably impact on the balance of the system, simply because of the size, population and material capacity of the two nations, especially if they were combined, which is precisely the implication of the term 'Chindia'. Can these two states combine? If they really address their bilateral problems, will they, as a combined force, challenge the current system?

The international system is often perceived as an organism that aspires to achieve a balance of power among its principal constituents. The post-Cold War period has witnessed a unique power equation, with the United States at the top, leading to a new equilibrium, but one whose stability and longevity have been debated heatedly. By common consent, equilibrium is built on the balance of power between dominant powers or blocs, as was the case during the Cold War. The absolute power of the United States in the international system seems, however, to have created an unseen equilibrium, which could maintain the stability of the system on the one hand, but which does not allow any other potential powers to challenge US dominance on the other. This is what the US global strategy is supposed to be about. In this context, the rise of China and India could present an intolerable challenge to the United States. Let's look into this issue by examining the debate about the US-dominated equilibrium before discussing China–India ties.

I

First of all, achieving systemic equilibrium can be supported on moral grounds. Despite the fact that all nation-states in the international system try to maximise their interests—and that this endeavour could readily lead to conflicts—few theories see conflict as a good thing. Systemic equilibrium is supposed to reduce the possibility of conflicts among nations and, therefore, the debate is not about whether equilibrium should be sustained, but what kind of equilibrium. Different nations had different opinions due to their respective interests, which was evident during the Cold War. For instance, the bipolar system was able to maintain basic stability in the international system, thus reflecting general equilibrium. Jawaharlal Nehru, however, the founding father of modern India, found so little to appreciate in this equilibrium that he and other leaders of developing countries who had no interest in joining either bloc looked for a 'third way' by establishing the Non-Alignment Movement, which was, by its nature, an attempt—though not necessarily successful—to create a new equilibrium, or to break down the general equilibrium.

When equilibrium is determined by the balance of power between the dominant players, those who do not have power might disagree with the situation, but it does not change the reality. Furthermore, in many cases, they could even benefit from the general equilibrium, because it helps maintain stability. They are thus described as free riders—a phenomenon that is discerned in many geopolitical games. India and China have have experienced this role. During the Cold War, even though India signed a security treaty with the Soviets, it remained neutral in East–West confrontations. In the meantime, the featured stability of the international system saw India acquire a favourable position from which to look for assistance from the two blocs when a crisis in its national security came up. [2] As for China, its late leader Deng Xiaoping was fully aware of the opportunities resulting from systemic stability long before the end of the Cold War. Deng's case for 'reform and opening up' stressed the importance of a stable environment to China's development and he argued that the Cold War stalemate provided that stability. Deng's new thinking thus paved the way for the adjustment of China's foreign policy.

Equilibrium thus presents two features. One is that it is not broken by those who are dissatisfied but who do not have the necessary power, and the other is that it can benefit many members of the international system, including those who are not satisfied with it. This point might contain some important implications when one considers the rise of China and India and their impact on the world system.

While equilibrium might be a universal feature of the international system, the dynamics inherent in the system will nevertheless bring about change, because the power of nations, especially the major players, changes. Therefore, judging from systemic evolution, the prospect that equilibrium could be broken exists, and the main driving force stems from nations' pursuit of their own interests, rendering moral judgment of the system less relevant. In other words, maintenance of the existing equilibrium and pressures to move to a new equilibrium result from the necessity to defend one's own interests. The key is whether the players have sufficient power to break the equilibrium and, further, whether this will benefit or hurt the interests of the players who have such power. It is precisely on this point that the rise of China and India could result in important new variables. Insofar as the power of China and India is concerned, they do not have the capabilities to alter the equilibrium, but the dominant power of the current system is not likely to estimate the prospect only by judging what China and India have and do now, but by what they will have and do in the future. This is the basis of the US strategic vision that focuses on prevention. One of the United States' preventive measures is, for instance, to make countries such as China and India 'stakeholders'. [3] In the US view, the countries that can challenge the existing system have to be integrated into it, thus preserving the dominance of the United States. From the American viewpoint, the existing power equation is rational, and the United States should do what it can to maintain and preserve equilibrium. It is therefore imperative to study whether the current equilibrium is desirable.

II

By common consent, equilibrium is realised through a sustainable balance of power. When ideology played a decisive role during the Cold War, East–West confrontation brought about a basic structure in the international system that was, in general, stable. The collapse of the Soviet Union—the so-called 'end of history'—ended this, with neo-liberalism prevailing. This does not, however, change the fact that equilibrium is necessary for international stability. In China, the debate turned out to be about the possible multi-polarisation of international politics, until the terrorist attacks of 11 September 2001 that saw the birth of neo-conservatism. Also, as a result, 'the clash of civilisations' seems to have been revived. The new form of confrontation, however, has only an ideological shell. Trying to make religion the real root of conflict in the post-Cold War ear is difficult, and the real issue is whether a new equilibrium under US dominance is possible. When the United States uses its power to strike its enemies, what it defends are US interests rather than religion and the maintenance of what the United States perceives as the rational equilibrium. Those forces that attack the United States in a non-traditional way do not constitute a real power to change the structure or create a new balance of power in the international system. That is why such confrontation could be described only as asymmetrical conflict. Non-traditional forces do not constitute elements decisive enough to change the fundamental structure of the international system.

The current system is thus characterised by a lack of significant power to parallel that of the United States. Because of this, debate has sprung up about whether the current system represents real equilibrium. By traditional assessment, it would be difficult to define the current system—with one absolute power—as equilibrium. Further, by a similar assessment, a system without equilibrium might not provide stability. The reality, however, seems different from the assessment—that is, the US-dominated system does not show much instability. Instead, because of its huge capability, the United States tries to build up a global framework with bilateral arrangements as its pillars. Needless to say, the United States takes the lead in such a system. The US approach has been well practised in the Asia-Pacific region and has won support particularly, of course, from its allies. The approach is now extending itself to South and Central Asia. As US President, George W. Bush, said during his visit to South Asia in March 2006, the United States wanted to help India rise to the status of a global power. President Bush did not say what kind of global power the United States wanted India to be, but it was certainly not one on par with the United States or one that enjoyed regional hegemony. The United States is unlikely to prefer to share its dominant position in the international system with any other power. Whether the US approach is successful, at least from the US perspective, the current system presents a favourable equilibrium, and the United States does not want to see any other real or potential power bloc to balance against it.

The issue here is whether other big powers such as China and India will accept such a US-dominated equilibrium. The answer lies in how they evaluate their own position and role in the international system and, more importantly, the judgment of their own interests.

III

Regarding the position and role of China and India in the international system, the first point could be relevant to their development vis-à-vis the systemic rules. The argument is that the rapid economic development of both countries cannot be separated from the basic stability of the international system—in other words, in terms of their economic development, they have benefited from the current system. Therefore, despite the fact that neither China nor India would agree with the unilateral behaviour of the United States in many instances, they do not have an oppositional position against the current international system, even though it is dominated by the United States. On the contrary, China and India stress the importance of integrating themselves into the system. This perhaps reflects, indirectly, a current preference to accept the system, and to distinguish between opposing unilateralism and objecting to the system.

Second, neither China nor India pursues a policy of breaking the current equilibrium as its priority because the consequences would bring about instability, even chaos, which could do enormous damage to their interests as they are in their respective economic take-off stages. As developing powers in the international system, they cannot be satisfied with the reality that they do not have much to say in nearly all the global institutions, but fundamentally changing the system is neither within their capacity nor in their interests. According to the principle of maximising one's interests, China and India would prefer a stable system rather than risking the instability that might flow from challenging it.

Third, China and India are rising powers and they certainly want to have a more significant position in the international system. In other words, with the increase of their capabilities, their dissatisfaction with the reality could be expressed in ways that are not yet obvious. Whether it will change the structure of the international system remains unknown. Precisely because of this uncertainty, the dominant power in today's world has to be ready to deal with any possible changes that could hurt its interests. In spite of the fact that neither China nor India really intends to challenge the international system, and that they both want to integrate themselves peacefully into it, the dominant power could determine its strategy on the basis of the 'worst-case scenario'. That is logical, just as China and India do not start from the 'best-case scenario' when they think about their interactions with the international system. This type of interaction could easily lead to the 'prisoner's dilemma'. While there is no confrontational element in the situation, the issue is that the rise of developing powers could change the international system and hurt the interests of others, especially the dominant power.

Moreover, if the manner in which the developing powers can change the system is not clear, even less clear is how China and India will deal with each other in the years to come. Discussing the impact of Chindia on the world system, one could put both countries in a similar category as a common variable, but this does not mean that the two countries share the same view of the system, nor does it mean they have already accepted each other completely or have solved their bilateral problems. One therefore needs to look into the real implications of the simultaneous rise of the two countries, and what is the essence of Chindia in a bilateral sense.

IV

Historically, China and India have found it difficult to handle each other's sensitivities. Because the two Asian powers are neighbours, there is a geopolitical element in their perceptions of one another. This problem existed when they were weak and it remains now that they are becoming more powerful. In fact, Nehru perceived it half a century ago. In November 1950, after China's army had been deployed in Tibet, Nehru wrote a note to his cabinet ministers in which he argued for a non-confrontational approach in their debates. Having said that India could not afford a conflict with China over Tibet and that India could not 'save Tibet' even if it had decided to fight China, Nehru pointed out that 'as two Asian powers with…[an expansionist] tendency, it would be difficult for them to deal with their relations'. [4] It is clear that Nehru's view could have stemmed from a geopolitical calculation. In the history of international relations, there are too many examples of difficulties in relations between two big neighbours.

In 1954, when Chinese Premier Zhou Enlai first visited New Delhi, the two sides determined to initiate the 'Five Principles of Peaceful Coexistence', which laid the foundation for sustainable development of the bilateral relationship. It was indeed a very idealistic framework for the two Asian giants, but the differences between the two sides in geopolitical interests that later events exposed reflected the fragility of the framework. If this was the situation when the two countries were very weak, what about now, when the two sides are rising rapidly in the international community?

Regarding the rise of Chindia, there are other things to be considered—and one is the two countries' comparative position in terms of economic power. Clearly, China's economic totality and growth rate exceed those of India. China's economic reform started more than 10 years earlier than India's, and, in the 15 years after India launched its economic reform, China's average annual growth rate was still much higher than that of India. These two factors indicate that, in terms of the general level of economic advancement, China has gone far ahead, whether in terms of gross domestic product (GDP) now, or its prospects for the future. [5] Even if India can sustain average annual growth of 8 per cent for the next 10 years, most predictions estimate that China will be able to match or exceed that rate. [6] That would make the disparity between China and India even larger in the years to come. In terms of trade, the disparity is even bigger, with China's total trade volume reaching US$1.7 trillion in 2006—making it the third-largest trading state in the world—while that of India reached about US$300 billion. These figures make the case for the simultaneous rise of China and India seem less convincing.

The rise of Chindia is a hot topic in the international media, which also focuses on comparison. India's potential is stressed, however, because India is believed to enjoy many advantages that China does not have, such as a multi-party political system, a fully competitive business environment, an independent judicial system, and so on. While India's democracy is appreciated, the more important point seems to lie at the strategic level. India attracts attention from the Western media not so much because of its economic power, but for its potential overall status in Asia vis-à-vis that of China. In Washington, this is elaborated as a counterweight against the rise of China. At this point, the simultaneous rise of China and India would be treated as a variable in the game of balance of power, for the two Asian giants have a number of unsolved problems and it is likely that India, like the Western powers, does not want to see a hegemonic China. Such a perception is perhaps well accepted in India, but not in the sense that India should follow a containment strategy; rather, India would like to use it for its own agenda. The worries that Western powers have about China are not a negative element as far as India's development is concerned. From the Chinese perspective, the key is, then, how to look at the rise of Chindia and whether it is a viable concept.

V

It should be clear in the first place that the simultaneous rise of China and India does not mean that they are in similar stages of development, or possess similar material capabilities. Compared with other developing countries, the rapid development of China and India—as states with large territories and populations—could impose significant change on the international system. The disparity between them is therefore less important than the prospect that their growth could have implications for the equilibrium of the international system. The rise of China and India is therefore discussed as the collective, Chindia, because China's development has already attracted extensive attention and India's rise, although starting later, has also shown strong momentum. More importantly, for more than half a century after World War II, China and India languished in very weak positions in the international system before finally rising up to the stage at which they could be defined as developing powers. Facing the Western-dominated system, they are in quite similar positions and are therefore likely to exert similar pressures on the system as they develop.

Bilaterally speaking, there is a historical legacy of severe and unresolved problems, but this does not render China and India hostile in the context of the international system. After their border conflict in 1962, the two countries had a painful period dealing with each other, but neither side was disposed to expand the dispute beyond the bilateral context. For instance, India never changed its position in support of China reclaiming its seat in the United Nations, nor did India regard China as an enemy in the international system because of the border conflict alone. By the same token, China was never hostile to the Non-Alignment Movement, which was founded by India with other nations. On the contrary, China fully supported developing countries including India and their great attempt to look for the 'third way'. In other words, although the 1962 war cast a heavy shadow on the bilateral relationship and changed the perceptions of the two peoples towards each other, it did not shift their position in the international system. Their status as developing countries decided their policies and behaviour within the system.

Now that China and India have acquired great momentum and are recognised as rising powers, this historical lesson is significant in policy making. One could argue that, even if they are not able to solve the boundary issue in the years ahead, this is unlikely to impose a significantly negative impact on their respective behaviour towards each other within the international system. This is precisely what has been observed in their policy regarding the other side, including India's participation in East Asian regional integration and China's engagement as an observer in the South Asia Association of Regional Cooperation

(SAARC). Despite the lingering suspicions stemming from their historical legacy, neither side has shifted its support in regional and global affairs. That could be seen as a result of the systemic constraints imposed on their behaviour, but such constraints are positive insofar as the rise of Chindia is concerned, because they will promote their cooperation as strategic partners.

In addition, the features of the current international system provide China and India with even more common ground. The supremacy of the United States has led to a significant imbalance of power in the system, and thus to incipient disequilibrium. To correct it requires a new formation of the power equation to incorporate other comprehensive powers. The rise of Chindia attracts attention precisely because it presents some uncertainties. No-one knows in what form China and India will become world-class nations, or even whether they will achieve this status. The potential their development has shown, however, and the status they have acquired in the international system indicate the possibility that they could change the fundamental structure of the system. Because of that uncertainty, the United States has listed them as rising powers at a strategic crossroads. After 11 September 2001, the Bush Administration stressed the importance of China and India in US global strategy, noting that the United States had to take them into account in its strategic thinking. American awareness of the potential challenges associated with the rise of Chindia is beyond doubt, even though, from the American perspective, their strategic significance can be differentiated, with India as a strategic, democratic partner.

VI

The commonality of China and India could help explain their impact on the world system, but it should not lead to a conclusion that they will retain their similarities and remain consistent within the international system. Negative elements in bilateral relations do play a role, and how to reduce them is a challenge.

First of all, concepts make the difference. In China–India relations, concepts such as 'hostile enemy' or 'good neighbour', competitor or collaborator and rival or partner are not clearly defined. In the past half-century, these concepts have come up, depending on specific situations. After the border conflict, for example, the concept of the other as the enemy prevailed for a long time, and, during and even after the Cold War, the concept of rivalry was applied despite the genuine progress of rapprochement. At a press conference in March 2004, Chinese Premier Wen Jiabao argued that, in more than 2000 years of exchanges between China and India, 99.9 per cent had been friendly, with conflict and tension prevailing for only a very short time. He thus strongly suggested a forward-looking vision for both sides. [7] Here, the Premier might have been referring to the importance of changing perceptions of each other. While the unpleasant episode was short indeed, [8] it might not be easily forgotten, because it took place not very long ago. More importantly, the unpleasant episode stemmed from geopolitical ideas, and they might not disappear with the rise of Chindia. It is therefore crucial for both sides to change their visions and perceptions and not allow notions of geopolitical rivalry to prevail.

Second, the disparity of China's and India's positions in the international system due to material capacity and the pace of growth could create new problems. For instance, in 2005, when efforts by the G4 (Germany, Japan, India and Brazil) to reform the UN Security Council failed, Indian media and academia alike presented lots of views, some of which attributed the failure to China's opposition and accused China of being unwilling to see India's rise as a global power. China was thus put into the category of a status-quo power rather than a rising power like India. This is not true, however, the key does not lie in how biased Indian media might have been or in the historical legacy. It is the disparity of their respective status in the international system that leads to different perceptions of interests when a crucial issue comes up. The same was true when India responded coldly to China's request for a seat in SAARC in the first Sino–Indian strategic dialogue in January 2005 in Delhi, though India finally accepted China as an observer at the SAARC Dhaka Summit in November the same year. That incident shows that India might not be comfortable sharing a forum in which it leads with a neighbour more powerful than itself. One could argue that the disparity between the two developing powers could lead to suspicion that the weaker party would regard the stronger party as a source of pressure or even an obstacle.

Third, in the political arena, there is another kind of disparity that favours India: the Western-dominated system apparently accepts democratic India more easily than it does China. For instance, in the US strategic blueprint, although China and India are identified as 'the big powers at a strategic crossroads', the American assessment of India tends to stress the positive. As President Bush said before and during his state visit to India in March 2006, the United States appreciated India's multicultural character and democracy and saw India as a strategic partner. The United States wanted to help India become a global power, though the President did not say what kind of global power the United States wanted India to be. With that appreciation, the United States decided to exempt India from the principles that guided its nuclear non-proliferation policy. [9] Compared with China, India apparently has a more favourable status. This political disparity might make India believe that it enjoys some sort of superiority, and to judge China as Western countries do. That would reduce the commonality of the two as developing countries in the international system, the impact of which would be negative as far as the rise of Chindia is concerned.

To sum up, the rise of China and India contains both positive and negative elements. For the purposes of this chapter, the issue is how the trajectory of these two states might affect the equilibrium of the international system.

VII

The existing international system is characterised by the sole superpower's dominance, presenting a unique equilibrium. It is unique because it differs from any other kind of equilibrium in history; however, it still has the general characteristic of maintaining basic stability. Historical experience since the birth of the nation-state suggests that the rise of other powers is likely to break such equilibrium and return the system to normal equilibrium. This development could be the default scenario for the impact of Chindia's rise on the international system, but it might not be something the current dominant power would like to see. Whatever its prospects, the United States is likely to do what it can to prevent it or delay its progress. The dominant power's logic lies in a vision that any attempt to restore the international system to 'normal' equilibrium will constitute a challenge to the United States, that normal equilibrium will hurt American interests, and therefore the United States should seek to prevent it from taking place. The two logics seem to be in conflict: first, the rise of Chindia will shatter the equilibrium of the international system; and second, the return to normal equilibrium will hurt the interests of the dominant power. This chapter tries to argue that the rise of Chindia might not destroy equilibrium. On the contrary, China and India will try their best to maintain equilibrium, thus promoting stability in the system—not because maintaining equilibrium is politically or morally correct, but because it fits their interests. In the process of resuming normal equilibrium in the international system, the rise of Chindia will not necessarily hurt US interests, and it could even promote American leadership in the world system in the years ahead.

That the rise of Chindia does not put at risk the equilibrium of the international system is based on three arguments. First, the equilibrium of current system is abnormal. It is a sort of absolute pyramid equilibrium with American power far superior to that of any other country or bloc. In historical terms, it is a temporary phenomenon, created by specific conditions, but this does not mean that the world can be expressed only in this way. In the meantime, the US-dominated system nevertheless maintains general stability, which in turn provides crucial conditions for China and India to pursue their own development. As Chinese leaders have reiterated, peace and development are the critical features of today's world. That definition is consistent with the equilibrium of the US-dominated system. Given this context, as long as other countries do not deliberately challenge the US-dominated system, with the rise of other nations that are qualified with fundamental conditions as big powers, the international system will shift from abnormal to normal equilibrium. If the rise of China and India does reach such a level as to contribute to a new power equation, it will only return the international system to its most familiar format, in which the big powers will present a new power structure, leading to a relative pyramid equilibrium. More importantly, economic globalisation has increased the pace of integration between nations, and interdependence between big powers is dramatically increasing. It is thus safe to predict that challenging systemic equilibrium will become an increasingly difficult option for China or India, and maintaining it will much better serve their interests.

Second, the rise of Chindia will be a gradual process. No-one really knows how long it will take for the two countries to reach such a level as to constitute a change in the equilibrium of the international system. Today, it is generally agreed that a nation's capacity is decided by comprehensive national power, not by GDP alone. At this point, China and India have a long way to go before becoming genuine global powers. In that long process, both have similar incentives and face similar constraints. Just as they cannot become successful overnight, there is nothing that can stop their development completely. In the meantime, the systemic force of the international regime will integrate them into the system gradually, and dampen any instincts to favour a different system. China's insistence on joining the World Trade Organisation (WTO) and India's painful efforts to achieve recognition from the international community as a legitimate nuclear-weapon state constitute cases in point. Whether or not they become global powers, their interests will drive them to integrate with the international system politically and economically, becoming stakeholders rather than challengers. The deeper they are integrated, the higher will be the stakes, and the stronger will be their interests in maintaining systemic stability rather than risking change to the system.

Third, the rise of Chindia is constrained not only by the dominant power in the current system, but by bilateral elements. While Sino–Indian relations have improved in the past couple of years, they are far from presenting a common force in the international system. At the conceptual and policy levels, there is still much inconsistency and divergence between the two countries. Moreover, it can be safely predicted that this will endure, and could even expand as a result of the disparity in interests and status. The higher the inconsistencies, the weaker the phenomenon of Chindia will remain and the smaller will be its impact on the prevailing international system. That will not be a destructive element as far as systemic stability is concerned, though it will be negative from the standpoint of their bilateral relationship.

In conclusion, the simultaneous rise of the two developing powers, which have various differences and difficulties, is an unprecedented phenomenon for the international system. Both powers share the ambition for and expectation of securing proper status in the system. Judged by their behaviour and policy, it could be said that both are expecting to be accepted as a global power in the US-dominated system. Their rapid growth is providing an increasingly solid basis for this expectation. In the meantime, their development is based on stability of the system, and they are thus the beneficiaries and keepers of systemic stability, which means that they will not challenge US dominance, because such a challenge will be destructive to stability. At this point, one could argue that China and India have already passed the crossroads, and are now in the process of integrating themselves into the international system by peaceful means through their development momentum. Their growth favours equilibrium of the international system and the role of the dominant power, as is demonstrated in their increasingly mature relationship with the United States in economic and trade exchanges, political interactions, security dialogues and so on. [10] The trends and prospects in this regard are quite positive, which will also help promote China–India relations. In final analysis, the rise of Chindia is not and cannot be a zero-sum game either to the international system or to Sino–Indian relations.

Reference

Shandilya, Charan 1999, *India–China Relations*, Supriya Art Press, India.

ENDNOTES

[1] Ramesh's book on Chindia was published in 2003, and the Congress won the general election in 2004. Ramesh himself joined the cabinet to take the post of State Minister for the Ministry of Commerce.

[2] The 1962 border conflict with China provided such a case, when India received support from the United States and the Soviet Union, further isolating China from the international community. Some Chinese scholars even argue that China's unilateral cease-fire during the war was partially attributed to this fact, despite China's military victory.

[3] The term was used by former Undersecretary Zollick to refer to the status of China. In the meantime, India's position is also changing fast. Since 2002, when the Bush Administration issued its first National Security Strategy, China and India were referred to in all US policy reviews and reports as rising powers that the United States should deal with cautiously, and they were further described as 'the nations at a strategic crossroads'.

[4] Prime Minister Jawaharlal Nehru's Note on China and Tibet (dated 18 November 1950, in Sardar Patel's Correspondence, pp. 342–47), indirectly quoted from Shandilya (1999:Appendix II).

[5] China's GDP in 2006 was about US$2.5 trillion, according to China's Central Bureau of Statistics—almost three times that of India, which produced about US$860 billion.

[6] After coming to power in May 2004, Prime Minister Manmohan Singh first set a growth target of 6–6.5 per cent for the next 5–10 years. He believed it would be a realistic goal. There are signs, however, that the Indian economic designer has upgraded his target. For instance, at an annual conference of the Asia Society of the United States in Mumbai on 18 March 2006, the Prime Minister delivered a keynote speech arguing that India's growth rate could be sustained at 9–10 per cent annually. Real growth in 2005, however, was 7.9 per cent, and 2006 saw a jump to 9.2 per cent, but there was debate about whether the Indian economy had been overheated.

[7] Premier Wen Jiabao's response at a press conference (*People's Daily*, Beijing, 24 March 2004).

[8] The Sino–Indian border conflict started on 20 October 1962, and China announced a unilateral cease-fire after only one month on 20 November the same year.

[9] The United States and India signed the civilian nuclear cooperation agreement during President Bush's visit to Delhi on 2 March 2006, which would have a significant impact on the non-proliferation regime because it indicated US recognition of India not only as a de facto but as a nearly de jure nuclear-weapon

state while India could maintain its status as a non-signatory of the nuclear Non-Proliferation Treaty (NPT). Secretary of State, Condoleezza Rice, provided two major reasons for this policy: India's nuclear weapon program was legal, as it had not signed the NPT, and India had a good record of non-proliferation. A huge debate followed, because the United States' new criteria might not help prevent other states going nuclear.

[10] With the United States, India has a defence dialogue and China conducts strategic dialogue in security and economic areas. All these mechanisms are regularised and institutionalised, reflecting a common desire between the three parties to seek better understanding on their strategic visions.

Chapter 7

Sino–Russian relations in the 'post'-Putin era

Yu Bin

Introduction: guns and games of August

August 2008 was quite eventful for Russia and China, as well as for their bilateral relations. Against all the odds (pro-Tibet protests and the devastating Sichuan earthquake in the second quarter), the twenty-ninth summer Olympic Games in Beijing opened and concluded with extravagant ceremonies and a record 51 gold medals for the host country. Shortly before the opening ceremony of the Beijing Olympics on 8 August, Georgia's attacks against South Ossetia and Abkhazia—two separatist regions of Georgia—led to a massive military response from Russia, a five-day war and Russia's recognition of the independence of the two disputed regions. Thus, the August guns and games brought the two strategic partners—China and Russia—back to the world stage, though through separate paths and with lasting geo-strategic implications for themselves and the rest of the world. One consequence of the Georgian–Russian war is that China's 'neutrality' is widely seen as a crisis in China's strategic relations with Russia.

For many in the West, China's cautious neutrality is a departure from, if not a betrayal of, its strategic partnership with Russia. China's 'strategic ambiguity' regarding the Georgian–Russian conflict has been the focus of the media and pundits ('China cannot back Russia in Georgia crisis: analysts', *AFP*, 28 August 2008, <http://afp.google.com/article/ALeqM5guAa5jCMIWCy-SMYWZY4-0451p5w>; Pronina and Alison 2008; Manthorpe 2008). Many observers tend to highlight the differences and conflicts of interest between China and Russia. China's move is seen as an effort to maximise its interests while Russia is going through difficult times with the West. China's own problem with Taiwan is perhaps one major reason why China cannot publicly support Russia on the South Ossetian issue (Hua 2008b). Most Central Asian states are also said to have reservations about Russia's policy due to the large number of ethnic Russians living in this 'near abroad' area and their cautious neutrality also shows the growing influence of China in this sphere of traditional Russian influence. These apparent differences between Russia and its Shanghai Cooperation Organisation (SCO) partners are indications, accordingly, of the fragility of this regional security group, and of the fact that many of its members simply dream different dreams while sleeping in the same 'bed' as Moscow (Hua 2008a). Georgia also lost no time thanking China for not taking sides in its most recent conflict with Russia (Hua 2008c).

This interpretation of reactions to the war in Georgia misreads the current state of the Sino–Russian relationship and lacks adequate understanding of its depth, breadth and complexity. As a result, the Western perception of the Beijing–Moscow relationship has swung from one of 'threat' against the West before the South Ossetian crisis, to the current premature celebration of the relationship's demise. Neither view is correct: both focus on the superficial and discount more substantive considerations.

This misperception of the Sino–Russian relationship took shape when the world was overwhelmed by dynamics and disorder in the second half of 2008. In East Asia, Pyongyang was finally on a path to de-nuclearisation after repeated threats to reverse this process; Japanese politics continued to fluctuate as Prime Minister Yasuo Fukuda was replaced by Taro Aso, who was far more hawkish than his predecessor on Japan's militarist past; and, coming on top of the successful Beijing Olympics, a 'taikonaut' from the People's Republic of China conducted that country's first space walk. Beyond East Asia and in addition to the US–Russian confrontation over South Ossetia, America's war on terror remained open-ended (now being conducted in the three separate theatres of Iraq, Afghanistan and Pakistan) six years after the Bush Doctrine of pre-emption made its debut. Moreover, the financial tsunami—originating in the United States—left no nation untouched and heightened the sense of a world far less secure than before. As Americans voted to put the first black president in the White House, the world's strongest power was losing influence among its friends and foes.

The nature and dynamics of the Moscow–Beijing strategic partnership, therefore, need to be comprehended within the broader context of a rapidly changing region and world. Specifically, this chapter will examine the Sino–Russian relationship by asking the following questions: what have been the patterns and trajectory of the Sino–Russian relationship since the normalisation of relations 20 years ago (in 1989)? How do the features of the current bilateral relationship compare with those in earlier periods? What are the prospects for Russian–Sino relations under Russian President, Dmitry Medvedev, and his 'copilot', Vladimir Putin? What are the areas of bilateral relations where cooperation outweighs competition? How will this relationship adapt to the ever-changing domestic and international environment? One could go on to ask how 'strategic' the current 'strategic partnership' really is. How and why did China opt for a posture of 'strategic ambiguity' over the conflict between Russia and the West? At the operational level, how will Moscow and Beijing continue and improve this 'best ever' relationship?

For this purpose, among others, this study begins with an overview of bilateral relations in the past 30 years. This is followed by an analysis of the nature of the two countries' 'strategic partnership'. With this in mind, recent developments in their bilateral ties will be examined, including Medvedev's May 2008 visit to Beijing, China–Russia interactions during and after the recent Russian–Georgian war, and their implications for relations between Russia and China.

Putin's eight years and beyond

By the end of Putin's presidency in March 2008, Sino–Russian relations had experienced almost two decades of stability since the historic normalisation of relations in 1989. [1] Few people at the time expected that the two countries would be able to live normally with one another for such a sustained period in the wake of three decades of intense rivalry across political, economic and military areas.

Under Putin, Russia and China managed to deepen and broaden their strategic partnership. As a result, bilateral relations have been transformed from the worst security nightmare to one of common strategic vision for regional and global stability; from a position of ideological rivalry within the communist world to coexistence between the two largest states on the Eurasian continent, with entirely different cultural and political systems; from an absence of any meaningful economic intercourse to rising trade relations (worth $48.2 billion in 2007); and from sharing the longest fortified border to a relationship of stability and flourishing economic interaction. In the past decade of their strategic partnership, the two continental powers have been taking joint action on various multilateral issues—including the United Nations, the SCO and the North Korean and Iranian nuclear talks—promoting a 'fair and rational world order' based on sovereignty, equality, dialogue and a new international security mechanism ('China–Russia joint statement regarding the international order of the 21st century', *Xinhua*, 1 July 2005).

About the time of the Russian presidential election in March 2008, 'continuity' was the buzzword for Russian domestic and foreign policies. Beijing, too, expected continuity for its bilateral relations and Chinese leaders were eager to invite Medvedev for an official visit as soon as the dust of the presidential election settled.

How strategic are Sino–Russian relations?

There has been, of late, a proliferation of so-called 'strategic' relationships among nation-states. China and Russia, for example, apply it to interstate relations vital for their national interests. [2] Such a relationship essentially means that the two sides attach great importance to their bilateral ties and share a strong willingness to commit to the enhancement of these ties. At the operational and functional level, it is largely a pragmatic approach to interact with one another on the basis of equality and with considerable freedom of action. According to Chinese analyst Cao Xin (2007), Beijing and Moscow conduct 'strategic coordination without alliance and [a] close relationship without excessive dependence'. A strategic partnership with these qualities is perhaps the result of the long and sometimes painful learning experience in the second half of the twentieth century: bilateral relations between Moscow and Beijing oscillated between excessive dependence (particularly of China on Russia) and almost no interaction. What is essential for today's Russian–Sino relationship is the absence of ideological factors and border disputes, which constantly besieged the two nations until the early 1990s. Moreover, there is a willingness to develop the more cooperative aspects of their relationship while managing issues of disagreement and competition.

In contrast, in the West, the term 'strategic relationship' is usually reserved for relations between members of a formal 'alliance', within which junior members are expected to come to a consensus with the leading state (the United States). Deviation from Washington's view is possible, but not encouraged. A typical case of this is the United States' fury over French and German opposition to its 2003 Iraq invasion, hence the famous dichotomy enunciated by Donald Rumsfield of the 'Old' versus the 'New' Europe ('Outrage at "old Europe" remarks', *BBC*, 23 January 2003, <http://news.bbc.co.uk/2/hi/europe/2687403.stm>). Regarding China, Washington has resisted characterising the relationship as 'strategic'. Instead, the United States insisted that a de facto 'strategic dialogue' between the two nations at the deputy foreign minister level, on 1–2 August 2005 in Beijing, was 'senior dialogue'.[3]

Regardless of the official pronouncement of their relationship as being the 'best ever', or the more cautious depiction of it as a 'marriage of convenience', the Sino–Russian strategic partnership since 1996 has essentially been a normal and stable relationship. This is substantially different to their highly volatile relations during the 'honeymoon' period (1949–60) and the period of hostility (1960–89), when problems and disagreements were either ignored or allowed to explode.

By no means should the Sino–Russian strategic relationship be idealised. At the operational level, it is a complex interactive process with elements of cooperation and competition at all levels and across all issues. Given the huge differences in their political, cultural, religious and socioeconomic developmental levels, the fact that the two countries' often have different perceptions of the same issue is natural if not desirable.

The complexities of their strategic relationship also mean that Moscow and Beijing are interrelated through a multidimensional (political, diplomatic, economic, security, societal, and so on) and multilevel (top leaders, governmental agencies and ordinary people) interface thanks to the broadening, deepening and institutionalisation of bilateral relations since normalisation in 1989. Within this web of interactions, policymaking and implementation may or may not lead to desirable outcomes. High-level trust and strategic cooperation, for example, might not preclude economic competition. Growing economic transactions frequently lead to more friction. Meanwhile, ordinary citizens do not know, let alone like, each other.

To a certain extent, the current strategic partnership between Beijing and Moscow may or may not be a reliable barometer for the future. For one thing, the current state of bilateral relations developed and was enhanced at a time when Russia was weak and disoriented after the disintegration of the Soviet empire. Now Russia is on its way back—not necessarily to the levels it attained as the core of the USSR, but to its traditional status as a major power on the Eurasian continent. China will—perhaps more than anyone else—have to deal with and adjust to such a changing reality.

It is within this context of their strategic partnership—featuring pragmatism, normalcy and complexity—that post-Putin era Sino–Russian relations are examined below.

The ordinariness and extraordinariness of Medvedev's visit

Perhaps more than anything else, President Medvedev's state visit to China on 23–24 May 2008 underscored the three 'Ss' for the two nations: strategic partnership, its stability and sustainability. It also means that Moscow and Beijing have managed to achieve policy stability and continuity through three leadership transitions: Boris Yeltsin, Putin and Medvedev for Russia; Deng Xiaoping, Jiang Zemin and Hu Jintao for China.

No matter how presidential Medvedev's appearance in Beijing was, his summit with his Chinese counterpart was considerably discounted in the West as routine, unsubstantial [4] and, of course, taking place in Putin's ubiquitous shadow (Erlanger 2008). This parallels a new trend in the West's Russia bashing, which has moved from mystifying Putin's 'soul' (Ignatius 2007) to minimising and even mocking his successor. The growing conflicts of interest between Russia and China—real or perceived—over various issues such as trade, energy, military sales, and so on, are also said to be eroding the strategic quality of relations between the two Eurasian giants (Marcus 2008; 'Chinese media reports only good things about Russia's president visit', *VOA*, 29 May 2008, <www.6park.com/news/messages/83390.html>).

While such assessments might touch on some of the technicalities of Moscow–Beijing ties, they nonetheless miss some important aspects of the evolving, deepening and broadening relations between the two largest nations on the Eurasian continent.

Perhaps more than anything else, Medvedev's two-day visit to China was to reaffirm the continuity and stability of Russia's China policy under the new president, with or without Putin's influence. In the past eight years, China gained considerable experience working with Putin when Medvedev served as head of Putin's 2000 presidential election campaign headquarters, as presidential chief of staff (2003–05) and as Deputy Prime Minister (2005–08). This time, the Chinese side would have taken a closer look at Medvedev as Russian President and at how he and Putin coordinated policies towards Beijing. In the longer run, Medvedev will have to put his own stamp on how to approach China and certain policy adjustments might be unavoidable. In the meantime, China wants to avoid surprises. [5] This is why China took the initiative to invite Medvedev as soon as he was officially elected Russian President in March. [6]

It so happened that China was Medvedev's first foreign visit outside the Commonwealth of Independent States (CIS); he was also the first foreign head of state to visit China after the Sichuan earthquake. The Russian military mounted the largest international relief effort in its history (Hongjian et al. 2008) when it sent a rescue team, which was among the first to arrive in the quake area, and was the only foreign search team to find any survivors. Once in China, Medvedev authorised additional assistance (eight cargo planes carrying 250 tonnes of goods) (Hongjian 2008; 'Medvedev orders more humanitarian aid to quake-stricken China', *Itar-Tass*, 24 May 2008). Before leaving China, Medvedev also suggested that Russia would host summer camps for dozens of Chinese children who had suffered as a result of the devastating earthquake ('Summer camps in Sverdlovsk region to receive Chinese children', *Itar-Tass*, 29 May 2008; 'Chinese children from quake-hit Sichuan to rehabilitate in Kemerovo', *Itar-Tass*, 7 June 2008). The real number of Chinese children going to Russia, however, quickly snowballed to more than 1000 as various Russian resort campuses competed to host Chinese children ('Russian President's representative visits students from China's quake-hit Sichuan Province', *Xinhua*, 26 July 2008). [7] The 'ordinariness' of Medvedev's first official visit to China as president assumed some degree of extraordinariness.

Medvedev's choice of China as the destination for his first foreign visit should not be overrated. It was, however, a quite different decision compared with Medvedev's two predecessors. In 2000, Putin chose Britain for his first foreign tour, despite the Kremlin's announcement shortly after Yeltsin's resignation that Beijing would be the first trip abroad for Putin and after China's repeated invitations in early 2000. In time, however, Putin became increasingly interested in the 'Euro–Asian dimension' (Palata 2008), which was quite different from the first few months of his presidency, when he toyed with the 'hypothetical' idea of Russia joining the North Atlantic Treaty Organisation (NATO) and when he 'confessed' to the visiting US Secretary of State his 'European essence' and his Asian superficiality (practicing judo and eating Chinese food) (Bin 2000).

Medvedev's explicit *'Ostpolitik'* at the onset of his presidency was also the opposite of Yeltsin, who was obsessed with Western-style political democratisation and economic 'shock therapy'. Before his sudden exit from power at the end of 1999, Yeltsin chose Beijing to remind the West of Russia's huge nuclear arsenal, in a manner more in keeping with 'a recidivist Soviet premier' (Wines 1999). In between, the father of the Russian Federation became progressively more disillusioned with the West.

Medvedev's *'Westpolitik'* through Beijing

Medvedev's visit occurred at a time when Moscow and Beijing were facing growing challenges from the West: for Russia, a new round of NATO expansion and missile defence; for China, mounting protectionism in the West and surging energy prices—not to mention Tibet and the Olympics. This led to the Joint Statement of the People's Republic of China (PRC) and the Russian Federation on Major International Issues, signed by the two heads of states. The 11-point declaration stressed common perceptions and preferences between Moscow and Beijing, ranging from the crucial role of the United Nations in peace, development, security and counter-terrorism to the need for a more equal, fair and multipolar world, concerns about missile defence and space weaponisation, cooperation on environmental protection and energy, negotiations and dialogue for regional issues such as the North Korean nuclear crisis, Iran, Sudan, and so on ('Full text of joint statement of the PRC and the Russian Federation on major international issues', *People's Daily*, 23 May 2008, <http://politics.people.com.cn/GB/1026/7290647.html>).

At the policy level, Beijing and Moscow have worked closely in creating a soft landing for regional crises such as North Korea and Iran; they co-sponsored a proposal in Geneva in February 2008 for an international treaty to ban weapon deployment in outer space; extended their eighth round of foreign ministerial meetings with India to a four-party dialogue including Brazil in May 2008; and vetoed a British-sponsored UN Security Council bill to apply sanctions against Zimbabwe in July 2008 ('China and Russia vetoed UNSC draft to sanction Zimbabwe, US and UK expressed disbelief', *Jiefang Net*, 12 July 2008, cited from <www.6park.com/news/messages/87718.html>).

Not everything was synchronised between Moscow and Beijing. By the end of Putin's presidency, Russia's reaction to NATO expansion and missile defence in Europe led to a series of confrontational responses from Russia, including the resumption of Russia's strategic bombers' routine patrols and military posturing in several 'near abroad' areas. Beijing shares Russia's concerns but might not want to see further deepening of the Russia–West breach to the point that it has to take sides (Hongfeng 2008). For the same reason, Beijing seems happy to see the SCO remain as it is—that is, a community of nations working for regional stability and economic development rather than an explicit counterforce to

NATO or the United States. Such a view also seems to be the consensus of most, if not all, of the other members and observers of the SCO. Short of a steep deterioration in the regional security situation, SCO members need to maintain working relations with Washington and the West, as much as they need each other. This could explain why the SCO's annual foreign ministerial meeting on 25 July in Dushanbe, Tajikistan, continued to uphold a moratorium regarding Iran's full SCO membership ('Shanghai ministerial session ends in Tajikistan', *Asia-Plus* [Online], 25 July 2008).

It appears that the more Russia wants to be identified with the West, the less likely it is that this will happen. Yeltsin and Putin tried to plant Russia fully inside Western civilisation, only to be dismayed by persistent Western policies ranging from NATO expansion and its stance on Kosovo, to missile defence and the 'colour revolutions'. At the end of their presidencies, both resorted to some high-profile strategic posturing, although Yeltsin's nuclear roar was somewhat hollow.

Medvedev's China trip should perhaps be understood in light of Russia's unrequited affection for the West. Medvedev was also widely believed to be 'liberal' and 'pro-West' before his presidency. This perception of Medvedev contrasted sharply with the image of Putin, who rose through the ranks of the KGB before the collapse of the Soviet Union. One of the goals of Medvedev's China 'detour' was, therefore, to promote Russia's '*Westpolitik*'. Indeed, 10 days after his visit to China, Medvedev was in Berlin unveiling his grand blueprint for a Euro–Atlantic community stretching from Vancouver to Vladivostok. Within this community, Russia and Europe would share common roots, history, values and thinking (Medvedev 2008). A month later, the Russian President again tossed around the same 'Medvedev doctrine' at the G8 summit in Japan. On the same day, however, the United States and the Czech Republic signed a missile defence agreement—to the dismay of Moscow (Gearan 2008). As a result of the five-day war over South Ossetia, the new Russian President did not even have a honeymoon period with the West—unlike his predecessor, Putin, in whose eyes US President, George W. Bush, saw the soul of the former KGB colonel.

China's 'old friend' and new challenges

Russia's enduring identity as a Eurasian power is its strength as well as its burden. Such a dichotomy could cast limits on its relations—as friend or foe—with the West and the East. After nearly 60 years of relations with the former Soviet Union and its successor, the Russian Federation, Chinese analysts seem to understand this well (Hongfeng 2008; Haiyun 2008).

Within the realm of feasibility, however, China has lost no time in stretching Medvedev's Orientalist temptation. Indeed, Medvedev, the new and young

Russian President, is perhaps quite unusual in that he became popular in China long before his Beijing summit in May 2008, thanks to his co-chairmanship of China's 'Russia Year' (2006) and Russia's 'China Year' (2007). The Russian President is described as China's 'old friend', despite his (relatively) young age and youthful appearance. As part of the China Year activities, Medvedev, then Vice-Prime Minister, even spent an hour and a half with Chinese 'netizens' (Internet surfers) from Moscow in February 2007. No top Chinese leader has ever done that with either Chinese or Russians. In the eyes of many Chinese, the young Russian President is indeed quite different from his predecessor in his familiarity and comfort with Chinese culture. Many times, including during his talk at Beijing University, Medvedev demonstrated his knowledge and appreciation of Chinese culture and philosophy ('Medvedev meets Chinese students, says he loves Chinese philosophy, culture', *Itar-Tass*, 24 May 2008). Putin, in comparison, is more interested in Chinese kung-fu ('"I've seen genuine Shaolin Kong Fu," Putin', *People's Daily* [Online], 24 March 2006).

Partly because of the two 'national years', mutual understanding between ordinary Chinese and Russians has improved. A national survey by the Russian Public Opinion Study Center in April 2008, a month before China's earthquake, showed that ordinary Russians believed that China was the country with which Russia had the best relations. [8] Separately, a poll in several major Chinese cities conducted by the Chinese Public Opinion Study Institute in Beijing for the same period indicated that more than 80 per cent of Chinese believed relations between Russia and China were very good ('Over 80 percent of Chinese believe relations with Russia very good', *Itar-Tass*, 16 May 2008).

These more positive mutual perceptions are occurring at a time when Russia and China are faced with several major bottlenecks in their bilateral relations. Under President Putin, frequent high-level interactions did not lead to tangible economic gains. In 1994, former President Yeltsin tossed around the idea of building an oil pipeline to China. To date, the world's emerging manufacturing giant (China) and its energy superpower neighbour (Russia) are still talking. Meanwhile, Russia is perhaps one of the few developed nations that benefits from current high energy prices. Ironically, Russia's declining manufacturing capability and reluctance to become China's 'raw material supplier' have led, at least partially, to its first trade deficit with China ($8 billion in 2007) since the collapse of the Soviet Union.

Even the once thriving Russian military sales to China have come to a standstill. Perhaps the time has passed for China to purchase from Russia large quantities of air and naval armaments based largely on Soviet research and development—unless Moscow is willing to elevate China to the level of India in military sales and technology transfer (Haiyun 2008). Without large-scale military sales to China, the 'trade structural problem'—meaning Russia as a raw material supplier to China—might not be easily resolved given the growing structural difference between China's manufacturing capability and Russia's raw material-based recovery.

These issues or bottlenecks, among others, are far from desirable for Russia and China, though none of them has spilled over to other issues or become politicised thanks to the thickening of the web of connections and institutionalisation of various governmental contacts. Their existence and deepening, however, are not in the interests of Russia or China. Working on these issues with China requires patience, perceptiveness and pragmatism. Medvedev's presidency seems to provide an opportunity for that.

South Ossetia and its fallout

In the early morning of 8 August 2008, when Medvedev was on vacation (Stanovaya 2008) [9] and Putin was in Beijing to attend the twenty-ninth Olympic Games, Georgia launched a military offensive to surround and capture Tskhinvali, the capital of South Ossetia. The Georgian assault started with a preparatory artillery attack from Georgian positions with fire support, including from notoriously imprecise truck-mounted multiple-barrelled rocket launchers (the LAR-160 rocket system, which fires 160mm unguided rockets). In the 14 hours before Russia's intervention, 1700 people were killed, including 12 Russian peace-keepers, and many parts of the region were devastated, according to Russia's account (Wang 2008). Prime Minister Putin blamed Washington for Georgia's war: 'If what I presume turns out [to be] true, then there is a suspicion that there are forces in Washington that deliberately fueled the tensions in order to create an advantage to one of the presidential challengers' ('Allies let him down—Moscow', *Kommersant.com*, 29 August 2008). After Georgian forces entered South Ossetia and initially seized the capital, Tskhinvali, in an attempt to subdue the separatist region, Russian forces responded—belatedly and awkwardly—with an overwhelming show of force. Although Russia eventually established air superiority, it did not achieve this until some unexpected losses of its ground-support jet-bombers and a Tu-22M3 strategic bomber, which should not even have been used in such limited warfare. [10] In five days, the war was over and Russian forces were in control, first of South Ossetia and then Abkhazia, plus the Georgian port city of Poti (Giragosian 2008; Stepanov 2008). On 12 August, President Medvedev and French President, Nicolas Sarkozy, reached a six-point plan for a cease-fire. This was followed by a visit by US Vice-President, Richard Cheney, to Tbilisi on 2–3 September and US$1 billion in economic assistance to Georgia ('Cheney attacks "illegitimate" Russian invasion on visit to Georgia, US vice-president holds talks with Georgian president, raising "grave doubts" about Russia's reliability as international partner', *The Guardian*, 4 September 2008, <http://www.guardian.co.uk/world/2008/sep/04/

georgia.russia>). A Russian–American confrontation loomed large on the horizon in the Caucasus.

Putin, who was in Beijing for the Olympics opening ceremony, immediately informed the Chinese side of the situation in his meeting with Chinese Premier, Wen Jiabao, on 8 August ('Russian PM Putin informs Chinese counterpart of situation in South Ossetia', *Vesti TV*, 8 August 2008). China's reaction to Georgia's assault, according to Putin, was that 'nobody needs the war', which was also US President Bush's reaction ('Russia: Putin says China, US against war in South Ossetia "unleashed by Georgia"', *Itar-Tass*, 8 August 2008). Meanwhile, China expressed serious concern about the escalated tensions and armed conflict in South Ossetia, and urged all sides to exercise restraint, institute an immediate cease-fire and resolve their dispute peacefully through dialogue ('Foreign Ministry spokesman: China urges various parties in the South Ossetia conflict to cease fire immediately', *Xinhua*, 9 August 2008). Beijing did not publicly and explicitly support Moscow.

A Chinese source pointed to a dilemma in that 'Russia and Georgia are countries with which China maintains diplomatic relations and friendly ties, hence it should hold a very cautious stance so as not to damage these relations' ('Chinese leader calls for ceasefire in South Ossetia', *Interfax*, 11 August 2008). What the sources did not say was that Washington, too, was part of this list of 'friendly' nations with whom China did not want to jeopardise relations. Strategic ambiguity, if not neutrality, is perhaps the only rational stance for Beijing. Moreover, Washington had been Tbilisi's strongest supporter. A more cautious approach to the still evolving situation was therefore entirely understandable.

There were some exceptions to China's carefully balanced posture of evenhandedness. One was China's decision to send $1 million in humanitarian aid to South Ossetia, for which the Russians publicly expressed appreciation ('China to send humanitarian aid to South Ossetia', *Itar-Tass*, 22 August 2008). Meanwhile, China's official ambiguity contrasted sharply with the critical views of Georgia and the United States in China's Internet chat rooms, including those run by official media outlets ('PRC netizens criticize US over Georgia's action in South Ossetia', China–OSC Summary, 15 August 2008, *Foreign Broadcasting Information Service*).

Six days after the Russian troops halted their military offensive on 12 August, the Russian Security Council Secretary, Nikolai Patrushev, arrived in Beijing for a 'working visit'. The situation in the Caucasus was discussed in his one-hour, closed-door meeting with his Chinese counterpart, State Councilor Dai Bingguo. Very little about this meeting has been disclosed to date ('Russian official meets Chinese state councilor, hails high-level Olympics', *Interfax*, 18 August 2008; <http://news.xinhuanet.com/english/2008-08/18/content_9490099.htm>). Two days after the end of the Beijing Olympics and two days before the SCO's annual summit in Tajikistan, President Medvedev declared that Moscow recognised the independence of South Ossetia and Abkhazia. Beijing's immediate reaction came in a news release by the official Xinhua News Agency, citing the negative reactions from various Western countries (the United States, the United Kingdom, France, Sweden and Germany). Towards the end of the story, this Xinhua news 'round-up' noted that 'the two regions broke from central Georgian rule during wars in the early 1990s after the collapse of the former Soviet Union, but their self-proclaimed independence is not recognized internationally' ('Some Western nations slam Russia's recognition of Georgian breakaway regions', *Xinhua Roundup*, 26 August 2008).

China did not immediately react to Moscow's recognition of the independence of South Ossetia and Abkhazia, with good reason: President Hu and President Medvedev were to meet the next day in Dushanbe, capital of Tajikistan, before the opening of the SCO's eighth annual summit. During the meeting, Medvedev briefed Hu on the situation in South Ossetia and Abkhazia and on Russia's stance. Hu said in this meeting that the Chinese side had noted the latest changes in South Ossetia and Abkhazia, and hoped that the relevant parties would resolve the problems appropriately through dialogue and consultation. A Chinese media report noted that Hu had also told Medvedev:

> At present, [the] China–Russia strategic cooperative partnership maintains a good development impetus. Not long ago, both sides exchanged in-depth views on major issues related to China–Russia energy negotiating mechanism and energy cooperation [sic], and *conducted explorations on the operation of the China–Russia strategic security consultation mechanism and the third round of consultations*. The smooth operation of the aforesaid two mechanisms and other mechanisms between the two countries will increase both sides' political mutual trust, strengthen the two countries' strategic cooperation, and play an important role in upgrading the level of [the] China–Russia strategic cooperative partnership. (Lei et al. 2008, emphasis added)

It is unclear exactly how the two sides 'explored' the 'operation of the China–Russia strategic security consultation mechanism'. The Patrushev–Dai talks on 18 August 2008 in Beijing did look like a 'strategic security consultation', but the Chinese media never referred to the meeting as 'the third round of consultations'. What was clear from the Hu–Medvedev meeting in Dushanbe was the lack of unambiguous Chinese public support for Moscow's policies towards South Ossetia and Abkhazia.

According to Chinese sources, the Russian Foreign Ministry presented a revised proposal for the Dushanbe Declaration, requesting that a statement be included on joint action on security and conflict-prevention issues, but China did not agree to the proposal ('HK commentator lauds PRC handling of SCO "embarrassment" over Georgia conflict, Chang Ching-wei: artfully defusing embarrassment of SCO summit meeting', *Ta Kung Pao* [Online], 11 September 2008). Chinese Foreign Ministry spokesman Qin Gang reiterated China's official position on 28 August that 'China assumes a principled position on analogous issues: all problems need to be resolved through dialogue and consultations' ('China confirms difference with Russia on Abkhazia, S. Ossetia independence updated version, amending tagging and precedence', *Interfax*, 28 August 2008). As a result, the Dushanbe Declaration essentially adopted a similar posture of 'neutrality' as its third clause states:

The member states of the SCO express their deep concern in connection with the recent tension around the issue of South Ossetia, and call on the relevant parties to resolve existing problems in a peaceful way through dialogue, to make efforts for reconciliation and facilitation of negotiations.

The same document reiterates:

In the 21st century interdependence of states has grown sharply, security and development are becoming inseparable. None of the modern international problems can be settled by force, the role of force [as a] factor in global and regional politics is diminishing objectively. Reliance on a solution based solely on the use of force faces no prospects, it hinders comprehensive settlement of local conflicts; effective resolution of existing problems can be possible only with due regard for the interests of all parties, through their involvement in a process of negotiations, not through isolation. Attempts to strengthen one's own security to the prejudice of [the] security of others do not assist the maintenance of global security and stability.

The participants of the Dushanbe meeting underline the need to respect historical and cultural traditions of every state and every people and the efforts aimed to preserve in accordance to international law unity and territorial integrity of states as well as to encourage good-neighbourly relations among peoples and their common development.

Aside from these familiar principles, the Dushanbe Declaration does contain a somewhat more comforting statement for Russia regarding the Georgian conflict: 'The member states of the SCO welcome the approval on 12 August 2008 in Moscow of the six principles of settling the conflict in South Ossetia, and support the active role of Russia in promoting peace and cooperation in the region' (Dushanbe Declaration of Heads of SCO Member States, 28 August 2008, <http://www.sectsco.org/news_detail.asp?id=2360&LanguageID=2>).

Russia's story

The SCO's position, along with that of China, was a disappointment for Russia, despite the effort of Russian leaders to explain it away. *Gazeta*, a Moscow-based daily, believed that the SCO has given Russia exactly the amount of support that corresponds to their interests in the international arena, without hurting their relationship with the United States and the European countries and without *seriously offending* Moscow. The joint declaration the SCO members adopted at the summit in Dushanbe on 28 August is a classic example of the art of diplomacy. (Shermatova 2008, emphasis added)

Separately, some Russian analysts equated the wording of the Dushanbe Declaration with the statements of many EU members after the Medvedev–Sarkozy plan was signed.

The SCO's apparent neutrality was, nonetheless, not necessarily a surprise for Moscow. Two days before the SCO summit, Russian analysts predicted such an outcome regarding China and the SCO's policies of neutrality. Political analyst Vyacheslav Nikonov argued that Russia should not expect China's support on this issue: 'China has domestic problems. This is not only Taiwan but also Xinjiang Uyghur Region and Tibet. This problem will be a barrier to approving Russia's decision to recognize Abkhazia and South Ossetia.' For the same reason, 'Russia cannot count on 100-percent support from SCO but [the] understanding of a considerable number of its members, or perhaps even all, is quite feasible. But there will be no formal support,' he said (Interview with *Interfax*, 26 August 2008).

Despite this lack of support, as well as lack of criticism, regarding Russia's policies, a source in the Russian delegation to Dushanbe revealed that the SCO leaders verbally expressed their approval of Moscow's line. Still, in its final declaration, the SCO supported the principle of territorial integrity and opposed the use of force in interstate relations. Before the summit, President Hu was quoted as saying that he 'understood the Russian position', but explained that 'we'll be unable to officially side with Moscow'. Later, the Kazakh President was quoted apologising for having failed to support Moscow due to different reasons.

To explain the discrepancies between the SCO's informal and formal positions, Russian Foreign Minister, Sergey Lavrov, in his press conference after the summit, said that 'Russia didn't seek to persuade its partners to recognize South Ossetia and Abkhazia'. 'Unlike certain Western partners, we prefer that every country should make [up] its mind with[out] any external pressure,' Lavrov said. Moscow knew about American envoys' visits to other states, during which they 'told them what to say regarding the problem'. 'Such sort of boorishness is not inherent in our political tradition,' the Russian minister told journalists. In his address, Medvedev was said to have even thanked his colleagues 'for the understanding and the unbiased assessment of Russia's peacekeeping role' ('Allies let him down—Moscow', *Kommersant.com*, 29 August 2008). A week after this, the Russian Ambassador to Beijing again expressed his 'appreciation' for China's 'understanding' of Russia's position (Wang 2008). Vitaliy Tretyakov (2008), Dean of the Moscow State University Higher School of Television, went a step further by claiming that the 'silence' of China was in fact recognition of Russia's right to do what it did, and that other factors, including its own worries about separatism, were not, in fact, the main reasons for China's stance.

In mid September, Prime Minister Putin also offered his own story. In an interview, he alluded to the flexibility inherent in the Sino–Russian strategic relationship in saying:

This [China's] position has absolutely not disappointed us. Moreover, we perfectly understand the People's Republic of China's foreign and home political priorities and do not want to put them in some uncomfortable situation. We have openly told our Chinese partners about this. I said it myself while attending the Olympic opening ceremony in Beijing. We relieved them from this responsibility in Russian–Chinese relations beforehand…In terms of international law, one country's recognition is enough for the appearance of a new entity under international law. ('Russia not disappointed by China's position on Abkhazia, S. Ossetia', *Interfax*, 13 September 2008)

The Russians, therefore, understood the limits of their strategic relations with China.

China's 'independent' foreign policy: beyond the Georgian–Russian conflict

Beyond bilateral relations, China's neutrality regarding the Georgian–Russian conflict derived from some other, perhaps more complex and deeper, underpinnings. To begin with, the timing of the conflict was an irritant for Beijing. China did not like any war at its historic moment of hosting the Olympics, whether Russia was part of the conflict or not. Given the complexities of the ethnic conflict, dating back to the 1920s ('Georgian–South Ossetian conflict', *Wikipedia*, <http://en.wikipedia.org/wiki/Georgian-Ossetian_conflict# Origins_of_the_conflict>), its evolving nature and the United States looming large in the background, China's cautious reaction was expected by, if not desirable for, Moscow.

Since the outbreak of the conflict, several leading Chinese analysts observed that the Georgian–Russian conflict was in essence between Russia and the United States. While there was finger pointing between Moscow, Washington and Tbilisi regarding who made the first move, it was inconceivable that a small state (Georgia) would dare to take on its giant neighbour (Russia) without explicit support from Washington. Indeed, Washington was not only aware of Georgian military action before it started, it explicitly sided with Tbilisi in the August surprise, [11] which could well have contributed to Georgian President Mikheil Saakashvili's recklessness and miscalculation (Whitmore 2008).

China's vision of a 'harmonious world' means stability of the existing international system, despite the fact that the West dominates that system. Indeed, China would like to see—as much as the West would—the stability and continuity of the existing international system, from which China has benefited enormously. Beijing has in fact been on good terms with all three players in the crisis—Moscow, Washington and Tbilisi—and does not want to choose sides. Doing so might please one side but inevitably at the expense of China's relations with the others. Maintaining amicable relations with all of them is perhaps the least harmful position for China.

That said, China has invested more heavily in its relations with Russia than with Georgia. Despite this investment, it is a relationship without the mutually binding commitment that is typically the case in a military alliance. As noted earlier, it is largely a pragmatic approach to 'conduct strategic coordination without alliance and [a] close relationship without excessive dependence' (Xin 2007).

Within the context of such a normal relationship, both sides retain a considerable degree of freedom of action. One typical case was Moscow's response in 2001 when a US spy plane (an EP-3) collided with a Chinese jet-fighter (J-8II) off China's coast, leading to a major crisis between China and the United States. During the crisis, Moscow remained neutral and even 'helpful' in that it opted to load the seriously damaged American spy plane onto a Russian military cargo plane and fly it back to the United States. China's current neutrality over the Georgian conflict is perhaps what Russia would do in a scenario of conflict between China and the United States over Taiwan—that is, Russia would be likely to remain neutral, though expressing sympathy for China.

Much of the 'normal' nature of the Sino–Russian strategic partnership also constitutes the reason behind the SCO's 'neutrality'. All of the SCO's Central Asian states are former Soviet republics, where many ethnic Russians still live and work. Most, if not all, of these states do not want to see any replay of the Georgian–Russian conflict in their part of the world. Such a concern among the Central Asian states, however, remains a distant possibility, given the fact that the SCO provides a framework for its members to resolve disputes and to achieve common purposes for security and development. The key to the SCO's stance towards the Georgian–Russian conflict, however, lies in the nature and structure of the regional security group. Far from becoming a military bloc such as NATO, in which members are obligated to defend one another, the SCO is a huge and diverse community of nations. If its observer members are included, the SCO comprises almost half of the world's population, the three largest nations (Russia, China and India) and almost all major civilisations: Christianity, Islam, Hinduism and Confucianism. The SCO's decision-making procedure of consensus building makes it very difficult for any single member to impose its will on the others. Meanwhile, the SCO's charter allows considerable space for individual members to pursue their own policies for their own interests. There is simply no obligation for SCO members to automatically commit themselves to support other members, as is usually the case in military alliances. For these reasons, Moscow perhaps never explicitly asked for or demanded public support from the SCO members over the South Ossetian conflict.

In these circumstances, the SCO's joint Dushanbe Declaration could mean quite a lot for the Russians, as it supports the 'active role of Russia in promoting peace and cooperation in the region'. The member states of the SCO also expressed 'their deep concern' over the tension around the issue of South Ossetia and called for dialogue for peaceful reconciliation and facilitation of negotiations (Dushanbe Declaration of Heads of SCO Member States, 28 August 2008, <http://www.sectsco.org/news_detail.asp?id=2360&LanguageID=2>). This could be seen as being directed towards both sides, but particularly Georgia, which started the ball rolling on 8 August.

The expectation that Beijing and Moscow are heading towards some sort of 'separation' is, therefore, an overstatement at best. It is also largely derived from the West's own experience and practice, which insists on unity because of (and for) uniformity. Hence, NATO members must be democracies and the members of the European Union must be European, Christian and perhaps white. Applying the same 'recipe' to the SCO and recent Sino–Russian relations, which have largely transcended the past practice of alliances, is quite inappropriate.

Last if not least, Beijing's public neutrality towards the Georgian–Russian conflict should not be a surprise in that it has been the pattern of China's diplomacy since the 1980s. In almost all cases, ranging from international crises (North Korea, Iran, Kashmir, and so on) to bilateral disputes (over the South China Sea with the Association of South-East Asian Nations, the East China Sea with Japan, border settlements with Russia, Vietnam and India), China has opted for dialogue and compromise, rather than confrontation or taking sides. The same operational principle has also been applied to difficult issues such as Taiwan and Hong Kong, for which China negotiated with Britain for the ending of colonialism there in the 1980s. In contrast, India, which is a democracy, used force to take back Goa from Portugal in December 1961 (see 'Goa', *Wikipedia*, <www.wikipedia.com>). Since the adoption of its 'independent foreign policy' in 1982, China has seldom judged others along the friend–foe fault line; rather, it has taken a more pragmatic, independent and case-by-case approach. Even with its allies such as North Korea, China will be critical of its neighbour's policy if it is destabilising. The Georgian–Russian crisis simply provided another opportunity for China to display the independent nature of its foreign policy.

Even if the Russians did not get all of what they wanted from China and the SCO summit in late August 2008, this was by no means the beginning of the end of their strategic partnership with China. In the past 30 years, China's diplomacy—particularly its relations with Russia—has become far more sophisticated, nuanced, measured and mature. To a large extent, China's foreign policy has gone back to its deeper philosophical underpinnings of 'unity/harmony with or without uniformity' ('*he er bu tong*'). This is also one of the psychological anchors for Sino–Russian strategic relations after the two rather extreme types of relationship of 'honeymoon' (1950s) and 'divorce' (1960s and 1970s) between Beijing and Moscow. What has happened in the past 60 years between the two largest Eurasian nations, and particularly in the past 20 years, is important to both sides.

The 'West's civil war' [12] again? Stupid!

The observations above on China's vision for a harmonious world, and its recognised dependence on the existing, Western-dominated international system made the Georgian conflict (particularly when seen as a thinly disguised US–Russian conflict) particularly troublesome for China. Whether the world is heading back to the Cold War (Bhadrakumar 2008) or pre-World War I settings, the ghost of the 'West's civil war'—which it was claimed ended with the collapse of the former Soviet Union in 1991—is being rekindled by the Georgian/US–Russian conflict. Given this spectre of general instability in the international system, [13] Beijing's cautious approach is perhaps quite natural.

'South Ossetia is a crisis with far reaching consequences,' declared veteran Chinese political commentator He Liangliang in early September. 'It is, nonetheless, a crisis of the West, not one for China.' He saw the root cause of the crisis as America's relentless effort to squeeze Russia's security space, which was necessary for any 'normal' major power. Ever since Peter the Great, according to He, Russia had pursued an unrequited desire to join Europe (the West). Such sentimentality is particularly keen at the moment when Russia has largely recovered from its difficult transition from the wreckage of the Soviet Union. Western policies such as NATO expansion, the 'colour revolutions' and missile defence have created in Russia feelings of betrayal and rage. South Ossetia was, therefore, Russia's strategic countermove. Unfortunately, He argued, neither the Russian-speaking Condoleezza Rice, who majored in Cold War history, nor German Chancellor, Angela Merkel, who grew up in a Soviet-type system, seems to have understood Russia's 'West complex' (Liangliang 2008).

Medvedev's predicament is, however, not new. Putin, like Yelsin before him, began his presidency with an unambiguous '*Westpolitik*' (visiting Britain for his first foreign tour as Russian President, toying with the idea of Russia joining NATO and confessing to visiting US Secretary of State, Madeleine Albright, of his 'European essence' and his Asian superficiality). In time, however, Putin adopted an increasingly Eurasian dimension, moving away from his Euro-centric stance.

Perhaps it is time for the West to reflect on its current '*Ostpolitik*' (missile defence, NATO expansion, and so on), not necessarily only for its own interests, but for those of the Russians. The alternative, of course, is to stay the course in making Russia a 'problem' for the twenty-first century.

When the 'Georgian dust' settles, the West could start to comprehend that the Sino–Russian strategic partnership is perhaps not as strong or as weak as it appears. It is still unclear how the current crisis between Washington and Moscow might play out. Washington has rushed $1 billion in aid, and Vice-President Cheney, to Georgia and NATO amassed warships in the Black Sea (Myers 2008). The US presidential candidates, too, rushed to demonise Russia and glorify Georgia as if there was no tomorrow. If this continues, the 'West's civil war' could well turn out to be a 'brave' new page for the twenty-first century, focusing on Russia as 'THE problem'. A key difference between this newfound obsession of the West and past stages of the West's civil war is that the world is now in an era of weapons of mass destruction. Already, pundits are talking about possible 'mushroom clouds' of World War III if Russia's rusting conventional military hardware fails to deter the other side (Sokov 2008). This scenario, no matter how distant, remains a possibility, which is qualitatively different from the nineteenth century, when the West dealt with the 'French problem' (the Napoleonic Wars), and of the twentieth century, with the 'German problem' (World War I and II). The latter sucked the whole world into the West's own senseless, mutual slaughter.

If this remains a possibility, China will be better off staying out. This neutrality, according to He Liangliang (2008), is an indicator of maturity—not crisis—in China's diplomacy.

References

Bhadrakumar, M. K. 2008, 'The end of the post-Cold War era', *Asia Times Online*, 13 August 2008, <http://www.atimes.com/atimes/Central_Asia/JH13Ag02.html>

Bin, Yu 2000, 'New century, new face, and China's "Putin puzzle"', *Comparative Connections*, First Quarter 2000.

Bin, Yu 2003, 'Party time!', *Comparative Connections*, vol. 5, no. 2, Second Quarter, July.

Erlanger, Steven 2008, 'Putin in Paris, not president but presidential', *New York Times*, 31 May 2008, <http://www.nytimes.com/2008/05/31/world/europe/31france.html?_r=1&ref=world&oref=slogin>

Gearan, Anne 2008, 'US, Czech Republic sign defense agreement', *Associated Press*, 8 July 2008, <http://ap.google.com/article/ ALeqM5gL5oQoIDzcGtENsih2jr24j6DDMwD91Q1SIG1>

Gharib, Ali 2008, 'Kosovo comes back to bite the US', *Asia Times Online*, 21 August 2008, <http://www.atimes.com/atimes/Central_Asia/JH21Ag02.html>

Giragosian, Richard 2008, 'Georgian planning flaws led to failure', *Asia Times Online*, 20 August 2008, <http://www.atimes.com/atimes/Central_Asia/JH20Ag01.html>

Haiyun, Wang 2008, 'Current trends in Russia's China policy and how to deepen bilateral relations', *People's Daily* (Online), 12 May 2008, <http://world.people.com.cn/GB/42032/7226448.html>

Hongfeng, Xu 2008, 'Four dilemmas in Russian–US relations Medvedev will face after his inauguration as Russian President', *People's Daily* [Online], 12 May 2008, <http://world.people.com.cn/GB/57507/7226820.html>

Hongjian, Yu 2008, 'Standing by the Chinese people', *People's Daily* (Online), 28 May 2008.

Hongjian, Yu, Guangzheng, Zhang and Xiaodong, Zhang 2008, 'Crisis led to genuine friendship: Russia disaster relief assistance to China', *People's Daily* (Online), <http://world.people.com.cn/GB/14549/7285875.html>

Hua, Bai 2008a, 'SCO summit did not support Russia's policy', *VOA*, 28 August 2008, <http://www.voanews.com/chinese/w2008-08-28-voa49.cfm>

Hua, Bai 2008b, 'Russia's confrontation with the West, China benefits from it?', *VOA*, 29 August 2008, <http://www.voanews.com/chinese/w2008-08-29-voa57.cfm>

Hua, Bai 2008c, 'Georgia praised China's position regarding Russia–Georgian conflict', *VOA*, 31 August 2008, <http://www.voanews.com/chinese/w2008-08-31-voa35.cfm>

Huntington, Samuel P. 1993, 'The clash of civilizations?', *Foreign Affairs*, vol. 72, no. 3, Summer 1993, p. 23.

Ignatius, Adi 2007, 'A tsar is born: Person of the Year 2007', *Time*, 4 December 2007, <www.time.com/time/specials/2007/personoftheyear/ article/0,28804,1690753_1690757_1690766,00.html>

Lei, Liao, Zuokui, Wang and Jingli, Lu 2008, 'President Hu Jintao meets Russian President Medvedev', *Xinhua*, 27 August 2008.

Liangliang, He 2008, 'Zhongguo gengjia chengshu, helai "zhongguo de nanao waijiao weiji"?', *Wenhui Bao*, 3 September 2008, <http://www.6park.com/news/messages/93953.html>

Manthorpe, Jonathan 2008, 'China plays it cool on Russia's escapade in Georgia', *The Vancouver Sun*, 22 August 2008, <http://www.canada.com/vancouversun/ news/editorial/story.html?id=75ea3659-7ab6-49dd-a9a1-1aa7f773cdb2>

Marcus, Jonathan 2008, 'Russian–Chinese message to US', *BBC*, 23 May 2008, <http://news.bbc.co.uk/2/hi/asia-pacific/7417400.stm>

Medvedev, Dmitry 2008, Statements on major issues, Speech at meeting with German political, parliamentary and civic leaders, Berlin, 5 June 2008, <http://www.kremlin.ru/eng/speeches/2008/06/05/ 2203_type82912type82914type84779_202153.shtm>

Myers, Steven Lee 2008, 'White House unveils $1 billion Georgia aid plan', *New York Times*, 3 September 2008, <http://www.nytimes.com/2008/09/04/world/europe/04cheney.html>

Palata, Lubos 2008, 'Russian Europe; divided Europe is not an equal partner for Russia, to our own and Russia's detriment', *Lidovky.cz*, 30 June 2008.

Pronina, Lyubov and Alison, Sebastian 2008, 'Medvedev seeks China's support on recognizing regions', (Update 2), *Bloomberg.com*, 27 August 2008, <www.bloomberg.com/apps/news?pid= 20601085&sid=aoZq9X9gOaKU&refer=europe>

Shermatova, Sanobar 2008, '"Diplomatic" SCO reaction to Russian recognition of breakaway republics analyzed', *Gazeta*, 8 September 2008.

Sokov, Nikolai 2008, 'Let's talk about World War III', *Asia Times Online*, 26 August 2008, <http://www.atimes.com/atimes/Central_Asia/JH26Ag03.html>

Stanovaya, Tatyana 2008, 'World seen supporting Saakashvili as Georgia attacks South Ossetia's Tskhinvali', *Politkom.ru*, 8 August 2008.

Stepanov, Anton 2008, 'Children under fire. Georgian army fired on civilians', *Tvoy Den*, 8 August 2008.

Tretyakov, Vitaliy 2008, '11 Sep; place not given: "August 2008: lessons and consequences"', *Izvestiya* (Moscow edition), 15 September 2008, RBIS.

Wang, Zhong Xin 2008, 'Russian ambassador to Beijing on Russian–Georgian conflict: Russia values China's understanding', 4 September 2008, <http://www.6park.com/news/messages/94019.html>

Whitmore, Brian 2008, 'Saakashvili overplays his hand', *Asia Times Online*, 12 August 2008, <http://www.atimes.com/atimes/Central_Asia/JH12Ag01.html>

Wines, Michael 1999, 'Yeltsin waves saber at West; his premier speaks softly', *New York Times*, 11 December 1999,

<http://query.nytimes.com/gst/fullpage.html?res=
9507E6DE1231F932A25751C1A96F958260>

Xin, Cao 2007, 'Russia into post-Putin era', *South China Weekend*, 10 October
2007, <http://www.infzm.com/content/5695>

ENDNOTES

[1] Previously, the 'honeymoon' between Beijing and Moscow lasted only 10 years (1949–59).

[2] Other nations, such as India and Pakistan, adopt a similar definition. The European Union, which is a non-military group, also elevated its relations with China to one of strategic partnership in 2005; see Joint Statement for the EU–China Summit (5 September 2005, < http://ec.europa.eu/external_relations/china/summit_0905/index.htm >).

[3] It was held between US Deputy Secretary of State, Robert B. Zoellick, and Chinese Executive Vice Foreign Minister, Dai Bingguo.

[4] The visit could have contributed to the West's assessment: no surprise, no breakthroughs, still no new large military contract, and no new paperwork for the long-talked-of Russian oil pipeline to China.

[5] China was quite surprised by Putin's succession arrangement.

[6] To a certain extent, Medvedev's choice of China as his first foreign visit in the capacity of Russian President was an act of reciprocity to Hu Jintao's visit to Russia in 2003 as his first foreign trip. See Bin (2003).

[7] The number of Chinese children who will travel to Russia for recuperation in 2008 and 2009 is expected to reach 1500; see 'First group of Chinese children affected by recent earthquake arrives in Russia' (*Interfax*, 20 July 2008).

[8] The poll showed that 23 per cent of the respondents named China as the country with which Russia had the best relations. This was followed by 17 per cent for Germany; 14 per cent for Belarus; 6–9 per cent for Kazakhstan, the United States, India and France; 4 per cent for the European Union; and 3 per cent for Bulgaria and Japan (see 'China is Russia's best friend: opinion poll', *Interfax*, 8 May 2008).

[9] Georgia began its military operation at about midnight on 7 August 2008. Beijing, which is four hours' ahead of Tbilisi time, was yet to wake up to the morning of 8 August for its Olympics opening ceremony that evening. Russian Prime Minister Putin arrived in Beijing on 7 August.

[10] In hindsight, many in Russia blamed bad intelligence and the Russian military's lack of preparation (< http://mil.news.sina.com.cn/p/2008-09-04/0833519716.html >).

[11] In July 2008, two US policies clearly emboldened Tbilisi. US Secretary of State, Condoleezza Rice, travelled first to Prague, where a treaty on the placement of radar was signed, and then to Tbilisi, where she precisely and unequivocally sided with Georgia in its conflicts with Russia.

[12] Lind cited in Huntington (1993).

[13] At the time of the Georgian–Russian crisis, circumstances on China's periphery had also become quite 'fluid': President Musharraf's resignation as Pakistani President; violent demonstrations in Thailand; the sudden exit of Japanese Prime Minister Fukuda, and the prospect of Taro Aso, then Secretary-General of the governing Liberal Democratic Party, becoming the next Prime Minister.

Alliances, military balances and strategic policy

Chapter 8

How China thinks about national security

Xia Liping

Introduction

Since the end of the Cold War, China's thinking about national security has changed greatly. During the Cold War, China viewed its national security mainly in terms of its struggles against the hegemony of one of the two superpowers or even against that of both superpowers and their followers. At present, China has been attaching most importance to the trend of globalisation, which has had positive and negative impacts on the country's national security. On the positive side, China's involvement in economic globalisation has increased its national strength and the range of interests it shares with other countries. On the negative side, China has faced a growing number of non-traditional threats, such as terrorism, the proliferation of weapons of mass destruction (WMD), global warming, environmental pollution, transnational crime, drug trafficking, HIV/AIDS, and so on. So, although military security is still very important for China, it is increasingly concerned about non-traditional security issues, such as energy, food and environmental security, financial security, information security, and so on. In order to resolve these issues, China and other countries have to cooperate more with each other.

During recent years, therefore, China has accepted some new concepts of security featuring mutual trust, mutual benefit, equality and coordination.

In December 2004, China formally put forward its national security strategy, which should be subordinated to and should serve its National Development Strategy (NDS). Since the early 1980s, China has been focusing its efforts on internal economic development in order to improve the living standard and educational levels of its people. China will continue to move forward in this way for some time. The long-term purpose of the NDS is to make China a mid-level developed country, which will be strong, democratic and civilised, by 2050 ('The report of Jiang Zemin at the 15th National Congress of the Chinese Communist Party', *People's Daily*, Beijing, 12 September 1997). To achieve this objective, China will continue to pursue its policy of reform and opening up, and it needs a peaceful international environment in the long term, particularly with respect to its immediate geographic surroundings. This means that China does not want to do anything to seriously disturb the current international economic and political mechanisms, except when its national interests are threatened. Even if China can achieve its planned objective, because of its large population and the fact that its economic development is very unbalanced, it will continue to focus its attention on internal issues. At the same time, the more prosperous China becomes, the more cooperative it will be with other countries, because, in such circumstances, China will be influenced more easily by the outside world.

China has been pursuing its independent foreign policy of peace since the mid 1980s. The objective of China's foreign policy is to maintain a peaceful international environment, which will be beneficial for China's long-term economic and social development. There are four outstanding characteristics in China's current foreign policy: peace, independence, mutual respect and cooperation. First, China's foreign policy is formulated from the viewpoint of whether it is beneficial to international and regional peace and stability, rather than from the viewpoint of achieving military superiority. Second, with regard to independence, China formulates its foreign policy according to its national interests and the common interests of the peoples of all the countries in the world. Mutual respect indicates that China would like to put its relations with other countries on a base of mutual respect, and would like to see international political, security and non-proliferation agreements based on mutual respect between the member parties. Cooperation indicates that China would like to continue its cooperation based on its 'Five Principles of Peaceful Coexistence' with all the countries in the world, including the United States, and would like to realise a concert between the major powers.

New thinking in China's national security strategy

China's leadership has formulated its national security strategy for the next 20 years. There is remarkable continuity in China's current foreign and security strategies. There is, however, also something new in them.

China's leadership has tried to put forward some creative and new concepts, which will become theories for guiding further economic and political reforms in China, and will lead China to further integrate itself into international society and become a responsible power in the world, especially with regard to its neighbours. Since China began its policy of reform and opening up at the end of 1970s, it has been making great progress in integrating itself into international economic and political mechanisms. The more closely China integrates itself into international mechanisms, the more willing it will be to play a responsible role in the international community.

In recent years, the Chinese economy has been developing steadily. If China can maintain the pace of economic development, it will be among the major powers in the world by the middle of the twenty-first century. Whether China can become a responsible great power or not will depend on internal and external factors. Those factors can be divided into subjective ones and objective ones, among which international mechanisms will play an important role. The world will benefit from the peaceful rise of China as a responsible power in the international community.

Three major tasks for China in the twenty-first century

In the twenty-first century, there are the three major tasks for China: to propel its drive for modernisation; to achieve national reunification; and to safeguard world peace and promote common development. [1]

Unlike China's three historical tasks in the twentieth century, as put forth by Deng Xiaoping in the 1980s, the three major tasks for this century make no mention of 'anti-hegemony'. The new formulation indicates that China has focused on safeguarding world peace and promoting common development in its foreign and security policies. This does not mean that China will not oppose hegemony. In the future, if a country pursues hegemonic policies or actions, China will oppose them. It does indicate, however, that in China's current political dictionary, 'hegemony' does not refer to a particular country, such as the United States.

Furthermore, the leadership of the Communist Party of China and the Chinese Government declared again that China would never seek hegemony and would never pursue expansion. Furthermore, China has constructively put forward the concept of the establishment of a harmonious world with lasting peace and universal prosperity as its long-term objective. At the same time, China has incorporated the concept of 'people first' into its diplomacy.

A period of important strategic opportunity

The first two decades of the twenty-first century will be a period of important strategic opportunity for China. During this period, China will focus its attention on building a prosperous society in a comprehensive manner. The objectives of China's modernisation are to quadruple the gross domestic product (GDP) of 2000 by 2020, and to become a mid-level developed country by 2050. In order to achieve these objectives, China needs a peaceful and stable international security environment beneficial for its economic development.

Although there are still some regional wars and armed conflicts in the world, such as the war in Iraq, peace and development remain the main themes of the era. At the same time, the trends of multipolarisation in the world and democracy in international relations have been playing an important role in restricting hegemony and power politics. These conditions will be conducive to the maintenance of a peaceful environment in the long-term, internationally and in China's periphery.

Keeping pace with global trends and safeguarding the common interests of all mankind

Due to economic globalisation, the common interests of all mankind have become more evident. China is ready to work with the international community to boost global multipolarisation, promote the harmonious coexistence of diverse forces and maintain stability in the international community. China will continue to improve and develop relations with developed countries. Proceeding from the fundamental interests of all countries concerned, China will broaden the converging points of common interests and properly settle differences on the basis of its Five Principles of Peaceful Coexistence, notwithstanding differences in social systems and ideologies. China has been cooperating with the United States and other countries in anti-terrorism efforts and in dealing with regional security problems, such as the North Korean nuclear crisis.

New concepts of security featuring mutual trust, mutual benefit, equality and coordination

Since the end of the Cold War, China has changed its security concepts greatly according to the new international situation and the interests of the Chinese people, as well as the aspirations of the peoples of the world for peace and development. China thinks that in order to obtain lasting peace, it is imperative to abandon the Cold War mentality, cultivate a new concept of security and seek a new way to safeguard peace. China holds that countries should trust one another, work together to maintain security and to resolve disputes through dialogue and cooperation, and should not resort to or threaten to use force. It has been proved that the new concepts of security are in keeping with the trends of the era and have great vitality.

China holds that the core of the new security concept should be mutual trust, mutual benefit, equality and coordination. [2] The new security concept should also be the guide for resolving disputes in international security.

The new security concepts China has adopted include the following.

1.   The concept of 'mutual security'. During the Cold War, the concept of 'zero-sum games' played the most important role in international politics. With the end of the Cold War, countries should accept the concept of 'mutual security' because of the changed situation. We should oppose any country building its absolute security on the insecurity of others.

1.   The concept of cooperative security. At present, all countries are facing many non-traditional security threats or transnational problems, such as

environmental problems, global warming, drug trafficking, terrorism, proliferation of WMD, severe acute respiratory syndrome (SARS), HIV/AIDS, and so on. They should make common efforts and cooperate to deal with these challenges.

1. The concept of comprehensive security rather than military security. Since the end of the Cold War, although geopolitical, military security and ideological factors still play important roles in some politicians' minds, the role of economic factors is becoming more prominent in international relations. Thus, all countries should make great efforts to settle divergences and disputes between them through peaceful means.

Cementing China's friendly ties with its neighbours and building good-neighbourly relations and partnerships with them

China regards this policy as an important part of its effort to maintain a long-term stable and peaceful international security environment. China will step up regional cooperation and increase exchanges and cooperation with surrounding countries.

China's peaceful rise

China's peaceful rise comprises the rise of peace, rise by peace and rise for peace. China needs long-term peace in the international environment for its economic and social development..

Since the early 1980s, China has been focusing its efforts on internal economic development in order to improve the living standards and educational levels of its people. China will continue to move forward in this way into the future. The mid-term purpose of China's NDS is to quadruple the GDP of 2000 by 2020. The first two decades of the twenty-first century will be a period of important strategic opportunity for China. During this period, China will focus its attention on building a prosperous society.

The long-term purpose of China's NDS is to make China a mid-level developed country, which will be strong, democratic, civilised and harmonious, by 2050. To achieve this objective, China will continue to pursue a policy of reform and opening up. The objective of China's national security strategy is to defend its national interests of sovereignty, security and development, and to maintain a long-term peaceful and stable international security environment beneficial to China's economic development. In order to achieve this objective, China will continue to follow the road of peaceful development, stick to the combination of development and security and strive for the enhancement of national strategic capability. China will also wield pluralistic means of security to deal with traditional and non-traditional security threats, and seek comprehensive national security of politics, economics, finance, the military and society. This means that China would like to continue its role as a responsible stakeholder in the international system.

China has been pursuing its independent foreign policy of peace since the mid 1980s. The objective of this policy is to strive for a peaceful international environment, which will be beneficial to China's long-term economic and social development. In recent years, China has held that safeguarding security requires new concepts. Thus, China advocates the 'new security concepts', which regard mutual trust, mutual benefit, equality and coordination as their core. At the same time, the purpose of the new security concepts is to improve mutual trust through dialogue and to spur common security through cooperation. [3] Recently, China put forward the concept of establishing a harmonious world with lasting peace and universal prosperity. [4] China also stressed its intention to go along the road of peace, development and cooperation as a member of the international community.

Chinese views on soft and hard power

In today's world, the concept of comprehensive national power has been extended to include:

- 'hard power', including population, land, natural resources, military forces, and so on
- 'soft power', including appeal to, cohesion and charm of civilisations and cultures, especially image, concepts of value, political stability and 'correct' policies of countries
- bonding power, including the capabilities of economics and trade to spur economic interdependence between countries
- creative power, including creative capabilities such as science, culture, management and the mechanisms and systems of countries
- national will power, including capabilities for strategic decision making and determination to pursue national strategies.

How will China work in the UN Security Council in the future?

From 1949 to the 1970s, China was outside the international system and even acted as a revolutionary against it. Since the beginning of China's reform and openness in the 1980s, it has gradually integrated itself into the current international economic and security system. Especially since late 1990s, China has been a responsible power in the international system. On 20 April 2006, US President George W. Bush said, 'We welcome the rise of a peaceful and prosperous China, which is also supportive of the international system. As the stakeholders of the international system, our two countries share many common strategic interests.' [5] China would like to continue its role as a responsible stakeholder. From the late 1980s to the early 2000s, China said that it favoured establishing a new international political and economic order that was fair and rational. Now China stresses that it stands for pushing the international order towards fairness and rationality.

The United Nations is still the core of the current international system. China will play a more positive and active role in the UN Security Council in the future, and will support the reform and strengthening of this core institution.

China's role in the UN Security Council in the future will be governed by the following principles:

1. China will play its role in international society not only according to its national interests, but in order to benefit regional and world peace, development, stability and prosperity
2. China will respond to its international obligations positively and actively
3. China will provide public goods in international and regional affairs.

Since the end of the Cold War, and especially since the terrorist attacks of 11 September 2001, there have been some new developments in the international strategic situation. First, non-state actors challenging sovereign states have become important factors, in which terrorism is the most salient threat in the international security and political fields. Second, non-traditional security problems, especially terrorism and the proliferation of WMD, have posed an increasingly serious threat to international society. Third, asymmetrical war has become one of the main forms of warfare. The conflict in Afghanistan between the coalition forces led by the United States and the Taliban along with al Qaeda and the Iraq war are examples of such asymmetrical war. The new developments in the international strategic situation have spurred the major powers to strengthen their cooperation to deal with the new threats and challenges.

The new framework for strategic cooperation and stability between the major powers in the twenty-first century should be established on a new theoretical foundation. At present, the international security situation is undergoing deep changes. The scope of security has been enlarged to encompass not only military issues, but those related to politics, economics, finance, science and technology, culture, and so on. The common interests between countries in the security field have greatly increased, and the interdependence between countries has been strengthened. The models of interaction between countries in the security field are also changing, turning from the original 'zero-sum' games to 'win-win' or 'win-win-win' models. Military means are not enough for dealing with varied security challenges, so it will be necessary to have new means and concepts to maintain stability and peace and to prevent nuclear proliferation.

The trend of globalisation has been imposing great pressure on the international system and has spurred potentially significant changes. The international system includes four major parts: major international actors, the international power structure, international regulation of interaction, and international institutions. In recent years, with the development of economic globalisation, multipolarisation and the democratisation of international relations, the four parts have been in transformation.

Although nation-states are still the major international actors, many non-state international actors have been greatly increasing their influence, including international intergovernmental organisations, transnational corporations and international non-governmental organisations. International terrorist organisations, such as al Qaeda, are also important international actors. These new non-state international actors have caused the diversification of the major international actors. On the one hand, new non-state international actors have offered new challenges to states and sovereignty, and international terrorist organisations have posed serious threats to international security and stability. On the other hand, new non-state international actors have also provided new opportunities for the international community. For example, international intergovernmental organisations have contributed to international and regional cooperation, and transnational corporations have been contributing to international trade and investment.

Since the end of the Cold War, the international power structure has been in significant and profound transformation. We should examine its evolution during the era of globalisation from a number of angles. On the whole, the international power structure has been trending towards multipolarity. In the world economy, the structural concept of a 'centre margin' has given way to the notion of 'tectonic plates'. The centre of gravity of world politics and economics has been shifting from the Atlantic to the Asia-Pacific area.

New thinking on international relations and new regulation of interactions, such as win-win or win-win-win models and the new security concepts, have been developing and colliding with the Cold War mentality and old thinking, such as zero-sum games, which run counter to current international trends. The results of these collisions will have important effects on the transformation of the international system.

International institutions have also been undergoing reform.

China's current policy towards East Asia

At present, cementing friendly ties with its neighbours is a priority of China's foreign policy. China is doing its best to build good-neighbourly relations and partnerships with them. East Asia is one of the most important areas for China. In recent years, China has sought not only to improve bilateral relations with other East Asian countries, but to place increasing importance on regionalism and regionalisation in East Asia. The Korean Peninsula is one of China's most important neighbouring areas and China deals with Korean issues from a regional or East Asian perspective.

Although the process of regional economic integration and security cooperation in East Asia, compared with the European Union, has had a late start, during recent years regional institutions have made significant progress, including the Association of South-East Asian Nations (ASEAN), ASEAN+3, ASEAN+1, the ASEAN Regional Forum (ARF), the East Asia Summit (EAS), Asia-Pacific Economic Cooperation (APEC) and the six-party talks on the North Korean nuclear issue. These regional institutions have been playing an increasingly important role in the economic and security arenas in East Asia.

These institutions can be divided into diverse types. The first type includes those institutions focused on economic issues, such as APEC. The second type includes those focused on security issues, such as the ARF. The third type are those that deal with economic and security issues, such as ASEAN, ASEAN+3, ASEAN+1 and the EAS.

These institutions are at different levels of development in terms of economic cooperation or security dialogue and cooperation. With regard to economic integration, ASEAN is more advanced than other institutions. Some institutions are still in the process of formation. For example, in North-East Asia, the six-party talks on North Korea could develop gradually into an important mechanism for subregional security dialogue and cooperation, if the North Korean nuclear issue can be resolved within its framework.

ASEAN+3 could develop into one of the most important institutions of regional economic integration and security cooperation. The Asian financial crisis of 1997 made ASEAN member states realise that it was necessary for them to promote regional cooperation with the rest of East Asia. This is because it is difficult for ASEAN, a group of developing countries with small markets and insufficient capital, to overcome crises simply by strengthening cohesiveness. So far, ASEAN has achieved economic development through participation in dynamic trade and investment relations in East Asia. Consequently, it is essential for ASEAN to strengthen cooperation with other East Asian countries, such as China, Japan and South Korea, to overcome its economic difficulties and achieve its long-term development. In November 1997, the first ASEAN+3 (China, Japan and South Korea) summit meeting was held. At the Manila meeting in November 1999, the leaders of ASEAN+3 issued a joint statement on East Asian cooperation, in which they agreed to strengthen cooperation in a broad range of fields, including politics, security, economics and culture. Cooperation in the economic and social fields was emphasised.

In line with these developments, at the first ASEAN+3 meeting of economic ministers held in Yangon, Myanmar, in May 2000, the ministers agreed to promote cooperation in nine specific fields, including expanded trade and investment, the information technology (IT) sector and Mekong Basin development. They shared the view that the meeting could provide a valuable opportunity for further collaboration, promote a cohesive response to the challenge of globalisation and consolidate the region's role as a world growth centre.

ASEAN+3 cooperation has made great strides in the financial field. In May 2000, the ASEAN+3 finance ministers gathered in Chiang Mai, Thailand, and agreed to promote measures to strengthen financial cooperation under the so-called Chiang Mai Initiative. Previously, Indonesia, Malaysia, the Philippines, Singapore and Thailand had concluded currency swap agreements worth US$40 million to prevent the recurrence of a currency crisis. Under the Chiang Mai Initiative, these agreements were expanded to include other ASEAN states and China, Japan and South Korea. In addition, the finance ministers agreed to build a 'repo' network of securities repurchasing agreements among ASEAN+3 members (National Institute for Defence Studies 2001:81). The progress of ASEAN+3 cooperation in the financial field reflects the fact that during the Asian financial crisis in 1997, East Asian countries were unable to receive meaningful assistance from the United States and the European Union. East Asian countries had little influence on the policy of the international financial institutions, especially the International Monetary Fund (IMF), which were under the strong influence of the United States and major European countries. In light of this experience, East Asian countries recognised the need to prepare their own countermeasures in case of another financial crisis.

At the fourth ASEAN+3 summit meeting, held in Singapore in November 2000, the leaders reaffirmed the importance of promoting the Chiang Mai Initiative and agreed to organise a study group with a view to creating an East Asian Free Trade Area (National Institute for Defence Studies 2001:81). Since then, a framework for cooperation in trade, as well as finance, has been developing among the ASEAN+3. With economic interdependence between countries in East Asia growing, ASEAN+3 cooperation in the economic field is expected to strengthen in the coming years.

The establishment of the new strategic stability framework between major powers will be beneficial for the long-term peaceful and stable international security environment, which is necessary for China's economic development and national interests. It will also be conducive to global stability and security, including in the Asia-Pacific region, and to China's continuing role as a responsible power, benefiting the interests of all other nations.

China's East Asian policy focuses on continuing to cement China's friendly ties with its neighbours, and persists in building good-neighbourly relations and partnerships with them. China regards this policy as an important part of its greater efforts to seek and maintain a stable and peaceful international security environment in the long term. China will step up regional cooperation, and increase its exchanges and cooperation with its surrounding countries to a new level.

China can cooperate with other countries through regional institutions

The ASEAN+3 framework has become the most important multilateralinstitution. It was established when there was growing momentum to strengthen regional cooperation among East Asian countries because of the experience of the Asian currency and financial crisis. Since 1997, the ASEAN+3 summit meeting has been held every year along with various ministerial meetings, such as foreign ministers' meetings, under the ASEAN+3 framework. Thus, the ASEAN+3 framework has acquired significant scope and depth.

Furthermore, since the beginning of the ASEAN+3 process, there have been those who believe that ASEAN+3 should deal not only with economic issues, but in the areas of politics and security, including transnational issues. At the ASEAN+3 summit meeting in Cambodia in November 2002, the leaders expressed their intention to develop counter-terrorism measures. At the same meeting, a clear message was issued in the Chairman's Press Statement urging North Korea to abandon its nuclear weapons development program.

China has made great efforts to strengthen economic cooperation and to maintain stability in East Asia through the ASEAN+3 and ASEAN+1 mechanisms. During the sixth ASEAN+3 summit meeting in November 2002, China put forward a 23-point proposal to promote regional cooperation and common prosperity in East Asia. Altogether, China signed or released 11 important documents, including the Framework Agreement on China–ASEAN Comprehensive Economic Cooperation, which launched the process towards a free trade area between the two sides; the national report on China's participation in the Greater Mekong River subregional development, which set in motion cooperation between China and ASEAN in the Mekong Basin; the joint declaration on non-traditional security issues, which broadened the scope of cooperation in this area; the declaration on a Code of Conduct of Parties in the South China Sea, which provided the political foundation for a stable South China Sea area; the memorandum of understanding on agricultural cooperation, which initiated moves towards China–ASEAN bilateral cooperation in priority areas; and the Asia Debt Reduction Plan to provide Laos, Cambodia and Myanmar with zero-tariff treatment for most of their exports to China, thus making tangible contributions to poverty eradication in the region. The Chinese leader also proposed a medium to long-term

IT cooperation program. ASEAN members unanimously endorsed his proposal. China–ASEAN cooperation in the priority fields is making solid progress.

Under the ASEAN+3 framework, China can cooperate with other countries on some important issues, such as economics and integration, anti-terrorism, anti-piracy, environmental protection, illegal immigration, drug trafficking, and so on.

Trilateral cooperation between China, South Korea and Japan provides a very importantmultilateral mechanism. Spurred by the first China–South Korea–Japan summit in 1999, trilateral cooperation has promoted cooperation centring on economic, financial and environmental areas towards improving prosperity in the region.

At the China–South Korea–Japan summit held in Cambodia in November 2002, the three countries expressed the view that, based on their relationship of trust, they would further deepen 'cooperation for prosperity' and promote trilateral cooperation in a wide range of areas. They also exchanged views regarding the situation on the Korean Peninsula. Furthermore, the three countries agreed that they would promote trilateral cooperation in the future, prioritising the five areas of economics and trade, information and telecommunications, environmental protection, human resources development and cultural cooperation.

During the summit meeting, some economic research institutions of the three countries submitted a report on a proposal for joint policies and proposed a feasibility study of a China–South Korea–Japan free trade zone and its possible economic impact. The leaders of the three countries endorsed this report in principle and supported the proposed feasibility study on the envisaged free trade zone.

At the China–South Korea–Japan summit held in October 2003, at the initiative of Chinese Premier, Wen Jiabao, the three countries issued a joint declaration on promoting trilateral cooperation, the first such document issued by the leaders of the three countries. The document defined the basic framework and future direction of trilateral cooperation. In December 2003, China, Japan and South Korea agreed to establish a trilateral committee, to be led by the foreign ministers of the three countries, to undertake research, planning and observation of trilateral cooperation in different fields so as to fulfil the objectives put forward in the joint declaration.

China and South Korea have also made significant progress in their bilateral economic cooperation. In 2002, China's trade with South Korea reached US$44.1 billion, up by 22.8 per cent from 2001. China (including the Hong Kong Special Administrative Region) has replaced the United States as South Korea's largest export market.

The advancement of China–South Korea–Japan trilateral cooperation in a wide range of areas, such as cooperation for prosperity and stability, is the driving force promoting East Asian cooperation. It is expected that China, Japan and South Korea will take the initiative to further advance specific cooperation with ASEAN countries so that this will lead to the expansion and deepening of regional cooperation in East Asia as a whole.

Through the mechanism of trilateral cooperation, China and South Korea can cooperate in the economic and security fields. At present, China, Japan and South Korea are facing many new security challenges, which can be classified into two fields: non-traditional and traditional.

In non-traditional security sectors, China, Japan and South Korea share many common interests and have to cooperate to deal with them. Furthermore, because these challenges are transnational or global problems, China, Japan and South Korea have also to rely on multilateral institutions.

China has become the biggest trading partner of South Korea and Japan. There is great potential for trade and economic cooperation between China, South Korea and Japan, which would be beneficial not only for the three countries, but for the world economy. In China–South Korea–Japan relations, economic exchange has always been at the forefront, and continues to expand and develop. In order to further speed up trilateral economic cooperation, it is necessary for them to develop a framework for a China–South Korea–Japan free trade area in the near future.

China views its relations with Japan and South Korea from a long-term standpoint, concluding that it is in China's national interest to cooperate actively and positively with other countries, especially its neighbours such as South Korea.

China and other countries share many common objectives and interests within the multilateral institutions of East Asia. Close cooperation between China and other countries will be one of the most important preconditions for the establishment of an East Asian free trade area, which will be one of the most important components of Asian security cooperation. US participation in Asian security cooperation is also necessary.

China's strategic culture and its impacts on China's security thinking

China's strategic culture can be divided into three levels. The highest level is Chinese philosophy. The middle level is China's national strategic culture. The third level is China's military strategic culture and foreign strategic culture.

Chinese philosophy

Chinese traditional philosophy is based on the belief that heaven and man should match well, which means that people must follow the objective laws or the thinking of heaven and must not violate them.

Chinese philosophy focuses on the concept of harmony, which means that people should live in harmony with other people, with the natural world and within themselves (by facilitating harmony between the mind and body).

Chinese philosophy has stressed peace despite differences, which means that different people can coexist peacefully even though they have different views.

Confucian philosophy stresses benevolence, which includes several important concepts, such as peace, harmony, propriety, righteousness, morality and love. Confucius said: 'Harmony is the right way of the world.' He also said: 'Harmony is precious.'

Mo Zi advocated universal love, which means people should love others without discrimination.

China's traditional national strategic culture

There are several important features of China's traditional national strategic culture.

- Decision makers should understand military issues, although they must not like war. Because sending troops to fight wars can cause a lot of casualties, they are very dangerous (Zhou 1996:16). Mo Zi even opposed all kind of offensive action.
- China should set an example of morality and excellent culture to neighbouring ethnic peoples and nations to attract them to present tribute to the Chinese emperor. Ancient Chinese thinkers advocated 'associating with benevolent gentlemen and befriending good neighbours'. During ancient times, therefore, China established a regional system of tribute within East Asia.
- Chinese civilisation was originally based on agriculture and farming, so one of its major characteristics was avoidance of expeditions of military force. Since ancient times, Chinese people have emphasised defence instead of offence. When the Chinese created the earliest written script, our ancestors used two pictographs to form the character 'force' (*wu*). One pictograph was 'stop' (*zhi*), the other was 'spear' (*ge*). The underlying logic was that wars should be abandoned as an instrument and the use of force could be justified to stop violence. Especially since the beginning of the Ming Dynasty, China has focused on its existing territory instead of on expansion. In the early fifteenth century, even before the period of Western 'geographic discovery', a great Chinese explorer and sailor named Zhen He led the largest fleet in the world on seven voyages westward. These voyages, reaching as far as the

eastern African coast and the entrance to the Red Sea, took Zhen He to more than 30 countries and regions. Unlike later Western explorers, who conquered the lands they discovered, this fleet did not subdue the newly discovered lands by force. This was not a voyage to plunder the local area for treasure, nor was it one to establish overseas colonies. As decreed by the Chinese Emperor, Zhen He's task was to convey friendship and goodwill and to promote economic and cultural exchanges between China and other Asian as well as African nations.

- Modest rulers can launch a just war against other countries (Zhou 1996:33). Some countries with arrogant rulers should be attacked, especially if they can't share their wealth with their neighbouring countries (Zhou 1996:33).
- Fighting for the reunification of China is justified.

China's military strategic culture

- Winning all wars is not the best; defeating the enemy without any war is the best (Zi 1999:35).
- The best way to defeat an enemy is to use stratagems; the second-best way is to use diplomacy; the third is to launch a war. The worst way is to attack castles, which should be a last resort, when no other alternatives are available (Zi 1999:35).
- Military commanders can use all kinds of stratagems to deceive enemies (Zi 1999:10).

China's foreign strategic culture

- Rulers of countries can make use of triangular relations, such as those during the Three Kingdoms of the Wei, the Shu Han and the Wu (AD 220–80).
- Rulers of countries can make use of marriage, benevolence, favour, trade or high-ranking official positions to attract the rulers of neighbouring ethnic groups or split up enemies.
- Countries can use armed forces as a deterrent for diplomatic purposes.

In sum, in China's strategic culture, at the top level, Chinese philosophy is peace loving. In China, there has been no war between religions, and the three major religions—namely, Buddhism, Taoism and Confucianism—coexist peacefully. At the middle level, China's traditional national strategic culture preferred defence over offence. If necessary, however, rulers of countries can launch military attacks to defend territory and people or to realise reunification. At the low level, China's military strategic culture and foreign strategic culture were realistic. Alastair Lain Johnston's viewpoint, therefore, that China's strategic culture was hard Realpolitik was wrong or only partly correct, because his research only touched on China's military strategic culture and foreign strategic culture during the Ming Dynasty.

The impact of China's strategic culture on China–US relations

Chinese philosophy has stressed peace despite differences. The philosophy of liberalism in the United States declares that every person is born equal. Liberalism is interested in multilateralism, international mechanisms and human rights in the international field, so if it becomes mainsteam in the United States, the possibility of military competition with China will be reduced and disputes between them over human rights could be increased. Neo-conservative thinking, on the other hand, stresses the rule of the jungle and when this philosophy is politically dominant, China and the United States could have some kind of military competition.

According to China's traditional national strategic culture, China would not challenge the leadership of the United States in the Asia-Pacific region and in the world, and would like to have a cooperative relationship with the United States, which would be beneficial for China–US relations.

Because China's military strategic and foreign strategic cultures are realistic, if the United States pursues policies of using military allies and sophisticated weapons against China, China will react. It could lead to a security dilemma between the two countries.

Reference

National Institute for Defence Studies 2001, *East Asian Strategic Review: 2001*, National Institute for Defence Studies, Tokyo, Japan.

Yi, Zhou 1996, *Collection of Five Classics*, Beijing Yanshan Publishing House.

Zi, Sun 1999, *Art of War of Sun Zi*, Shanxi Ancient Books Publishing House.

ENDNOTES

[1] *Documents of the 16th National Congress of the Communist Party of China*, 2002, Foreign Language Press, Beijing, China, p. 2.

[2] China's document on its position regarding New Security Concepts, put forward by the Chinese delegation at the meeting of the ASEAN Regional Forum, 31 July 2002, Seri Begawan, Brunei (*People's Daily*, Beijing, 2 August 2002, p. 3).

[3] A speech by Tang Jiaxuan, then Chinese Foreign Minister, at the fifty-seventh UN General Assembly, 13 December 2002, New York (*People's Daily*, 16 September 2002, p. 7).

[4] Speech by Hu Jintao, Chinese President, at the Summit Meeting of the United Nations' Sixtieth Anniversary, 15 September 2005 (*People's Daily*, 16 September 2005, p. 1).

[5] Speech by US President, George W. Bush, at the ceremony welcoming Chinese President, Hu Jintao, to the White House, 20 April 2006 (*People's Daily*, Beijing, 21 April 2006, p. 1).

Chapter 9

China's national defence: challenges and responses

Fan Gaoyue

This chapter is organised into three parts, covering: the main bases and principles of China's national defence policy, the main challenges China's national defence is facing and the responses of China's national defence policy.

The main bases and principles of China's national defence policy

Since 1998, China has issued national defence white papers biannually to expound its national defence policy to the world. With the changing international security situation and environment, China's national defence policy in different historical periods has been adjusted accordingly, but the basics remain unchanged. These basics are: China's national laws (the *Constitution of the People's Republic of China* and the National Defense Law), international relations principles, international security situations, national security interests, big countries' responsibilities, China's national, historical and cultural traditions, and the basic patterns of warfare.

Analysing New China's national defence policy in different historical periods, we discover that China always adheres to the following basic principles: first, strategic defence—that is, it always sticks to the tenet 'if you don't attack me, I will not attack you; if you attack me, I will surely attack you'; second, self-reliance—that is, China does not seek alliances with any big country or bloc, nor does it participate in any military bloc, and it handles all national defence and security matters independently; third, self-defence by the whole population—that is, to combine a streamlined standing army with a powerful reserve force and bring the integrated power of 'people's war' into full play; fourth, coordinated development—that is, national defence construction must be subordinated to and serve economic construction; fifth, safeguarding peace—that is, to safeguard world peace and oppose aggression and expansion.

The main challenges facing China's national defence

The world is undergoing major changes and readjustments. Peace and development remain the dominant themes of our era. Multi-polarisation and economic globalisation have accelerated and the serious imbalance in international strategic alignments is improving. Interdependence among countries is increasing. The duality of competition and cooperation among major powers becomes more obvious. At present, China does not face a realistic danger of being invaded by external enemies and its overall national strength and international influence are increasing. China's practical cooperation with major powers continues to grow, its friendly relations with its neighbouring countries and other developing countries have improved steadily. Although China enjoys a sound security environment, its national defence still faces the following challenges.

Challenge one

The international security environment has become more complicated. In 2006, the US Department of Defence (DoD) issued its Quadrennial Defence Review report, which observed that 'China has the greatest potential to compete militarily with the United States and field disruptive military technologies that could over time offset traditional US military advantages absent US counter strategies'. In the same year, the United States began to adjust its global military deployments and to enhance its military presence in the Asia-Pacific area by enlarging its military base on Guam, augmenting its forces in the Western Pacific, increasing special operations forces in East Asia's coastal areas and moving the First Corps headquarters from its homeland to Japan, and striving to station its forces permanently in the Middle East and Central Asia. Considering the United States' promise to defend Taiwan, these adjustments to a certain extent constitute a realistic threat to China's security. The military alliances between the United States, Japan and South Korea have been enhanced. The American–Japanese cooperation on missile defence has made great progress and the balance of strategic force in the Asia-Pacific area began to tilt towards the American–Japanese side. The United States plans to build global missile defence systems by deploying intercept missiles on its western coast and in Europe, and it is developing and deploying theatre missile defence systems with its allies, which will further unsettle the strategic balance among the big powers.

Challenge two

The activities of internal separatist forces run rampant. In Taiwan, with the change of leaders on 20 May 2008, some relaxation of tensions has been brought about in relations across the Taiwan Strait. The separatists advocating 'independence' for Taiwan are, however, not reconciled with their setbacks and have continued making efforts to promote Taiwanese independence, which is a live volcano that could influence the stability of the region. In Tibet, the separatists advocating Tibetan 'independence' stirred up the '3.14 Riot' and created a tense atmosphere by beating, smashing, robbing, burning and killing. In Xinjiang Uygur Autonomous Region, the Uygurs advocating independence for 'Eastern Turkestan' plotted several terrorist attacks. On 4 August 2008, they openly attacked an armed police unit undertaking its morning drill, causing 16 dead and 16 wounded. How to prevent and control various sabotage activities by separatist forces and maintain social stability in China are arduous tasks for the Chinese armed forces.

Challenge three

Territorial disputes remain. China has more than 20 neighbouring countries, with a land border of 22 000 km and a coastal border of 18 000 km. China has already settled demarcation of its land boundaries with 10 neighbouring countries, including Russia, Nepal and Myanmar, but still has disputes over land borders with India and Bhutan. China also has disputes over territorial waters or islands with eight countries, including Japan, South Korea, Vietnam and the Philippines. The disputes over land borders, territorial waters and islands have complicated historical causes and cannot be solved effectively within a short time. If not well handled, they could harm peace and stability in the region.

Challenge four

Military competition is intensifying. As military transformation develops in depth, each country has increased its military input, the quest to research and produce new high-tech weapons and equipment has accelerated and military competition characterised by 'informationisation' is intensifying. In 2008, the defence expenditure of the United States was US$607.26 billion, while Russia's was 959.6 billion roubles, an increase of 9.9 per cent and 16.7 per cent, respectively from the previous year. In recent years, China's defence expenditure has kept increasing but, compared with the United States, Russia and some other countries, it is still at a relatively low level. The growth in China's defence expenditure is due primarily to the following factors: increasing salaries and allowances for military personnel and improvements in their living conditions; increasing investment in weaponry, equipment and infrastructure; supporting the training of military personnel; compensating for price rises; and increasing expenses for international cooperation in non-traditional security fields. At present, in comparison with the armies of developed countries, the Chinese military's informationisation of weapons and equipment lags far behind. As military transformation deepens in developed countries, the gaps between the Chinese armed forces and those of developed countries in weapons and equipment will not be narrowed, but, on the contrary, could widen.

Challenge five

Diversified military tasks keep increasing. In the 1990s, the Chinese army began to take part in international peacekeeping operations led by the United Nations. At the same time, military operations other than war (MOOTW), such as relief efforts after floods and earthquakes, have increased substantially. The range of MOOTW has been widened and the scale of forces employed has been enlarged. In 1998, when floods hit the Yangtze, Songhuajiang and Nenjiang Rivers, 300 000 officers and soldiers rushed to the disaster-hit areas. In early 2008, when an extraordinarily serious disaster of snow and freezing rain hit southern China, about 100 000 People's Liberation Army (PLA) soldiers and armed policemen were deployed to the affected area. On 12 May 2008, when a huge earthquake measuring 8.0 on the Richter scale hit Wenchuan County, Sichuan Province, about 150 000 PLA soldiers and armed policemen rushed to the area to rescue those buried and care for the injured. During these MOOTW, PLA soldiers and armed policemen, fearing neither death nor hardships and tiredness, fought day and night to save lives and properties and were highly praised, loved and respected by the people. Owing to the lack of MOOTW theory, however, related professional training and special equipment, the Chinese army cannot adapt itself to diversified military tasks very well. At the end of 2004, when a tsunami occurred in the Indian Ocean, China did not send military forces to provide assistance or carry out rescues on a large scale. When the earthquake struck Wenchuan in May, the disaster-relief forces did not have the necessary heavy machinery for rescue. How to raise its capabilities to execute diversified military tasks is therefore an urgent task for the Chinese military.

The responses of China's national defence policy

In response to the complicated international security situation and ever changing grave challenges, China has continuously adjusted its national defence policy. To sum up, the responses of China's national defence policy include four aspects.

Response one

Preventing separation and safeguarding state sovereignty and territorial integrity are designated as the primary missions of the PLA. In June 1996, during his visit to Cornell University in the United States, Taiwan's leader Li Denghui expressed his desire to separate Taiwan from China. In 1999, Li officially put forth the fallacy of 'two sides, two countries'. In March 2000, the Democratic Progressive Party, which advocated Taiwanese independence, won the so-called 'presidential election' and became the ruling party. After Chen Shuibian came into power, he broke his promise of 'four nos and one without', pursued a radical policy for Taiwanese independence and launched 'de jure Taiwanese independence' activities such as constitutional reform, a referendum on joining the United Nations, and so on. The separation of Taiwan thus became China's gravest and most imminent threat. China's national defence policy has therefore designated 'counter-separation' as the primary mission of the PLA, and construction of the PLA has also been carried out around this mission. The purpose of China's development of military power is not, however, to attack Taiwan, but to maintain peace and stability across the Taiwan Strait because, only backed by powerful military strength can we deter the forces pushing for Taiwanese independence and avoid conflict. As Sun Zi in *The Art of War* says, 'To subdue the enemy without fighting is the supreme excellence.'

Response two

The second response emphasises the development of the navy, air force and second artillery capabilities. As the PLA originated from the army, the army is the 'elder brother' in the military and enjoys great advantages in scale and defence expenditure. With the advent of high-tech and 'informationised' warfare, the strategic status of the navy, air force and second artillery force began to rise and China's national defence policy began to show them more concern. In 1985, 1997 and 2003, China cut the size of the PLA by one million, 500 000 and 200 000 people respectively, with the army suffering the largest cut. The navy, air force and second artillery force suffered smaller cuts and some even had a small increase. Through restructuring, the proportions of the navy, air force and second artillery force in the PLA have been raised by 3.8 per cent, while that of the army has been lowered by 1.5 per cent. The input of defence expenditure for the navy, air force and second artillery force has also been increased.

Response three

The third response emphasises winning local wars under conditions of informationisation. With the rapid development of science and technology (information technology in particular) and their extensive application in the military field, the patterns of warfare have begun to change. Although China has always had a basically defensive military strategy, there have been changes of emphasis over time. During the 1980s, China's military strategy emphasised 'active defence and luring the enemy in deep' to win the 'people's war' under modern conditions. The 1990–91 Gulf War demonstrated in an all-round way the power, role and status of high-tech weapons and equipment and also predicted the trend of future warfare. China's national defence policy therefore shifted its emphasis from military preparation to winning local wars under the conditions of high technology. With the advent of the information era and large quantities of informationised weapons and equipment being used on the battlefield, the patterns of mechanised warfare of the industrial era began to evolve into those of informationised warfare.

Response four

The fourth response places stress on international cooperation. China's reform and open-door policy began in 1978, but its international security cooperation did not unfold until the 1990s. In April 1992, China formally organised its first 'blue helmet' troops and sent them to Cambodia to execute tasks. In May 1997,

China agreed to join the UN 'peacekeeping on-call arrangement'. By November 2007, China had sent a total of 9040 people to participate in 18 UN peacekeeping operations and became the largest contributor among the five permanent members of UN Security Council.

In addition, China has significantly expanded its involvement in international cooperation in non-traditional security fields such as counter-terrorism, cracking down on drug production and trafficking, non-proliferation, maritime search and rescue, severe acute respiratory syndrome (SARS), avian influenza and so on. The 2004 edition of China's national defence white paper lists carrying 'out military exchanges and cooperation' as a formal component of its national defence policy.

Chapter 10

China's defence industries: change and continuity

Richard A. Bitzinger and J. D. Kenneth Boutin

China's defence-industrial sector is being transformed by reforms introduced in the interest of enhancing its competitiveness and capacity to meet the ambitious conventional arms requirements of the People's Liberation Army (PLA). China's defence-industrial base is becoming more decentralised, with increasing scope for local state-owned enterprises (SOEs) and privately owned enterprises to contribute to research and development (R&D) and production. This chapter assesses the long-term implications of this structural transformation. The progressive 'marketisation' of R&D and production is strengthening China's capacity for sustained defence-industrial development and helping to narrow its capability gap with major industrialised states, but ingrained attitudes and procedures and enduring concern about the political implications of defence-industrial dependence limit the scope for structural reform. China is not in a position to exploit the full defence potential of its impressive industrial and technological progress in the near term, but its long-term prospects are more positive.

Defence-industrial development in China

Defence-industrial development has figured prominently in China's efforts to enhance its security in the face of perceived threats to its sovereignty, territorial integrity and national interests. The development of indigenous defence industries capable of supplying modern arms constituted a central pillar of the self-strengthening movement pursued by the Qing Dynasty in the late nineteenth and early twentieth centuries. Similar efforts were a feature of the 1916–28 'warlord period', when competing military leaders struggled for local and national power, and the Nationalist Government of the Republic of China devoted considerable resources to defence-industrial development during World War II.

The new Chinese Government moved quickly to restore and expand the defence-industrial base after 1949. Technological development 'to serve construction of…national defense' was enshrined in Article 43 of the Common Program of 1950, which constituted the initial de facto constitution of the People's Republic of China (Wang 1993:37). By 1950, the defence-industrial sector encompassed 45 factories employing some 100 000 workers (Shambaugh 2002:226). By the end of the decade, China was self-sufficient in terms of a comprehensive range of arms required by the land, air and naval branches of the PLA, with notable exceptions such as major surface combatants and long-range strike aircraft. Though the level of support for defence R&D and production has waxed and waned under the People's Republic and there have been a number of major policy shifts, the need to maintain key defence-industrial capabilities has never been in doubt.

The established Chinese defence-industrial model

China's post-1949 defence-industrial model was broadly similar to that of the Soviet Union. Defence-industrial activity was the exclusive domain of the State and China's defence-industrial base featured highly centralised control and a very bureaucratic structure. All arms production undertaken by SOEs and defence-related R&D were either allocated to a research institute answering to one of the Ministries of Machine Building responsible for various aspects of China's arms programs or undertaken by academic institutions that answered to the State. There was no apparent requirement to ensure that arms production was economically viable, though the substantial arms requirements of the PLA undoubtedly often resulted in considerable economies of scale. Since the 1950s, for example, China has produced more than 14 000 military aircraft and 50 000 aircraft engines, mostly for the PLA (Matthews and Bo 2002:36). The absence of a profit motive meant that no resources were devoted to developing arms tailored to the particular requirements of export customers.

Where the Chinese defence-industrial model differed from that of the Soviet Union was with respect to the importance attached to technological progress. Defence R&D and production in China were characterised by modest technological objectives. While the Soviet defence industry was geared to the requirements of providing a comprehensive range of arms that was relatively technologically advanced, if not necessarily on a par with comparable Western systems, China's sights were set on much less ambitious requirements. At no point did China strive to even approach foreign arms in qualitative terms, choosing instead to focus on the large-scale production of relatively unsophisticated arms. The Chinese defence industry established a reputation for the quantity of production of arms that were obsolescent, if not obsolete, and for progressing to new product generations long after their introduction elsewhere.

Defence industrialisation and autonomy

The objective of autonomy has been central to Chinese defence industrialisation. In this, China is by no means unique, but the form that this takes here has been distinct, and reflects China's particular security imperatives and policy objectives. These have been conditioned by its past difficulties in securing arms supplies and by the ideological basis of the ruling Chinese Communist Party. China was the subject of a Western arms embargo between the early 1950s and 1980s and, after 1960, was the target of what effectively constituted a Soviet arms embargo as well. The characteristic features of China's established defence-industrial model testify to the importance attached to self-reliance ('*zili gengsheng*'), which is seen in China as an 'indispensable component…of national security' (Park and Park 1988:119). China long pursued a general developmental approach summed up by the slogan of 'walking on two legs'. This emphasised the importance of relying on China's own capabilities, regardless of the level of efficiency or even the effectiveness that this involved.

The defence-industrial strategy of the People's Republic has been distinguished by the dedication and persistence with which the objective of autonomy has been pursued. In many states, practical efforts to promote defence-industrial autonomy are restricted to production capacity, but in China the long-term development of autonomy with respect to R&D and production is considered crucial. This has involved developing and maintaining a capacity to supply the complete range of arms required by the PLA, including in terms of the local production of all arms components. Studies of the Chinese defence industry generally see its defence industrialisation as being driven by the objective of maximising self-sufficiency (see, for example, Shambaugh 2002:226). It is noteworthy, for example, that China moved to reconstitute its defence-industrial capabilities in the 1950s despite its success in securing large-scale arms transfers from the Soviet Union. China developed its defence industries as a means of ensuring a domestic capacity to meet the material requirements of the PLA. Interest in providing arms as military assistance to friendly states constituted an objective of secondary importance, and there was no apparent interest in the commercial opportunities of arms exports until the 1980s, when China emerged as a major supplier of arms to the Middle East.

The importance attached to defence-industrial autonomy was manifest in the relative isolation of Chinese R&D processes. Defence-related R&D in China did benefit from foreign input, but technological flows were unidirectional and did not involve arrangements that had the potential to generate long-term dependent ties, including collaborative R&D arrangements. This included technology transfers from the Soviet Union during the 1950s. After the termination of Soviet defence-industrial support in 1960, China continued to exploit foreign sources of arms-related technology, but this was limited to the reverse engineering of arms and components, either in terms of the outright copying of foreign designs or the derivation of technological insights contributing to the development of more advanced arms in China. This involved the opportunistic exploitation of opportunities as they arose, rather than any regularised ties. Only towards the end of the Cold War did China supplement such efforts with selective purchases of technology and subsystems from other states. Until recently, none of China's external defence-industrial arrangements threatened its efforts to maintain independent arms R&D and production capabilities. The effective isolation of China's defence-industrial base eliminated the prospect of dependence on potential adversaries, which China had been unable to overcome despite its best efforts during the self-strengthening movement.

China's defence-industrial approach came at some cost. China's reluctance to engage other states on defence-industrial issues other than the terms that it did was inherently limiting in qualitative terms, particularly given China's relatively low technological base and the limited resources it was in a position to devote to defence-industrial development. That China was able to meet its defence-industrial needs with so little foreign support was due in large part to its unique arms requirements. For most of the history of the People's Republic, China pursued a strategy of 'people's war', which emphasised drawing an attacker deep into the Chinese hinterland, where superior numbers and geography could be exploited to China's advantage. This approach obviated the requirement for conventional arms that were on a qualitative par with those of China's potential adversaries. This factor, along with the difficulty involved in supplying China's large military establishment with sophisticated arms and developing the logistical capacity to support them, meant that less-advanced arms that were within the developmental and production capacity of Chinese industry were sufficient.

Even so, China struggled to meet its limited requirements in terms of more complex categories of arms such as combat aircraft. Here, while there was progress in absolute terms, in relative terms China's defence-industrial capacity regressed over time. The 1960s saw China producing the J-6 fighter, which was a derivative of the early 1950s-vintage Soviet MiG-19, but 20 years later it had advanced only to the point where it was producing the J-7, based on the Soviet MiG-21 design from the late 1950s. While the leap involved in progressing from the technological generation of the MiG-19 to that of the MiG-21 was considerable, its failure to advance further than this meant that China steadily fell behind its potential adversaries. China's struggle to advance technologically in areas such as aerospace was exacerbated by the severe anti-intellectualism of the Cultural Revolution, which saw the closure of many academic institutions.

China's defence-industrial approach came under threat only when it became apparent that it was incapable of meeting its changing arms requirements, which resulted from its evolving military strategy. By the 1980s, the utility of the strategy of people's war was being questioned. Its limitations were demonstrated by the Gulf War of 1990–91, when American-led forces soundly defeated numerically superior, relatively well-equipped Iraqi forces within a matter of days. This highlighted the potential conferred by conventional military capabilities that were beyond the scope of China's defence industries to support.

The Chinese military-industrial complex in the late 1990s

By the late 1990s, China still possessed one of the most technologically backward defence industries in the world; most indigenously developed weapons systems were at least 15 to 20 years behind those of the West—basically comparable with 1970s or (at best) early 1980s-era technology—and quality control was consistently poor. China's defence R&D base was regarded to be deficient in several critical areas, including aeronautics, propulsion (such as jet engines), microelectronics, computers, avionics, sensors and seekers, electronic warfare and advanced materials. Furthermore, the Chinese military-industrial complex remains weak in the area of systems integration—that is, the ability to design and develop a piece of military equipment that integrates hundreds or even thousands of disparate components and subsystems and have it function effectively as a single unit (Medeiros et al. 2005:4–18).

Consequently, aside from a few 'pockets of excellence' such as ballistic missiles, the Chinese military-industrial complex appeared to demonstrate few capacities for designing and producing relatively advanced conventional weapon systems. China generally confronted considerable difficulties in moving prototypes into production, resulting in extended development phases, frequent program delays and limited production runs. For example, the J-10 fighter jet—China's premier fourth-generation-plus combat aircraft—took more than a decade to move from program start to first flight, and more than 20 years before it entered operational service with the PLA Air Force (Medeiros et al. 2005:161–2; Shambaugh 2002:261–2). Even after the Chinese began building a weapon system, production runs were often small and fitful. According to Western estimates, during much of the 1990s the entire Chinese aircraft industry of about 600 000 workers manufactured only a few dozen fighter aircraft a year, mainly 1960s and 1970s-vintage J-8 IIs and J-7s (Allen 1997:244). According to the authoritative *Jane's Fighting Ships*, China launched only three destroyers and nine frigates between 1990 and 1999—a little more than one major surface combatant a year. Moreover, the lead boat in the Song-class submarine program—China's first indigenously designed diesel–electric submarine—was commissioned only in 1999, eight years after construction began (Jane's Information Group 1999:119–20, 124–5).

Consequently, despite years of arduous efforts, the inability of China's domestic defence industry to generate the necessary technological breakthroughs for advanced arms production meant that Beijing continued to rely heavily—even increasingly—on direct foreign technological inputs in critical areas. It is believed that the J-10 fighter, for example, is based heavily on technology derived from Israel's cancelled Lavi fighter-jet program. Chinese dependency is especially acute when it comes to jet engines, marine diesel engines and fire-control radar and other avionics. For example, endemic 'technical difficulties' surrounding the JH-7 fighter-bomber's indigenous engine resulted in significant program delays, forcing the Chinese to approach the British in the late 1990s about acquiring additional Spey engines in order to keep the aircraft's production line going; additionally, current versions of the J-10 are being outfitted with a Russian engine, until the Chinese aviation industry is able to perfect an indigenous replacement (Medeiros et al. 2005:170–1). The new Song-class submarine uses a German-supplied diesel engine, while the Ming and Han-class submarines have reportedly been upgraded with a French sonar and combat system. Chinese surface combatants incorporate a number of foreign-supplied systems, including Ukrainian gas-turbine engines, French surface-to-air missiles, Italian torpedoes and Russian naval helicopters.

Finally, and perhaps most significant, in the past decade—and particularly since the turn of the century—the PLA has increasingly favoured imported weapons platforms over locally built counterparts. From this, one can infer that the Chinese military remains dissatisfied with the quality and capabilities of weapon systems coming out of domestic arms factories, or that local industry is unable to produce sufficient numbers of the kinds of weapons required by the PLA. In the early 1990s, for example, despite the fact that China already had four fighter aircraft programs either in production or development—the J-7, J-8 II, JH-7 and J-10—the PLA nevertheless decided to buy several dozen Su-27 fighters; this purchase was later supplemented by an agreement to license-produce 200 Su-27s and a subsequent purchase of approximately 100 more advanced Su-30 strike aircraft. The PLA Navy (PLAN) is currently acquiring 12 Kilo-class submarines and four Sovremennyy-class destroyers (armed with supersonic SS-N-22 anti-ship cruise missiles), even though Chinese shipyards are building the Song and several new types of destroyers. In addition, China has reportedly purchased precision-guided munitions, advanced air-to-air missiles, airborne warning and control aircraft and transport aircraft from Russia, as well as acquiring several hundred S-300 and SA-15 surface-to-air missiles. Consequently, China has become one of the world's largest arms importers, and, between 1998 and 2005, Beijing signed new arms import agreements worth some US$16.7 billion; in 2005 alone, it purchased US$2.8 billion worth of foreign weapon systems (Grimmett 2006:56, 57).

Compounding these technological deficiencies was a number of structural and organisational/cultural deficiencies that impeded the design, development and manufacture of advanced conventional arms. Overall, arms production in China has largely been an inefficient, wasteful and unprofitable affair. One reason for this was over-capacity: quite simply, China possessed far too many workers, too many factories and too much productive capacity for what few weapons it produced, resulting in redundancy and a significant duplication of effort, inefficient production and wasted resources. The Chinese aircraft industry, for example, was estimated in the late 1990s to possess a workforce nearly three times as large as it required (*China Daily*, 3 October 1997). Within the shipbuilding industry, output during the same period was only 17 tonnes a person a year, compared with about 700 tonnes a person in shipyards in more advanced countries (Gangcan 1998:17).

By the mid 1990s, at least 70 per cent of China's state-run factories were thought to be operating at a loss, and the arms industries were reportedly among the biggest money-losers. As a result, most defence firms were burdened with considerable debt, much of it owed to state-run banks (which were obliged to lend money to state-owned firms); at the same time, arms factories were owed money, which was nearly uncollectible, by other unprofitable state-owned companies (Frankenstein 1999:197–9; 'Industry embraces market forces', *Jane's Defence Weekly*, 16 December 1998, p. 28; Jencks 1999:617).

The creation of China's 'third-line' defence industries—that is, the establishment of redundant centres of armaments production in the remote interior of southern and western China—in the 1960s and 1970s only added to the overcapacity, underutilisation and unprofitability of the Chinese military-industrial complex. Estimates are that from 1966 to 1975, third-line construction consumed perhaps two-thirds of all industrial investment. Even by the late 1990s, approximately 55 per cent of China's defence industries were located within the third line, yet most of these industries were much less productive than coastal factories and continued to operate in the red (Shambaugh 2002:277; Frankenstein and Gill 1996:403).

Another structural impediment affecting the Chinese defence-industrial complex was the emergence of a highly compartmentalised and vertically integrated defence-industrial base. Such a stratified environment had several repercussions for the local defence industry. It restricted the diffusion of advanced, relevant civilian technologies to the defence sector. It also limited communications between the R&D institutes that designed the weapons and the factories that produced them, between defence enterprises when it came to collaborating on weapons projects and even between the defence industry and its major consumer, the PLA, when it came to requirements and specifications. It also exacerbated redundancy and the duplication of effort within the arms industry, as each defence enterprise tried to 'do it all', resulting in the maintenance of expensive but under-utilised manufacturing processes, such as dedicated second and third-tier supplier networks and the establishment of in-house machine shops for parts production, instead of outsourcing such manufacturing to other firms.

Finally, China's military-industrial complex functioned for a long time under an organisational and managerial culture that, in a manner typical of most SOEs, was highly centralised, hierarchical, bureaucratic and risk averse. This stymied innovation, retarded R&D and further added to program delays. In a study on Chinese capacities for innovation, two Western analysts (Arayama and

Mourdoukoutas 1999) argued that 'Chinese managers do not have the will, the expertise, or the freedom to take the risks and make the adjustment associated with innovations'. Consequently, production management was often highly centralised and 'personality-centric', with most critical project decisions being made by a single chief engineer. At the same time, lower-level managers tended to be 'conformist, adhering to standard rules and procedures rather than to personal judgments based on their professional experiences'. Hence, they were usually reluctant to make 'learning mistakes' or to act on their own to deal with problems that might arise on the factory floor, thereby inhibiting experimentation and innovation (Arayama and Mourdoukoutas 1999).

An American aerospace industry representative best summed up China's problems with armaments production in the 1990s, writing that:

> Part of the problem with Chinese [aircraft] manufacturing…is that industrial management in China still relies on 1950s Soviet styles. This involves 'batch-building' a full order of aircraft in advance based on state-planned and dictated order[s] for parts and materials. As a consequence of this system, there are no direct lines of accountability for quality control, and no cost-cutting discussions or steps available to mid-level management. There is no competitive bidding for contracts, workers are redundant, and schedules continually slip because state planning doesn't have a fixed required-delivery date for products…Young managers stay risk-averse and are reluctant to change or improve the system. (Quoted in Wortzel 1998:20)

Reforming China's defence industry, 1997 to the present

Chinese authorities have long been aware of the deficiencies in their defence industry and have undertaken several rounds of reform to improve and upgrade their R&D and production processes. The intention of this overall restructuring effort was to spur the defence SOEs to act as true industrial enterprises and therefore be more responsive to their customer base (that is, the PLA), and to reform, modernise and 'marketise' their business operations.

These goals are central to the PLA's new modernisation strategy, as laid out in China's 2004 defence white paper, of 'generation leap'—that is, to skip or shorten stages of R&D and generations of weapons systems. This process, in turn, entails a 'double construction' approach of mechanisation and 'informisation' in order to concurrently upgrade and digitise the PLA. Part of this strategy also depends on China's 'latecomer advantage' of being able to more quickly exploit technological trails blazed by others, as well as avoiding their mistakes and technological dead ends (Ji 2004).

In the early 1990s, in an effort to 'corporatise' the defence-industrial base, the Chinese transformed their military-industrial complex from a series of machine-building ministries into large SOEs. The Ministry of Aerospace, for example, was broken up into the Aviation Industries of China (AVIC; aircraft) and the China Aerospace Corporation (CASC; missiles and space), while the Ministry of Atomic Energy was converted into the China National Nuclear Corporation (CNNC). Other 'super SOEs' within the defence industry included the China Ordnance Industry Corporation (COIC, often referred to as Norinco; ground combat systems) and the China State Shipbuilding Corporation (CSSC; naval systems). At the same time, control of individual production facilities, research units and trading companies was transferred to these new corporations.

The most recent round of defence industry reforms began more than a decade ago, in September 1997, when the Fifteenth Communist Party Congress laid out an ambitious agenda for restructuring and downsizing the SOE sector (including the defence industries) and for opening up SOEs to free-market forces—that is, supply-and-demand dynamics, competitive products, quality assurance and fiscal self-responsibility. In March 1998, the Ninth National People's Congress further refined this agenda by announcing plans to reorganise the government's defence industry oversight and control apparatus and to establish new defence enterprise groups.

One of the most important decisions to come out of the 1998 congress was the creation of a new PLA-run General Armaments Department (GAD), acting as the primary purchasing agent for the PLA, overseeing defence procurement and new weapons programs. As a 2005 RAND report put it, the GAD is part of a process 'to create [a] system that will unify, standardize, and legalize the [Chinese] weapons procurement process' (Crane et al. 2005:165). In particular, the GAD is supposed to ensure that local arms producers meet PLA requirements when it comes to capabilities, quality, costs and program milestones.

Another key element of current defence reforms was the creation in July 1999 of 10 new defence industry enterprise groups (DIEGs) (Table 1). These DIEGs were supposed to function as true conglomerates, integrating R&D, production and marketing. Breaking up the old SOEs was also intended to encourage the new industry enterprise groups to compete with each other for PLA procurement contracts, which it was hoped would pressure them to be more efficient and technologically innovative. At the same time, the government's role in the daily operations of the defence industry was to be greatly reduced, and these new enterprise groups were given the authority to manage their own operations as well as to take responsibility for their own profits and losses.

Another crucial aspect of these new reform initiatives was the declared intent to significantly downsize the Chinese military-industrial complex, including eliminating (through retirement, attrition or even lay-offs) as much as one-third of its workforce. The aircraft industry, for example, intended to downsize by 200 000 workers. The rationalisation of the defence industry was also supposed to include factory closings and consolidation as a result of government-encouraged mergers, as part of the policy of 'letting the strong annex the weak'.

Table 10.1 China defence industry restructuring, July 1999

Old corporate entity	New enterprise group	Major products
Aviation Industries of China (AVIC)	China Aviation Industry Corp. I (AVIC I)	Fighter aircraft, bombers, transports, advanced trainers, commercial airliners
	China Aviation Industry Corp. II (AVIC II)	Helicopters, attack aircraft, light trainers, UAVs
China Aerospace Corporation (CASC)	China Aerospace Science and Technology Corporation (CASC)	Space-launch vehicles, satellites, missiles
	China Aerospace Science and Industry Corporation (CASIC)	Missiles, electronics, other equipment
China Ordnance Industry Corporation (COIC/Norinco)	China North Industries Group Corporation	Tanks, armoured vehicles, artillery, ordnance
	China South Industries Group Corporation	Miscellaneous ordnance, automobiles, motorcycles
China State Shipbuilding Corporation (CSSC)	China State Shipbuilding Corporation (CSSC)	Destroyers, frigates, commercial ships
	China State Shipbuilding Industry Corporation (CSIC)	Destroyers, commercial ships
China National Nuclear Corporation (CNNC)	China National Nuclear Corporation (CNNC)	Nuclear energy development, nuclear fuel and equipment
	China Nuclear Engineering and Construction Group Corporation (CNECC)	Construction of nuclear power plants, other heavy construction

At the same time, Beijing prodded defence industries to undertake more civilian production as a means of acquiring dual-use technologies that could also be used to support arms production. This strategy goes back to the late 1970s and the enunciation of Deng Xiaoping's so-called 16-character slogan: 'Combine the military and civil/combine peace and war/give priority to military products/let the civil support the military.' Whereas earlier efforts at civil–military integration (CMI) tended to revolve mostly around conversion—that is, switching military factories over to civilian use—China's approach to CMI after 1997 entailed a critical shift in policy towards promoting integrated dual-use industrial systems capable of developing and manufacturing defence and military goods; or, as one Western analyst (Folta 1992:1) put it, 'swords into plowshares…and better swords'. This new strategy was embodied and made a priority in the defence industry's tenth Five-Year Plan for 2001–05, which emphasised the dual importance of the transfer of military technologies to commercial use and the transfer of commercial technologies to military use, and which therefore called for the Chinese arms industry to not only develop dual-use technologies but to actively promote joint civil–military technological cooperation. Consequently, the spin-on of advanced commercial technologies to the Chinese military-industrial complex and in support of the overall modernisation of the PLA was made explicit policy.

The key areas of China's new focus on dual-use technological development and subsequent spin-on include microelectronics, space systems, new materials (such as composites and alloys), propulsion, missiles, computer-aided manufacturing and particularly information technologies. In the past decade, Beijing has worked hard to encourage further domestic development and growth in these sectors *and* to expand linkages and collaboration between China's military-industrial complex and civilian high-technology sectors. In 2002, for example, the Chinese Government created a new industry enterprise group, the China Electronics Technology Corporation, to promote national technological and industrial developments in the area of defence-related electronics. Under the tenth Five-Year Plan, many technology breakthroughs generated under the so-called '863' science and technology program, initiated in March 1986, were finally slated for development and industrialisation. Defence enterprises have formed partnerships with Chinese universities and civilian research institutes to establish technology incubators and undertake cooperative R&D on dual-use technologies. Additionally, foreign high-technology firms wishing to invest in China have been pressured to set up joint R&D centres and to transfer more technology to China.

In this regard, China's military shipbuilding appears particularly to have benefited from CMI efforts in the past decade. After an initial period of basically low-end commercial shipbuilding—such as bulk carriers and container ships—China's shipyards have, since the mid 1990s, progressed towards more sophisticated ship design and construction work. In particular, moving into commercial shipbuilding began to bear considerable fruit beginning in the late 1990s, as Chinese shipyards modernised and expanded operations, building huge new dry docks, acquiring heavy-lift cranes and computerised cutting and welding tools, and more than doubling their shipbuilding capacity. At the same time, Chinese shipbuilders entered into a number of technical cooperation agreements and joint ventures with shipbuilding firms in Japan, South Korea, Germany and other countries, which gave them access to advanced ship designs and manufacturing technologies—in particular, computer-assisted design and manufacturing, modular construction techniques, advanced ship-propulsion systems and numerically controlled processing and testing equipment. As a result, military shipbuilding programs co-located at Chinese shipyards have been able to leverage these considerable infrastructure and software improvements when it comes to design, development and construction (Medeiros et al. 2005:140–52).

China's nascent space industry has also spurred the development and application of dual-use technologies. This includes telecommunications satellites, as well as China's rudimentary Beidou navigation satellite system and its Ziyuan-1 and Ziyuan-2 Earth-observation satellites. In addition, many of the technologies being developed for commercial reconnaissance satellites, such as charge-coupled device cameras, multispectral scanners and synthetic aperture radar imagers, have obvious spin-on potential for military systems.

Finally, the PLA has clearly profited from exploiting the development and growth of the country's commercial information technology (IT) industry. The PLA is striving to expand and improve its capacities for command, control and communications, information processing and information warfare, and it has been able to enlist local IT firms—many of which have close ties with China's military-industrial complex and were even founded by former PLA officers—in support of its efforts. Consequently, the PLA has developed its own separate military communications network, utilising fibre-optic cable, cellular and wireless systems, microwave relays and long-range high-frequency radios, as well as computer local area networks.

A disappointing track record

Nevertheless, Chinese efforts to reform its military-industrial complex have been disappointing. If the intention of creating new industrial enterprise groups was to inject greater competition into China's military-industrial complex—and therefore spur innovation and greater responsiveness to PLA systems requirements—these restructuring efforts have largely been a failure. The GAD, for example, has yet to implement competitive bidding and market pricing into the overall arms procurement process; in particular, competitive bidding is apparently still not used when it comes to major weapons programs, as any purchases of more than CNY2 million (less than US$250 000) are exempt (Crane et al. 2005:167).

There is also little evidence to suggest that recent institutional reforms have strengthened PLA oversight of armaments manufacturing, particularly when it comes to quality control. RAND notes that the military has long had a Military Representative Office (MRO) system in place in many factories to watch over production, but even it admits that this system is woefully understaffed and ineffective when it comes to overseeing armaments production and quality control, and that the effectiveness of current reform efforts is 'far from clear' (Medeiros et al. 2005:45–6).

Moreover, at one time it was expected that the Chinese would create large, trans-sectoral, cross-competing defence conglomerates, similar to the South Korean *chaebols* or, more specifically, to horizontally integrated mega-defence companies such as Lockheed Martin or Britain's BAE Systems. Such a strategy would have entailed a much more complicated restructuring of the defence industry, crafting enterprise groups that would have competed with each other to produce a broad array of weaponry. Instead, all Beijing did was break up each of its former defence corporations into smaller groups.

With few exceptions, too, China's new DIEGs still do not compete with each other when it comes to defence materiel. Of the two new enterprise groups replacing the old AVIC, for example, all fighter aircraft production is concentrated within one DIEG, while all helicopter and trainer-jet production is centred in the other. The nuclear industry will be split into separate enterprises for either construction or nuclear energy development, while Norinco appears to have been subdivided into one enterprise group concerned mostly with armoured vehicles and ground ordnance, while the other is almost entirely civilianised, specialising in automobile and motorcycle production. In fact, Beijing appears to have *intended* that these new defence industries not vie directly with each other. For example, the two new aerospace (missile) enterprise groups do not compete in terms of products, but rather 'in terms of their systems of organization and their operational mechanisms' ('Applying technology to national defence', *China Space News*, 26 May 1999). Naval construction is the only defence sector that appears to be truly competitive in that both major shipbuilding companies (CSSC and CSIC) vie with each other for PLAN contracts.

It could even be that the Chinese have abandoned the idea of competing defence firms: in 2008, Beijing announced that AVIC I and AVIC II would merge, creating, again, a single aviation company. This new, reunited AVIC will also establish a cross-corporate subsidiary, similar to Europe's Airbus, dedicated to developing and manufacturing large passenger jets (Minnick 2008).

Rationalisation of the defence industry has also been much slower than expected. Details are sketchy, but according to one Western estimate, no more than 20 per cent of the labour force in the overall defence sector has been laid off ('Chinese defence industry: Chinese puzzle', *Jane's Defence Weekly*, 21 January 2004). AVIC, for example, had downsized by only 10 per cent overall, and this was likely accomplished through retirement and job leavers ('Chinese defence industry: Chinese puzzle', *Jane's Defence Weekly*, 21 January 2004). At the same time, there have been few cases of arms factories being closed or merged. Much of the defence industry therefore appears to still suffer from excess capacity, in terms of the workforce and redundant manufacturing capacity.

It is also unclear how independent these new defence enterprises will be of government control or how responsible they will ultimately be for their own profits and losses. Beijing made it clear from the beginning that arms production was a strategic industry too critical to national security to be privatised, and that it would keep the new DIEGs under much stricter supervision than other types of reformed SOEs. At the same time, these same rules will work in favour of the arms industries, as Beijing will likely feel pressured to continue to prop up unprofitable defence enterprises in order to preserve key arms programs.

Above all, the reform initiatives implemented so far do not directly address those impediments affecting technology absorption and upgrading of China's defence industry—that is, the lack of advanced technical skills and expertise, compartmentalisation and redundancy within the industrial base and a bureaucratic/risk-averse corporate culture. As a result, it is doubtful that these reforms will go very far in injecting market forces that will, in turn, drive the modernisation of the Chinese military-industrial complex and affect China's ability to develop and manufacture highly advanced conventional weapons systems. It is also doubtful whether there really exists much of a latecomer advantage when it comes to extremely esoteric high-tech sectors such as arms production, where the technological demands are very high and the economic pay-offs are very low. Even RAND noted that while 'the technological gap between China's military aviation industry and that of the United States and other major aviation producers will likely narrow in coming years, [it] will still remain significant unless China makes fundamental changes in contracting and enterprise management' (Crane et al. 2005:180).

Chinese arms production: success in spite of failed reforms?

Despite reforms making little apparent progress, the Chinese defence industry appears to be booming. Production and sales are up—by 19 per cent and 14 per cent, respectively, in 2001 (the last year for which we have reliable data)—and China's military-industrial complex technically broke even in 2002 after eight straight years of losses. The missile and shipbuilding sectors have been particularly profitable in recent years ('Chinese defence industry: Chinese puzzle', *Jane's Defence Weekly*, 21 January 2004; Medeiros et al. 2005:8).

It is also increasingly evident that the Chinese have in recent years greatly added to their military capabilities in terms of power projection, stand-off precision strike and improved command, control, communications, computing, intelligence, surveillance and reconnaissance (C4ISR). China's defence industry has begun manufacturing and delivering to the PLA several new types of advanced weapons systems, including the fourth-generation J-10 fighter, an upgraded version of its JH-7 fighter-bomber, the HQ-9 long-range surface-to-air missile (akin to the US Patriot air-defence missile), the improved Song-class diesel–electric submarine and the Type-052C destroyer (which incorporates low-observable features and an Aegis-type phased-array air defence radar into its design). Moreover, the quality and capabilities of *some* Chinese weaponry have also apparently improved. Recent versions of the Song-class submarine, for example, are outfitted with a skewed propeller for improved quieting and are capable of carrying an encapsulated anti-ship cruise missile that can be launched underwater.

The shipbuilding industry has made particular progress in modernising its design and manufacturing capabilities and in spinning-on commercial shipbuilding technologies to its naval construction side. Chinese shipbuilding is competitive domestically and globally (at least, at the low end of the technology scale), and it also appears to be profitable—so much so that it is the only sector in the defence industry that is actually *adding* productive capacity (that is, new shipyards and more workers). This in turn has permitted a significant expansion in naval-ship construction since the turn of the century, and, since 2000, China has begun construction of at least six new destroyers, seven frigates and eight diesel-powered submarines—more than double the rate of naval-ship construction during the 1990s.

Nevertheless, most progress in expanding armaments production, quantitatively and qualitatively, seems to have come about *despite* defence industry reforms—or at least the more recent attempts at reform—rather than *because* of them. Many of the so-called successes in generating new-generation weapon systems actually have their genesis in design and development decisions made years, even decades, ago—that is, long before the reforms of the late 1990s were inaugurated. These weapons programs were already in the pipeline and on schedule to enter production in the late 1990s and the first decade of the twenty-first century, and while the most recent reform efforts could have helped to accelerate or expand production of these weapons systems, they certainly did not play any key role in their initiation. For example, the success of the Chinese shipbuilding industry appears to be the result mostly of decisions made back in the early 1980s to commercialise the shipbuilding sector, to open up the industry to foreign technology inputs and to compete on the global market.

In addition, it is perhaps premature to make overly optimistic and sweeping statements about recent progress in modernising the Chinese defence-industrial base. In particular, the continuing lack of transparency on the part of the Chinese forces Western analysts to rely too much on scanty, often anecdotal, evidence and inference. Some new weapons systems and platforms could *appear* to be more modern and more capable, but in the absence of sufficient and reliable information (which is perhaps collectable only by covert means), one can only speculate about any true increase in the capabilities and quality of weapons systems presently coming off Chinese assembly lines. We also continue to lack detailed and consistent economic data regarding the Chinese defence industry (such as sales, profits, capacity utilisation, productivity, and so on) when it comes to assessing the success of defence-sector market reforms.

Moreover, rising defence spending also likely has had as much to do with the recent expansion in Chinese arms production as any reform efforts. Chinese military expenditure has nearly quadrupled in real terms since the mid 1990s. China's official 2007 defence budget was CNY350 billion (US$45 billion)—an increase of nearly 18 per cent from the previous year and thus continuing a trend of double-digit real increases in Chinese military spending extending back more than a decade. PLA annual spending on equipment increased from US$3.1 billion in 1997 to an estimated US$12.3 billion in 2006—a fourfold increase in real spending; at this rate, the 2007 equipment budget would total about US$15 billion (not including likely extra-budgetary funding for foreign arms purchases, which was running at about US$1.5–2 billion a year). It could be argued, therefore, that simply throwing more money at the problem has had the most impact on the local defence industry—that is, in increasing procurement spending and therefore production, and by providing more funding for R&D.

It also is important to note that the sharpest edges of the pointy end of the PLA spear are still mostly foreign—and particularly Russian—sourced, such as the Su-27 and Su-30 fighters, the Sovremennyy-class destroyers and S-300 surface-to-air missiles. They are, with few exceptions (such as tactical ballistic missiles or nuclear submarines), still the most critical force multipliers when it comes to calculating Chinese military power.

Overall, it appears that Beijing's formal strategy regarding its defence sector still relies on minor structural tinkering, a healthy increase in defence spending and a continuing reliance on 'pockets of excellence'. While past reform efforts have resulted in some technological and structural improvements in weapons R&D and manufacturing, China's military-industrial complex remains in many respects an inefficient and less-than-optimal production model. This will continue to exert a drag on the Chinese military modernisation process and make it harder for the PLA to close technology and capability gaps with its rivals.

It is important to note, however, the long-term potential of China's general industrial transformation. The growing scope for non-state economic activities in China extends to militarily relevant high-technology industries, and there are numerous indications that the private sector is eager to avail itself of the opportunity to develop and produce arms for the PLA and for export. There is some recognition of this potential on the part of Chinese authorities, who are permitting non-state enterprises to enter the defence market. In 2006, for example, it was announced that the State was prepared to subsidise private-sector arms production (Vogel 2006:18). It remains to be seen how this trend will develop or what impact it will have, but if China is able to effectively harness the potential inherent in its dynamic industrialised economy, this could help to offset the limitations of the state defence-industrial sector outlined above.

Conclusions

China faces major obstacles in developing its defence-industrial capabilities. These stem from its structural basis and its political requirements, which will continue to encourage extensive reliance on autonomous national industries under the close supervision—if not the direct control—of the State. China can, however, be expected to continue to seek foreign technological inputs to help address particular equipment requirements and even to import arms when these could be developed locally, in cases where this is seen as justified by the capability difference involved.

The transformation of China's defence-industrial sector likely will continue to be a gradual, incremental process that is beset by major difficulties. The principal features of China's emerging defence-industrial model are continued strong state direction and a continued reliance on SOEs for a considerable amount of R&D and production, but some acceptance of a defence-industrial role for private enterprise, in terms of meeting China's requirements and those of other states.

China could, in the long term, be in a much better position to provide the PLA with the advanced arms it requires, and to do so in a much more timely manner than currently is the case. How successful its efforts are will depend in no small part on the extent to which it is prepared to adhere to established objectives of defence-industrial autonomy. Opening up defence-related R&D and production to market forces holds great promise, but this will force political authorities in China to carefully consider which sovereign capabilities are crucial and which are not.

References

Allen, Ken 1997, 'PLAAF modernization: an assessment', in James Lilly and Chuck Downs (eds), *Crisis in the Taiwan Strait*, NDU Press, Washington, DC.

Arayama, Yuko and Mourdoukoutas, Panos 1999, *China Against Herself: Innovation or imitation in global business?*, Quorum, Westport, Conn.

Crane, Keith et al. 2005, *Modernizing China's Military*, RAND.

Folta, Paul H. 1992, *From Swords to Plowshares? Defence Industry Reform in the PRC*, Westview, Boulder, Colo.

Frankenstein, John 1999, 'China's defense industries: a new course?', in James C. Mulvenon and Richard H. Yang (eds), *The People's Liberation Army in the Information Age*, RAND, Santa Monica, Calif.

Frankenstein, John and Gill, Bates 1996, 'Current and future challenges facing Chinese defense industries', *China Quarterly*, June.

Gangcan, Rao 1998, Development and outlook in new building technology in China, Manuscript.

Grimmett, Richard F. 2006, *Conventional Arms Transfers to Developing Nations, 1998–2005*, 23 October 2006, United States Congressional Research Service, Washington, DC.

Jane's Information Group 1999, *Jane's Fighting Ships, 1999–2000*, Jane's Information Group, London.

Jencks, Harlan 1999, 'COSTIND is dead, long live COSTIND! Restructuring China's defence scientific, technical, and industrial sector', in James C. Mulvenon and Richard H. Yang (eds), *The People's Liberation Army in the Information Age*, RAND, Santa Monica, Calif.

Ji, You 2004, 'China's emerging national strategy', *China Brief*, 24 November 2004.

Matthews, Ron and Bo, Xu 2002, 'China's aerospace self-reliance still elusive', *Asia-Pacific Defence Reporter*, vol. 28, no. 6, p. 36.

Medeiros, Evan S., Cliff, Roger, Crane, Keith and Mulvenon, James C. 2005, *A New Direction for China's Defense Industry*, RAND, Santa Monica, Calif.

Minnick, Wendell 2008, 'Chinese aviation may portend military applications', *Defence News*, 4 August 2008.

Park, Han S. and Park, Kyung A. 1988, 'Ideology and security: self-reliance in China and North Korea', in Edward E. Azar and Chung-In Moon (eds), *National Security in the Third World: The management of internal and external threats*, Edward Elgar Publishing, Aldershot.

Shambaugh, David 2002, *Modernizing China's Military: Progress, problems, and prospects*, University of California Press, Berkeley, Calif.

Shichor, Yitzhak 1998, 'Conversion and diversion: the politics of China's military industry after Mao', in Efraim Inbar and Benzion Zilbergfarb (eds), *The Politics and Economics of Defence Industries*, Frank Cass, London.

Vogel, Ben 2006, 'China to subsidise private sector defence activities', *Jane's Defence Weekly*, vol. 43, no. 33, 16 August 2006, p. 18.

Wang, Yeu-Farn 1993, *China's Science and Technology Policy: 1949–1989*, Avebury, Aldershot.

Wortzel, Larry M. 1998, *China's Military Potential*, October, US Army War College, Carlisle, Pa.

Multilateral processes: countering or reflecting regional cleavages?

Chapter 11

China's participation in Asian multilateralism: pragmatism prevails

Mingjiang Li

Introduction

China started to truly participate in various multilateral regimes after it was admitted into the United Nations (UN) and became a permanent member of the UN Security Council in the early 1970s. Its involvement in international economic institutions intensified as its reform and opening-up program was initiated in the early 1980s and deepened in the 1990s. China's participation in Asian regional multilateralism, however, lagged behind its presence in regimes at the global level. It was really in the late 1990s that China started to take an active stance towards multilateralism in Asia, partly because of the belated development of multilateralism in the region. Beijing now regards multilateral diplomacy as an integral and important part of its foreign policy.

It now seems a cliché to say that China no longer shuns multilateralism in the Asian region. Not only is China a participant in almost all official and track-two institutions and forums, it has played a leading role in creating one of the most influential regional organisations: the Shanghai Cooperation Organisation (SCO). China is now not only involved in all these processes, it actively makes proposals on all sorts of issues of regional concern. In recent years, Beijing has even shown some signs of confidence in participating in multilateral security activities—for example, joint military exercises. On the South China Sea issue, which is a highly contentious one in East Asia, China has changed its previous callous position of adhering to bilateral talks and now at least grudgingly agrees to multilateral discussions. In fact, in the past few years, China has conscientiously pushed for trilateral cooperation—with the Philippines and Vietnam—on resource exploration in the South China Sea.

Why has China become so active in multilateralism? What are the most notable Chinese concerns about regional multilateralism? This chapter, extensively utilising various Chinese sources and interviews, attempts to address these questions. I seek some answers by looking at the track record of China's participation in regional multilateral processes and comparing the differences in China's participation and role in the three subregions in Asia: South-East Asia,

North-East Asia and Central Asia. I conclude that China has not yet developed a grand vision for regional multilateralism and integration. China's behaviour in Asian multilateralism has been driven largely by pragmatism: the pursuit of short-term national interests in accordance with changes in regional political and economic circumstances. This pragmatism is revealed in China's super-activism in economic multilateralism, enthusiasm for non-traditional security cooperation and differentiated approaches to conflict prevention in East and Central Asia.

China assesses the prospect of East Asian multilateralism

It goes without saying that China attaches great importance to its relations with countries in its neighbourhood. In fact, Chinese analysts propose that as part of its strategy to ensure its own rise, China should regard East Asia as its strategic hinterland and should actively participate in regional institution building as a fundamental policy (Angang and Honghua 2005). The Chinese Communist Party's sixteenth congress report in 2002, for the first time, juxtaposed regional multilateral cooperation with bilateral relations—a clear indication that Beijing had begun to attach greater importance to multilateralism (Honghua 2008). Five years later, Chinese leaders reaffirmed this position at the Seventeenth Party Congress. In recent years, China has regarded good relations with its contiguous neighbours and multilateralism as two of its four basic foreign policy guidelines.
1

This section describes China's overall assessment of the ultimate prospect of various multilateral mechanisms in Asia. Even though China has willingly accepted multilateralism as an approach in its international relations in Asia, it is not clear what Beijing regards as the ultimate goal or what kind of regional community all these multilateral mechanisms should eventually lead to. In 1999, at the landmark third '10+3' summit, leaders of the 13 countries agreed on the principles, direction and key areas for East Asian cooperation. Together with other members of the 10+3 framework, at the sixth 10+3 summit, China approved the report drafted by the East Asian Vision Group in 2002. The report proposed an East Asian free trade agreement (FTA) and an East Asian community. Despite clear support for an East Asian FTA, Beijing has offered no clear blueprint of its own version of an East Asian community.

In fact, there is profound scepticism among Chinese decision makers and analysts with regard to the prospect of East Asian regionalism. In the Chinese understanding, many challenges remain with regard to the further development of regionalism in East Asia. One of the challenges is the geographical expansion of regional cooperation and forums—for example, the East Asian Summit (10+6), which also includes India, Australia and New Zealand. Many Chinese analysts regard the East Asian Summit (EAS) as a setback or at least a new barrier to the growth of East Asian multilateralism. They believe such expansion has made forming a common geographical identity (related to cultural identity and common values)—an essential element in any regionalism—more difficult, if not impossible (Jianren 2008). Chinese analysts also take note of the fact that the Association of South-East Asian Nations (ASEAN), currently the driver of East Asian regionalism, has no consensus on the geographical boundary of regional multilateral processes. For instance, two of the three conditions required by ASEAN for other states to become EAS–ASEAN dialogue partners—signing ASEAN's Treaty of Amity and Cooperation (TAC) and substantive interactions with ASEAN—have no specific geographic limitation. According to Chinese analysts, this vision of a borderless regional community would only compound the growth of multilateralism in the region given the fact that even within the 10+3 framework, differences in cultural identities and values are already a huge challenge.

Related to this concern, and perhaps a much more important factor in China's assessment of Asian multilateralism, is the role of the United States. Many analysts in China simply do not believe that the United States will play a constructive role in promoting East Asian integration. Many believe that US supremacy in East Asia is not good for regional integration. They argue that since many East Asian countries still depend on the United States for political, economic and security interests, they have little incentive to further enhance multilateral cooperation within the region. Regional states still have to pay respect to US preferences when it comes to regional multilateralism. For instance, during the East Asian financial crisis, Japan proposed setting up an Asian monetary fund to cope with future financial problems in the region. Japan had to drop the idea, however, when the United States strongly opposed it (Hongsong 2006).

Beijing also believes that the traditional US 'hub and spokes' security arrangements are not conducive to the growth of new security modes in East Asia—for example, cooperative security. The popular expectation among regional states of US security protection does not provide any incentive to push for new security arrangements. Given the fact that US predominance and its bilateral security ties with various regional states are perceived as effective in maintaining regional security, cooperative security in East Asia is not likely to take shape in the foreseeable future (Fan 2005).

In the Chinese understanding, the United States can live with an East Asian regionalism that is open, inclusive and capable of solving all problems, including security issues, but Washington is opposed to a stronger Chinese role in any regional grouping. Washington once favoured Japan as the leader in spearheading East Asian multilateralism, but in recent years it has realised that there are many restraining factors for Japan: its relations with neighbouring countries and its declining economic importance as China's economy continues to grow. The United States is, however, not ready to accept any Chinese leadership role in pushing for East Asian regionalism, fearing that the rise of Chinese influence might diminish American clout in the region. By default, Washington continues to support ASEAN remaining in the driver's seat. The United States is also concerned about the function of a future East Asian community, fearing that it might marginalise the Asia Pacific Economic Cooperation (APEC) group and the ASEAN Regional Forum (ARF), two institutions that Washington has a lot of complaints about yet still regards as useful tools to advance its interests in East Asia (Xinbo 2007).

In addition to these factors, Beijing takes note of conflicting policy pronouncements from Washington and believes that American policy on East Asian multilateralism is uncertain. Former Secretary of State Colin Powell (2004) commented that the United States regarded an East Asian community as unnecessary and warned that any effort towards such a community should not be carried out at the expense of Washington's good and stable relations with its Asian friends. In early 2006, US APEC senior official Michael Michalak (2006) commented on East Asian regional processes by saying that the United States did not think the ASEAN+3 or EAS would harm American interests but, at the same time, he unequivocally reiterated the importance of cross-Pacific institutions and organisations. In May 2006, Assistant Secretary of State Christopher Hill (2006) said that America understood Asian countries' consideration for regional architecture, which was largely a reflection of the economic and financial integration among these nations. The United States welcomed that effort.

Some Chinese scholars believe that the uncertainty in American policy is reflected in its conditional support for and selective participation in East Asian multilateralism. They argue that the United States should further adjust its policy to become a constructive force in East Asian integration (Rongsheng 2007). On the part of China, despite profound suspicion of US intentions, there has been growing awareness that Beijing will ultimately have to recognise US preponderance in the region even in the long run and accommodate US interests in any future East Asian multilateral mechanisms. Lin Limin, a strategic analyst at the China Institute of Contemporary International Relations (CICIR) argues that the United States is a 'special' external power to East Asia due to all the political, economic, historical and emotional ties it has with many countries in the region. He argues that US policy towards East Asian regionalism is at a crossroads. The United States should support and participate in the process of East Asian integration and be a responsible member of the grouping. East Asia, in return, should adopt a 'grand' scheme of integration to incorporate the United States (Limin 2007).

In the Chinese perception, Japan's policy on regional multilateralism has also been inconsistent. This is largely a result of Japan's uncertain orientation—whether it should identify itself as one of the Western powers or root itself in East Asia. Chinese analysts detect some sort of oscillation in Japanese strategy in regional multilateralism between strengthening its alliance with the United States as its key international strategy and pushing for a leadership role in regional integration. They believe that currently Japan does not have a coherent regional integration plan, which does not bode well for a Japanese leadership role in furthering regional multilateralism (Shichun 2007).

Many Chinese analysts believe that Japan, nevertheless, intends to strive for a leadership role and restrain China and forestall China's dominance in East Asia, which is likely to work against a smooth development of multilateral cooperation in the region (Hongling 2006). They point to many instances in Japan's policy moves in South-East Asia to demonstrate Japan's intention of trying to outrun China. For instance, in 2002, when former Japanese Prime Minister Junichiro Koizumi proposed the idea of an 'expanded East Asian community', he had in mind a leading role for Japan, with support from ASEAN, to include extra-regional states such as Australia. China believed Koizumi's plan was an obvious initiative to check growing Chinese influence in East Asia (Honghua 2008). Another example frequently mentioned in China is Japanese reaction to China's signing of the TAC. Two months after China acceded to the ASEAN TAC, Japan decided to sign the treaty as well—a clear indication of a Japanese response to China's proactive engagement in South-East Asia. Beijing maintains that Japan's insistence on incorporating India, Australia and New Zealand in the East Asian Summit is simply another major Japanese step to restrain Chinese influence in East Asia (Zhilai 2006).

More recently, in 2006, Japan proposed an East Asian Economic Partnership Agreement (EPA), envisioning concluding an economic partnership agreement among ASEAN countries: Japan, China, South Korea, India, Australia and New Zealand (Junhong 2006). This EPA proposal would far surpass a regional FTA to include arrangements for investment, services and human flows. Chinese reports claimed that the Japanese proposal was intended to put Japan in a leadership position in East Asian regionalism and to restrain the rise of China ('Japan intends to promote "East Asia economic partnership agreement" to check China's rise', *China News Service*, viewed 7 August 2008, <http://world.people.com.cn/GB/1029/42354/4271464.html>). Since the second half of 2006, China and Japan have made many efforts to improve their strategic trust, but Japan's intention to constrain China on political and security issues in the region has not dwindled (Honghua 2008). The Sino–Japanese competition for leadership in East Asian multilateralism, in particular the Chinese perception of an assertive Japan, is another factor that has contributed to China's lack of confidence in a bright future of regional multilateralism.

China is also not sure how ASEAN is going to readjust its policy on East Asian multilateralism. China takes note of ASEAN's volatile positions on the geographic boundary of regional integration. The chairman's statement of the twelfth ASEAN Summit in January 2007 insisted that 10+3 should be the main approach to an East Asian community, but in the chairman's statement from the thirteenth ASEAN summit, there was no mention of using 10+3 as the main channel; it instead emphasised the complementarities of 10+3 and EAS. At the third EAS, ASEAN Secretary-General, Ong Keng Yong, noted that 'ASEAN has reached a consensus regarding Japan's proposal of including Australia, New Zealand, and India into [an] East Asian community' ('East Asia community to accept New Zealand, Australia, and India', *Central News Agency*, 20 November 2007). Beijing closely watches these subtle changes in ASEAN's position and is likely to regard ASEAN's vacillation as further evidence that continuing substantive growth of multilateralism in Asia is still inopportune. In the long run, China might not have confidence in ASEAN's ability to lead multilateralism in East Asia. According to one Chinese observer (Xiaosong 2008), if multilateralism in this region is going to lead to further regional integration, the leadership role will have to be exercised by a three-power consortium: China, the United States and Japan. Given the above evidence of the relations among these three powers, however, such a consortium might not be feasible in the foreseeable future.

In response to all these challenges, China steadfastly insists on relying on the 10+3 as the main framework for regional economic cooperation, it supports ASEAN's role in the driver's seat and maintains a gradualist approach to East Asian regional multilateralism. China believes that the 10+6 should not replace the 10+3 and that conditions for an FTA among the 10+6 countries are not yet mature (Jianren 2008). In order not to appear obstructionist, China has tried to downplay the importance of the EAS instead of refusing to be part of it, arguing that the EAS should more properly serve as a strategic platform for the exchange of ideas and facilitation of cooperation ('Premier Wen Jiabao's speech at the second EAS', *Xinhua News Agency*, 15 January 2007). In practice, Beijing still values 10+3 and 10+1 mechanisms for substantive cooperation.

In sum, in spite of active participation in all regional institutions and emphasis on 10+3 and 10+1, China believes that the prospect that various regional multilateral processes will lead to a discernable East Asian community is not good in the near future. Many factors are restraining the growth of such a community, including regional states' reluctance to relinquish their sovereignty, cultural differences, historical problems and the still-dominant position of the United States (Hongsong 2006). Because of the United States' hegemonic presence and the rivalry between China and Japan in East Asia, East Asia can develop only limited regionalism, an incomplete regional security architecture and security community (Zhongqi 2006). Due to these factors, China has not clearly defined its role and position in the East Asian community (Xintian 2008). In the meantime, China seems unconcerned by the pessimistic estimation of the prospect of East Asian multilateralism. What it intends to focus on now is pragmatic cooperation in areas of Chinese concern. Former Deputy Foreign Minister Wang Yi (2004) once noted that China pursued an open regionalism to carry out practical cooperation with regional states and at the same time did not exclude the United States and other external powers.

China's super-activism in economic multilateralism

Despite the fact that China is not exceptionally sanguine about the prospect of East Asian integration, it has taken a proactive stance on bilateral and multilateral economic cooperation. China has worked hard to push for bilateral FTAs with various East Asian states—for example, South Korea and Japan—but at the same time has strenuously pushed for economic collaboration at the multilateral level. Some Chinese analysts believe that bilateral FTAs could be beneficial to parties in the bilateral frameworks, but bilateral agreements that work parallel to each other could bring about various costs—for instance, policymaking and administrative expenditure, industrial readjustment costs and increased trade transfers that could offset the benefits of comparative advantage (Ronglin 2005). Thus, Beijing favours liberal multilateral economic cooperation.

China's early interest in economic multilateralism had its origin in political considerations. When the former Malaysian leader Mahathir bin Mohamad made the proposal to set up an East Asian economic group in December 1990 during a visit to Beijing, then Chinese Premier Li Peng immediately responded positively, indicating that China's consent was largely a political decision instead of one made after careful deliberation of economic costs and benefits. Former Chinese Presidents Yang Shangkun and Jiang Zemin on different occasions between 1992 and 1994 expressed China's support for such an idea, showing China's enthusiasm for such a regional economic grouping (Jianren 2008). China's early interest in economic multilateralism was related partly to its desire to end its diplomatic isolation in the aftermath of the Tiananmen Square episode.

Over the years, China's growing interest in multilateral economic regimes has been a reflection of a mixture of economic and political interests. In 2001, Beijing proposed the FTA with ASEAN together with some flexible measures such as the early harvest scheme. This move was seen widely as being driven partially by China's political goal of reassuring ASEAN countries of its benevolence and further defusing the 'China threat' in the region. There are, of course, other multilateral projects in South-East Asia in which China plays an active role—for instance, the Greater Mekong River Basin project and the emerging pan-Tonkin Gulf regional economic zone. The Kunming Initiative, although supported by China, has, for various reasons, not made much progress.

In North-East Asia, China is also engaged in a number of multilateral economic projects, the largest of which is the Tumen River regional development, initiated by the UN Development Program (UNDP) in 1991. This project covers a wide range of areas, including investment, trade, transportation, environmental protection, tourism, human resources, communications and energy. Japan, however, has not participated fully, but has instead joined as an observer only (Guoping 2007). Chinese scholars have also been advocating the Bohai economic circle in order to further develop the economy in northern China and to revitalise the industrial base in north-eastern China. This subregional economic zone would require the participation of South Korea and Japan (Ziheng 2004).

China is also enthusiastic about a trilateral FTA between China, South Korea and Japan. In 2002, China made an informal proposal for such an FTA. A joint research group completed a feasibility study in 2003, concluding that a trilateral FTA would be very beneficial to the three economies. The group also conducted a feasibility study on possible modes of trilateral investment arrangements and concluded that such arrangements would contribute to economic growth in the three countries. At the informal meeting in Bali, Indonesia, in 2003, leaders of the three countries signed a joint statement on the promotion of trilateral cooperation on trade and investment facilitation. Since then, the three parties have made some progress in adopting facilitation measures in customs, networking of ports, communications and environmental protection.

In official Chinese planning, an FTA among the 10+3 countries should ultimately take shape. A Chinese study concluded that a 10+3 FTA would contribute economic growth of 1.96 per cent and 0.34 per cent to China and Japan respectively (Lijun 2007). At the 2004 ASEAN–China summit, Chinese Premier Wen Jiabao called for an FTA in East Asia and an East Asian community based on such an FTA. This clearly shows China's strong desire to push for broader economic multilateralism in East Asia. The incentive for such preference is derived increasingly from the inherent need of China's domestic economic growth. China is increasingly becoming the trading and production centre of East Asia. According to some estimates, the volume of China's foreign trade is likely to overtake that of Japan and be close to that of the United States by 2020. By then, more than half of China's imports will come from other East Asian countries. In the coming 20 years, China is likely to maintain notable surpluses in its trade with the United States and Europe and large-scale deficits with East Asian countries. On the basis of the expected economic interdependence, Chinese analysts recommend that a future East Asian FTA could be formed on the basis of China–ASEAN, South Korea–ASEAN and Japan–ASEAN FTAs (Yunling 2006). Likewise, in Central Asia, China has exhibited much interest in multilateral economic cooperation. At the 2003 SCO summit, Premier Wen proposed setting up a free-trade area among member states of the organisation. China's active involvement in Central Asia has stemmed largely from its need for secure and diversified energy supplies to safeguard its rapidly developing economy (Andrews-Speed and Vinogradov 2000).

China's enthusiasm for NTS multilateralism

In the past decade or so, China has demonstrated enthusiasm towards non-traditional security (NTS) cooperation in Asia. Chinese analysts believe that cooperation on NTS helps enhance mutual understanding and trust among regional states, cultivates the growth of regional identity and deepens and broadens regional cooperation mechanisms. All these are helpful for gradual integration in the region (Shengrong 2008). In recent years, many Chinese analysts have been proposing a larger role for the military in multilateral cooperation on NTS issues in East Asia. [2]

China has cooperated extensively on NTS issues with other countries in Asia. In 2000, bilaterally with ASEAN, China signed an action plan on countering drug trafficking. In the same year, China participated in the Chiang Mai initiative for East Asian cooperation on financial security. In 2001, China, Laos, Myanmar and Thailand held a ministerial-level meeting on fighting drug trafficking and published the 'Beijing Declaration'. In 2002, China and ASEAN signed a joint declaration that specified issues of cooperation between the two sides in the NTS area: drug and human trafficking, piracy, terrorism, arms trafficking, money laundering, other international economic crimes and Internet crime. China pledged to cooperate with various parties concerned on marine environmental protection, search and rescue and anti-piracy. In 2003, China and ASEAN held a special summit meeting to tackle severe acute respiratory syndrome (SARS) and initiated a cooperation mechanism on public health. In 2004, China signed a memorandum of understanding with ASEAN on NTS cooperation, which further emphasised the need for Sino–ASEAN cooperation on NTS matters.

In North-East Asia, China, South Korea and Japan have also taken some steps to strengthen their cooperation on NTS issues. These measures include environmental protection, earthquake relief and tackling transnational crime. Starting from 1999, the three countries launched a ministerial-level meeting on the environment and various concrete proposals on sandstorms and marine environmental protection were carried out. In 2004, the authorities monitoring earthquakes in the three countries agreed to share seismic information and technology. The immigration authorities of the three countries have also held workshops on countering terrorism, drug trafficking and human trafficking in North-East Asia.

In the larger context of East Asia, China's posture towards NTS has also been quite positive. In 2004, ASEAN+3 held its first ministerial-level meeting on fighting transnational crime. In 2005, ASEAN+3 signed an agreement on cooperation among their capital police agencies to jointly fight various NTS challenges. China also has no problem working on NTS issues within the ARF. China did not lodge any opposition to the 2002 ARF joint statement that called for enhanced cooperation on fighting drug trafficking, illegal immigration, money laundering and piracy at sea. The 2005 ARF joint declaration stressed regional coordination and cooperation on disaster relief and other measures for emergencies.

In APEC, in which China has quite vehemently opposed any inclusion of discussions of security matters, Beijing has not blocked multilateral efforts on fighting NTS issues. The APEC summits in 2001 and 2002 published two statements on counter-terrorism. The 2003 and 2004 declarations further emphasised multilateral cooperation to fight terrorism and other transnational crimes. China also agreed to the APEC initiative to deal jointly with various transnational health epidemics, such as HIV/AIDS, SARS and avian influenza.

In Central Asia, China has an impressive record of working with other SCO members to meet various NTS challenges—primarily the so-called 'three evil forces': separatism, religious extremism and terrorism. The SCO has set up various institutions and signed many legal documents on all sorts of NTS threats.

China's different approaches to preventive measures on security

China's policy stance on traditional security issues is in sharp contrast with its attitude towards economic and NTS cooperation. Overall, China is still reluctant to work multilaterally on sources of potential interstate military conflicts. In particular, China has been opposing quite strongly any preventive measure that would impinge on domestic issues. There are, however, some notable differences in China's stance across various regions. In South-East Asia, China has been quite adamant in opposing the further institutionalisation of preventive measures on traditional security issues. In North-East Asia, China has taken an active role in helping solve the North Korean nuclear crisis. China is also open to the discussion of a security framework in North-East Asia. [3] In Central Asia, China has been more willing to engage member states of the SCO on preventive measures to deal with traditional and non-traditional security issues.

Overall, China's reluctance to agree to more substantive multilateral preventive measures is a reflection of its concerns about US predominance and what it perceives as the United States' hostile security policy towards China in East Asia. The most alarming assessment of American intention in East Asia is that Washington plans to establish and consolidate a strategic encirclement of China from East Asia, South-East Asia, South Asia and extending to Central Asia. China believes that various military exercises that the United States conducts with China's neighbouring states are intended to put pressure on China and provide more leverage to states in China's neighbourhood (Deqi 2006). For many years, China did not participate in the Shangri-la security dialogue, the primary reason being its belief that the dialogue was influenced too excessively by Washington from behind the scenes. The forum was perceived as a mechanism to constrain China strategically. [4]

In the first years of China's participation in the ARF, China was afraid that the United States and its allies would use the forum as a tool to harm China's security interests. Beijing understood that one of the original goals of setting up the ARF was to restrain and socialise China. In 1995, at the second ARF meeting, China expressed its reservations with regard to the norms and principles on regional security proposed by other participating countries. At the 1996 ARF meeting, former Chinese Foreign Minister Qian Qichen elaborated China's 'new security concept', urging states to solve security problems through dialogue and consultation. China hoped to expand confidence among major powers in the Asia-Pacific, strengthen ASEAN's understanding of China and thus reduce the influence of the perception of the 'China threat'. China also found out that the ARF could be a good forum in which to fight the Cold War mentality of some external powers (Yanbing 2000). All these demonstrate China's pragmatism in security cooperation.

For China, participation in the ARF has been both an opportunity and a challenge. China can utilise the forum to explain its policies and stances so as to reduce misunderstanding and influence the perceptions of other states towards it. Participation also means, however, that China will have to face up to the collective pressures of ASEAN and other countries. Chinese analysts list China's concessions on the South China Sea issue as examples of the negative consequences of China's participation. Some of the major concessions include agreeing to multilateralism as a means to deal with the dispute instead of the previous bilateral approach, China's agreement to use international law as a basis for a solution to the problem and the signing of the declaration of cooperation (Changsen 2000).

In 1997, China sent a delegation to various Asian countries to lobby for the abrogation of bilateral and multilateral security alliances. The focus was of course on persuading various countries in East Asia to forgo their bilateral security ties with the United States. That effort was not successful. ASEAN countries indicated their disapproval of the Chinese suggestion. China, in return, understood better the concerns of ASEAN countries and has not since openly pursued this issue. It was a turning point for China to accept at least implicitly US military presence as a balancing force in East Asia (Xiaopeng 2006).

Still, the biggest challenge for China is how to cope with the security environment in East Asia. On one hand, there is the reality of the US-centred bilateral security arrangements that still serve as the backbone for security in the region. On the other hand, the bilateral arrangements seem to be expanding at the expense of Chinese security interests. For instance, in the past few years, there has been growing interest among the neo-conservative thinkers in Washington in constructing an Asian version of the North Atlantic Treaty Organisation (NATO).

In March 2007, Japan and Australia signed a joint declaration on security cooperation in which the two countries pledged to enhance cooperation and consultation on issues of common strategic interest including regularly holding the '2+2' defence and foreign ministers' talks. In the past few years, efforts have also been made to bring India in to form some sort of quadrilateral security mechanism in East Asia. Although leadership changes in Japan and Australia made the possibility of forming a quadrilateral security mechanism less likely, to Chinese decision makers, all these efforts reinforced their perception that other regional powers had the intention, no matter how volatile, to gang up on China.

These perceptions and beliefs explain why, in the ARF, China, together with ASEAN countries, belongs to the group of 'reluctant' countries that has not been enthusiastic about preventive diplomacy. China's unwillingness to move towards preventive diplomacy in the ARF is a reflection of its concern that any problem in the South China Sea or the Taiwan Strait would allow international interference (Yuzawa 2006). Beijing maintains that there is still a lot of work that needs to be done to enhance confidence-building measures in the region, which are at their most primitive stage in East Asia. Pushing to enter a stage of preventive diplomacy would not be good for the development of the ARF (Kuisong 1998).

China realises that Asia-Pacific is an area in which major powers have significant interests. The primary goal for China's security strategy in the region is to maintain at least normal and functioning relations with all other major powers so that China is not isolated by other powers. China's second goal is to try its best to maintain friendly relations with other regional states to forestall the possibility of any containment alliance supported by other major powers. China increasingly realises that economic interdependence creates common interests and is conducive to the prevention of conflicts. Beijing believes that the best strategy is to become the provider of markets, investment and technology for regional states to transform China into the engine of regional economic growth (Shiping and Yunling 2004).

One area in which China has been trying to play a role is its proposal of a 'new security concept'. Official rhetoric in Beijing constantly emphasises 'mutual trust, mutual benefit, equality and coordination' as the principles of practising a new security mode. According to the Chinese interpretation, the gist of a new security concept is to pursue cooperative security. China's preference for cooperative security is perhaps one of necessity. In today's East Asia, there are three primary modes of security arrangements: US hegemony, the traditional balance of power and various loose multilateral security forums. China pushes strongly for cooperative security simply because the first two security modes work against its security interests. Advocating cooperative security serves many Chinese security goals. First, it helps alleviate the China threat. Second, it conforms to China's interest in maintaining a stable regional environment. Third, it serves as a check to the first two security modes, thus improving China's strategic security position in East Asia. The challenge for the future is for China to come up with concrete proposals to make cooperative security really work in East Asia.

China's security policy and practice in Central Asia are notably different from those in East Asia. China demonstrates much more confidence in dealing with security issues in Central Asia, as shown in the high level of institutionalisation of the SCO and its willingness to embrace preventive measures.

According to Chinese analysts, China's security policy in the SCO is intended as a contrast to US security policy in East Asia, which is underpinned by bilateral alliances and 'forward deployment'. Chinese analysts argue that in the SCO, China and Russia have been working on cooperation and dialogue as the main means for security building and reducing the military presence in border areas (Kuisong 1998). Confidence-building measures have been and appear to continue to be a key area for the SCO, as evidenced in the two treaties regarding border security signed in 1996 and 1997, and the recently signed treaty among SCO member states on good neighbourly relations, friendship and cooperation.

The SCO has, however, gradually taken on the concept of preventive diplomacy. Currently, preventive diplomacy in the SCO is essentially carried out in areas of NTS by a wide range of agencies, including the military. There are, however, signs that the SCO is increasingly moving towards a more substantive practice of preventive diplomacy. The SCO is likely to meaningfully discuss preventive diplomacy in tackling traditional security issues, including dealing with domestic crises. A few recent SCO official documents clearly refer to this possible development.

The 'Declaration on the Fifth Anniversary of Shanghai Cooperation Organisation' mentions that the SCO has the potential to play an independent role in safeguarding stability and security in this region. The document points out that in case of emergencies that threaten regional peace, stability and security, SCO member states will have immediate consultation on responding effectively to fully protect the interests of the SCO and its member states. The paper calls for member states to study the possibility of establishing a regional conflict-prevention mechanism within the SCO framework. The 2007 *Joint Communiqué of the Meeting of the Council of Heads of SCO Member States* proclaims that it is vital to implement preventive measures against the processes and phenomena causing instability in SCO territory. The document calls for the process of creating a mechanism of joint responses to situations threatening peace, stability and security in the region to be expedited. In the recently concluded SCO summit in Dushanbe, the member states once again proclaimed that the SCO would conduct preventive diplomacy to safeguard peace and security in the region. [5]

A few scholars at various Chinese government-sponsored institutions have conducted studies on the need for and feasibility of some formal preventive diplomacy measures in the SCO. They justify the establishment of such formal mechanisms on the grounds that the SCO will not be able to grow further without preventive diplomacy given the fact that the Euro-Asian region is so complicated in cultural, ethnic and geo-strategic contentions, and because of potential conflicts among those Central Asian states in terms of territorial borders, water and other resources and internal socio-political instability in the smaller members of the SCO. They conclude that all these contentions and internal instability have the potential to not only hamper the further progress of the SCO but to derail the SCO process (Tao 2006).

Conclusion

China's policy towards Asian multilateralism pretty much reflects the overall 'low-profile' foreign policy line that was set by the late leader Deng Xiaoping. Deng, back in the early 1990s, advised that China should not act aggressively as a leader in international politics to avoid too much international attention while it was rising. At the same time, he admonished other leaders that China had to play a role ('*you suo zuo wei*'). Playing a role is particularly important in issues of concern to China and relevant to Chinese interests. Deng's foreign policy line was deeply rooted in pragmatism. Chinese policy on various multilateral processes reflects that pragmatic consideration.

In addition to the perceived attitudes of other major players, part of the reason why China lacks a grand vision of regional multilateralism has to do with the fear that any Chinese effort to lay out a blueprint for regional integration will only invite suspicion on the part of other major powers, further complicating China's strategic position in East Asia and the world. China has not openly or strongly opposed matters that it does not favour. Instead, Beijing has made its reservations known and has worked subtly to reduce the negative impact on its interests. This is clearly the case with regard to the EAS. Chinese officials now recognise that it is unwise for China to openly obstruct the EAS. Instead, they maintain that China could go along with any policy proposal that works to the benefit of all participants. [6]

Emphasising multilateral cooperation on economic and NTS issues is also a clear demonstration of Chinese pragmatism in practice. It helps build a better image of China in the region—a more benign and cooperative China. It helps create a friendlier environment for China's rise in the long run. Economic multilateralism is also necessary for the sustained growth of the Chinese economy. Cooperating on NTS issues is highly desirable simply because all these non-traditional challenges have transnational roots and impacts. China stands to benefit from all these multilateral mechanisms in dealing with NTS threats.

Beijing's different positions on preventive measures in East and Central Asia also have to do with its pragmatic response to the different regional political and strategic contexts. In East Asia, the strategic rivalry is much higher than other areas; China's position has to be largely defensive. In Central Asia, however, China enjoys much stronger political power and less strategic competition. As long as China can accommodate Russia's core interests, Beijing will find much room to be flexible in embracing preventive measures.

References

Andrews-Speed, Philip and Vinogradov, Sergei 2000, 'China's involvement in Central Asian petroleum: convergent or divergent interests?', *Asian Survey*, vol. 40, no. 2, March–April.

Angang, Hu and Honghua, Men 2005, 'Yanjiu zhongguo dongya yitihua zhanlue de zhongyao yiyi [The significance of studying China's East Asian integration strategy]', *Guoji Guancha* [*International Observation*], issue 3, 2005, pp. 26–35.

Changsen, Yu 2000, 'Dongmeng diqu luntan de mubiao yu daguo de lichang [ARF's goals and the positions of major powers]', *Dong Nan ya Yanjiu* [*Southeast Asian Studies*], issue 4, 2000, pp. 22–6.

Danzhi, Yang 2007, 'Shang ge li la duihua: yuanqi,tezheng ji qi dui yatai anquan de yingxiang [Shangri-la dialogue: origin, characteristics, and its impact on Asia-Pacific security]', *Xiandai Guoji Guanxi* [*Contemporary International Relations*], issue 2, 2007, pp. 8–13.

Deqi, Jiang 2006, 'Meiguo yatai anquan zhanlue tiaozheng de zhongguo bianliang [The China factor in US readjustment in security strategy in Asia-Pacific]', *Dangdai Shijie* [*Contemporary World*], issue 1, 2006.

Fan, Wang 2005, 'Dong ya anquan moshi: gongcun, bingxing haishi zhihuan [East Asian security modes: coexistence, juxtaposition or replacement]', *Shijie Jingji yu Zhengzhi* [*World Economics and Politics*], issue 11, 2005, pp. 16–21.

Guoping, Wang 2007, 'Dongmeng yu dongya xin diqu zhuyi [ASEAN and East Asian new regionalism]', *Dangdai Yatai* [*Contemporary Asia-Pacific*], vol. 7, 2007, pp. 18–23.

Hill, Christopher 2006, The US and South-East Asia, Remarks to the Lee Kuan Yew School of Public Policy, 22 May 2006, Singapore, <http://www.state.gov/p/eap/rls/rm/66646.htm>

Honghua, Men 2008, 'Zhongguo jueqi yu dongya anquan zhixu de biange [China's rise and the evolution of East Asian security order]', *Guoji Guancha [International Observation]*, issue 2, 2008, pp. 16–25.

Hongling, Cao 2006, 'Dongya jingji yitihua de guoji guanxi lilun jiedu [An analysis of East Asian economic integration from IR theories]', *Guoji Guancha [International Observation]*, vol. 6, 2006, pp. 70–7.

Hongsong, Liu 2006, 'Dongya jingji yitihua de yueshu tiaojian yu dangqian moshi xuanze [Restraining factors in East Asian economic integration and current choice of a model]', *Yatai Jingji [Asia-Pacific Economic Review]*, issue 3, 2006, pp. 10–13.

Jianren, Lu 2008, 'Cong dongmeng yitihua jincheng kan dongya yitihua fangxiang [Direction of East Asian integration seen from ASEAN integration process]', *Dangdai Yatai [Contemporary Asia-Pacific]*, vol. 1, 2008, pp. 21–35.

Junhong, Liu 2006, 'Riben jiyu dajian dongya gongtongti', *Shijie Xinwen Bao [World News]*, 6 April 2006.

Kuisong, Ding 1998, 'Dongmeng diqu luntan yu yatai anquan hezuo [ARF and Asia-Pacific security cooperation]', *Xiandai Guoji Guanxi [Contemporary International Relations]*, issue 7, 1998, pp. 7–12.

Lijun, Jia 2007, 'Dongya jingji yitihua jincheng zhong de zhong ri boyi fenyi [A game theory analysis between China and Japan in East Asian economic integration]', *Riben Yanjiu [Japanese Studies]*, vol. 2, 2007, pp. 24–9.

Limin, Lin 2007, 'Meiguo yu dongya yitihua de guanxi xilun [An analysis of the US and East Asian integration]', *Xiandai Guoji Guanxi [Contemporary International Relations]*, issue 11, 2007, pp. 1–6.

Michalak, Michael 2006, Remarks at the International Institute of Monetary Affairs, Michael Michalak, US Senior Official for APEC, 25 January 2006, Tokyo, Japan, <http://www.state.gov/p/eap/rls/rm/60355.htm>

Powell, Colin L. 2004, Roundtable with Japanese Journalists, 12 August 2004, Washington, DC, <http://www.state.gov/secretary/former/powell/remarks/35204.htm>

Ronglin, Li 2005, 'Zhongguo–Dongmeng ziyou maoyi qu yu dongya quyu jingji yitihua [China–ASEAN FTA and regional economic integration in East Asia]', *Dangdai Yatai [Contemporary Asia-Pacific]*, vol. 8, 2005, pp. 19–23.

Rongsheng, Ma 2007, 'Meiguo zai dongya yitihua zhong de juese banyan [The role the US plays in East Asian integration]', *Guoji Luntan [International Forum]*, vol. 9, no. 3, 2007, pp. 20–5.

Shengrong, Ma 2008, 'Tiaozhan yu jiyu: dongya yitihua shijiao zhong de fei chuantong anquan hezuo [Challenge and opportunity: cooperation in non-traditional security in the perspective of East Asian integration]', *Dong Bei Ya Luntan [Northeast Asia Forum]*, vol. 17, no. 2, 2008, pp. 44–8.

Shichun, Sun 2007, 'Riben de FTA zhanlue yu dongya jingji yitihua [Japan's FTA strategy and East Asian economic integration]', *Riben Yanjiu [Japanese Studies]*, issue 4, 2007, pp. 36–42.

Shiping, Tang and Yunling, Zhang 2004, 'Zhongguo de diqu zhanlue [China's regional strategy]', *Shijie Jingji yu Zhengzhi [World Economics and Politics]*, issue 6, 2004, pp. 8–13.

Tao, Xu 2006, 'Shang he zhuzhi jianli yufang diqu chongtu jizhi de shijian yiyi [The practical implications of establishing regional conflict-prevention mechanisms in the SCO]', *Xiandai Guoji Guanxi [Contemporary International Relations]*, issue 12, 2006, pp. 12–22.

Xiaopeng, Xue 2006, 'Zhongguo dui dongya diqu zhuyi guannian de zhuanbian [Changes in Chinese perceptions of East Asian regionalism]', *Foreign Affairs Review*, vol. 89, June 2006, pp. 28–33.

Xiaosong, Tang 2008, 'San qiang gong zhi: dongya quyu yitihua de biran xuanze [Three-power consortium: the inevitable choice for East Asian regional integration]', *Xiandai Guoji Guanxi [Contemporary International Relations]*, issue 2, 2008, pp. 10–15.

Xinbo, Wu 2007, 'Meiguo yu dongya yitihua [US and East Asian integration]', *Guoji Wenti Yanjiu [International Studies]*, issue 5, 2007, pp. 47–53.

Xintian, Yu 2008, 'Zhongguo peiyu dongya rentong de sikao [Thoughts on China's role in East Asian identity formation]', *Dangdai Yatai [Journal of Contemporary Asia-Pacific Studies]*, issue 3, 2008, pp. 21–35.

Yanbing, Ma 2000, 'Dongmeng diqu luntan de chuangjian, fazhan ji qianjing [ARF: creation, development, and prospects]', *Heping yu Fazhan [Peace and Development]*, issue 4, 2000, pp. 8–15.

Yi, Wang 2004, 'Quan qiu hua jincheng zhong de yazhou quyu hezuo [Asian regional cooperation in the process of globalisation]', *People's Daily*, 30 April 2004.

Yunling, Zhang 2006, 'Zhongguo tong dongya de jingji yitihua yu hezuo [China and East Asian economic integration and cooperation]', *Dangdai Yatai [Contemporary Asia-Pacific]*, vol. 1, 2006, pp. 3–12.

Yuzawa, Takeshi 2006, 'The evolution of preventive diplomacy in the ASEAN Regional Forum', *Asian Survey*, vol. 46, issue 5, 2006, pp. 785–804.

Zhilai, Qin 2006, 'Jiexi shou jie dongya fenghui de kaifang xing "diqu zhuyi" [Explaining the open "regionalism" of the first East Asian summit]', *Xueyi Yuekan* [*Study Monthly*], vol. 259, issue 2, 2006, pp. 36–7.

Zhongqi, Pan 2006, 'Baquan gashe,daguo duikang yu dongya diqu anquan de goujian [Hegemonic intervention, major powers' rivalry and East Asia regional security building]', *Shijie Jingji yu Zhengzhi* [*World Economics and Politics*], issue 6, 2006, pp. 38–44.

Ziheng, Zhou 2004, 'Zhongguo jingji fazhan de diyuan zhanlue yu dongya jingji yitihua [The geopolitical strategy of China's economic development and East Asian economic integration]', *Shijie Jingji yu Zhengzhi* [*World Economics and Politics*], issue 2, 2004, pp. 67–71.

ENDNOTES

[1] The four guidelines include: major powers are the key, neighbouring regions should receive more attention, the developing world is the foundation and multilateralism serves as the stage.

[2] Author's interviews with various Chinese analysts in the past two years.

[3] Chinese Foreign Ministry spokesman Qin Gang's remarks at a press briefing, 27 May 2008, viewed 3 September 2008, <http://www.fmprc.gov.cn/chn/xwfw/fyrth/t440969.htm>

[4] Author's interview with Chinese official, July 2008; Danzhi (2007).

[5] SCO Summit 'Dushanbe Declaration', viewed 5 September 2008, <http://news.xinhuanet.com/world/2008-08/28/content_9731209.htm>

[6] Author's interview with Chinese Foreign Ministry officials, July 2008.

Chapter 12

The perils and prospects of dragon riding: reassurance and 'costly signals' in China–ASEAN relations

See Seng Tan

From any vantage point, the shift in relations between China and the Association of South-East Asian Nations (ASEAN) in the past four decades has been nothing less than remarkable. Branded by Beijing at its inception in 1967 as an anti-China and anti-communist regional grouping, ASEAN, in 2007, was openly acknowledging 'the important role that China has been playing in regional and global affairs' and the 'significant' contributions that close China–ASEAN relations had brought 'to peace, stability and prosperity in the region and the world at large' (ASEAN 2007).

At the risk of oversimplification, contemporary theoretical assessments of the evolution of China–ASEAN relations largely coalesce around two main propositions. On one hand, social constructivists argue that normative suasion and change as well as regional identity formation have taken place as a result of efforts by both parties at complex engagement with one another (Acharya 1996; Ba 2006; Johnston and Evans 1999). By and large, these efforts in part attribute the stabilisation and enhancement of China–ASEAN ties to the shared reliance on the non-contractual, non-confrontational, consensus-seeking and process-oriented diplomatic convention advanced by ASEAN—namely, the so-called 'ASEAN way'. They highlight China's transition from its initial mistrust of regional arrangements, such as the ASEAN Regional Forum (ARF) and the Asia-Pacific Economic Cooperation (APEC) forum, as nefarious strategies aimed at encircling China, to its keen embrace of such and of multilateral diplomacy at large (Johnston 2003; Kuik 2005). For social constructivists, the ASEAN way constitutes a 'counter-Realpolitik' philosophy of regional security, which promotes reassuring behaviour over traditional Realpolitik approaches that emphasise competition and coercion (Acharya 1997; Johnston 2003:123). [1]

On the other hand, realists and English School pluralists are considerably less sanguine about prospects for regional peace. They see rising China's external security calculations as symptomatic of an emerging grand strategy, the key aim of which is to diminish the prospect of its ascent being hindered by other powers in a multipolar strategic environment (Swaine and Tellis 2000; Goldstein 2005). Thus understood, despite China's 'acquiescence' to membership in ASEAN-centred regional arrangements, they question ASEAN's ability to elicit collaborative behaviour from a hegemonic China that will not bow easily to external pressure (Emmers 2001; Leifer 1996; Lim 1998). Others question the potential gains purportedly accruable to China from its participation in ASEAN-based regionalism and multilateral diplomacy in general (Wang 2000). For them, the ASEAN way is not without merit, having provided, in a limited fashion, a relatively useful 'rudimentary code of interstate conduct' that for all intents and purposes continues to guide regional relations (Leifer 1986:151–2). It remains, however, essentially an avoidance strategy for holding at bay ambitious regional aspirations for cooperation and integration that encourage interventionism and emasculate sovereignty norms (Jones and Smith 2007).

Against this backdrop, characterisations of China–ASEAN relations that treat power and reassurance as mutually exclusive categories are unlikely to be helpful for grasping a fuller picture of that complex and nuanced relationship. To be sure, social constructivists do not discount material power, nor do realists and English School pluralists disregard reassurance. That said, in advancing the ASEAN way as 'counter-Realpolitik', social constructivists inadvertently play down the softer aspects of power-balancing behaviour, which could assume the form of political balancing and/or communal/cooperative balancing (Emmers 2003; Khong 2004; Tan with Cossa 2001). Such balancing does not necessarily have to involve China and ASEAN—at least not directly. More likely, ASEAN could tacitly use surrogates—for instance, the United States and/or India—to politically balance China (Batabyal 2006; Goh 2007–08). By reducing China's strategy of reassurance and accommodation—and, of course, 'soft power'—to purely utilitarian calculation and instrumental logic, realist explanations tend to presuppose reassurance as an essentially short to intermediate-term approach, which Beijing will conceivably discard for an aggressive approach once it has acquired material power capabilities commensurate with its deeper (and possibly darker) strategic aspirations.

Without taking anything away from these important insights, this chapter offers a modest proposition that seeks to avoid exclusive treatments of power, on one hand, and reassurance on the other. In this respect, the notion of 'security seeking', despite its conceptual problems, seems a useful framework from which to analyse the evolution of China–ASEAN relations, especially because of the concept's sensitivity to power and reassurance. As part of their efforts to reassure other states about the nature of their intentions, security-seeking states implement a policy of 'costly signalling' (Kydd 2005). Costly signalling is the key mechanism that makes reassurance possible through the making of significant gestures by the parties involved that serve to prove to all each other's trustworthiness. In the context of multilateral regional arrangements that are not defined by a malign hegemony, interstate security cooperation will likely result only if an element of trust is present. It has been argued that states can and do cooperate solely on the basis of self-interest (Oye 1986), although the strength of such utilitarianism-based claims tends to falter especially vis-à-vis Asia, where longstanding cultural enmities and negative historical memories combine with existing security dilemmas to render the pursuit of security cooperation therein difficult. Further, the region's enduring preoccupation with confidence building—and apparent inability or unwillingness to move towards preventive diplomacy, in the case of the ARF (Garofano 2002)—underscores the significance trust and reassurance have to Asia's international relations, and specifically China–ASEAN relations.

In this respect, it could be argued that China has done a fair bit of signalling to its Asian neighbours, especially via its concerted 'charm offensive', although whether that has been a costly endeavour for China is debatable. [2] To the extent that China's participation in ASEAN–centred regionalisms is emblematic of strategic restraint on Beijing's part, it could be said that Chinese assurance has indeed been costly. [3] For its part, ASEAN has also sought to reassure China, chiefly through a longstanding engagement that relies on the ASEAN way. Some of the signals that ASEAN members issued could be construed as potentially costly to their respective national situations, although these could also have been offset by other considerations (Goh 2005, 2007–08).

ASEAN's engagement of China: from the cold to the fold?

Getting the People's Republic in from the revolutionary cold and into the regional fold, as it were, has long been ASEAN's regional 'game plan'. The strategy (to the extent it can be so called) has essentially involved extending the ASEAN model of regional security—the ASEAN modus operandi of soft regionalism and process-driven institutionalism—to the wider Asia-Pacific region, and providing great and regional powers a stake in the preservation and promotion of the peace and prosperity of Asia (Indorf 1987; Leifer 1996). ASEAN's regionalist approach to engaging China has been informed in part by the collective historical experience of the ASEAN member states in engaging post-'Confrontation' Indonesia. In this regard, the association's model of security regionalism can be understood as a historically tried-and-tested strategy that committed New Order Indonesia to the region through an ASEAN framework that not only provided Jakarta a regional leadership role but concomitantly assured recognition of sovereignty and non-interference for the other member nations. In like fashion, the ASEAN model would permit the endorsement of China as a status-quo leader—though not necessarily ahead of America in the power hierarchy—and responsible power/stakeholder in the web of regional institutions and ties within which it is enmeshed (Foot 2006; Goh 2005, 2007–08).

Perhaps more than any other region, South-East Asia has long been susceptible to the influence of and intrusion by the great powers. Although the end of the Cold War brought relative peace and security to South-East Asia, the geopolitical milieu of the region since the early 1990s has been shaped largely by several key developments—namely, American ambivalence regarding its strategic commitments to the region (Acharya and Tan 2006) and the rise of China as an economic, diplomatic and, somewhat less convincingly, military power (Goldstein 2005; Loo 2007; Shambaugh 2002; Swaine and Tellis 2000). A third development is the rise of regionalism in the form of ASEAN. A crucial part of the association's story has been about facilitating regional ties with external powers as much as it has been about ensuring intraregional stability (Emmers 2003; Goh 2007–08). In this regard, ASEAN regionalism has been shaped by the tension between its internal and external dimensions, and nowhere is this more apparent than in the association's longstanding efforts to engage China.

It has been argued that the contemporary Asian security order is hegemonic in kind, with China at its epicentre and ASEAN as well as other Asian countries relating to Beijing in suzerain-vassal terms (Kang 2003). Such an interpretation presupposes an effective 'bandwagoning', en masse, by Asian states with China—a claim contested by others, who point to efforts by Asian states to balance China or enmesh it within a multilateral web of regional relations and architectures (Acharya 2003–04; Goh 2005, 2007–08). Crucially, if the extant regional security discourse is anything to go by, it is more likely that ASEAN member states, despite their shared acknowledgment and relative 'acceptance' of China's growing power and influence, see China's rise as a major economic and security concern, and concur on the need for the United States—despite rising anti-Americanism within some South-East Asian societies in recent times (Liow and Tan 2008)—to remain actively involved in Asia and maintain a stable balance of power therein, provided America's efforts complement and enhance ASEAN's own initiatives on regional security (Acharya 1996). Thus understood, the association's engagement of China is essentially provisional in that it involves the integration of China into an ASEAN-defined regional order, one in which the United States plays a leading role. In this respect, while the notion of China as a 'responsible stakeholder' of the international system originated with the Americans—former US Deputy Secretary of State Robert Zoellick, to be exact—it is an orientation with which ASEAN security planners can agree, as long as it coheres with their own regional ideas and praxis.

It is likely that ASEAN's complex yet provisional engagement of China has had a part to play in facilitating China's successive permutations from revolutionary regime to normal state to, if only embryonic, responsible great power. This qualified contention does not insist that ontological priority be granted ASEAN as the causal agent of change. Reciprocity played a significant part as both parties learned to accommodate one another. By the 1970s onwards, China had, in fits and starts, volitionally begun its incremental shift away from ideology and towards pragmatism in its conduct in international affairs. This transition has more or less continued throughout the post-Cold War period to the present. In theoretical terms, it could be said that the evolution of Chinese foreign policy through successive political leadership—from that of Mao Zedong and Deng Xiaopeng to Jiang Zemin and now Hu Jintao—reflects a China in transition from a quasi-expansionist state, at least in terms of its ideological support for communist movements throughout South-East Asia during the Cold War, to a 'security seeker' rather than an 'offensive realist' aggrandiser (Li 2004; Tang 2007). Arguably, ASEAN's 'China policy'—at times robust and concerted, at other times ambivalent and disjointed—played a relatively significant role in assuaging China's concerns about perceived risks of its assimilation into the post-Cold War regional order. To be sure, other factors were equally important, not least China's changing assessment, under Deng's leadership, that nuclear war with America was not inevitable, and its pragmatic emphasis on national economic development, which essentially denoted a growing reliance on and support for the US-led liberal international economic order (Chen 2008). Indeed, other than occasional hints of bellicosity where cross-straits affairs are concerned, China clearly prizes the stability and prosperity of the region, and to that extent it has largely supported the regional status quo.

In this respect, insofar as ASEAN regionalism has principally been about accommodation rather than exclusion, confidence building rather than the enforcement of rules and reassurance rather than confrontation, it is a brand of regionalism that, at least in rhetoric, resonates positively with Beijing's own 'five principles of coexistence' first articulated at the Asian–African Conference in 1955, and, of considerably more recent vintage, its 'new security concept', formally introduced to South-East Asians at an ASEAN meeting in Bandar Seri Begawan in 2002 (Deng and Wang 2005; Tan and Acharya 2008). The ASEAN way of consensus, consultation and non-interference has been celebrated—at least until the region-wide financial crisis of 1997—as a brand of regionalism that works, even though it has also gained notoriety as a poor excuse for a persistent lack of political will among member nations to advance and implement express regional goals (Jones and Smith 2007). Elsewhere it has been branded as chimerical (Nischalke 2000). It is this very model of regional security—a diplomatic approach predicated on accommodation and 'argumentative persuasion' (Adler 1997; Antolik 1990; Ba 2006; Checkel 2001; Risse 2000)—that hitherto has arguably succeeded in allaying Chinese suspicions and convincing Beijing of the ostensible value and virtue of ASEAN-based regionalism.

That said, bumps and potholes of all sorts line that road and it remains to be seen how successfully ASEAN and China can negotiate these obstacles as they arise. Further, the ASEAN way is itself evolving—ironically, in response to new challenges confronting the region, not least the rise of China—which could complicate future China–ASEAN ties. In this respect, how the advent of the ASEAN Charter, unveiled in November 2007, and the continuing evolution of the South-East Asian region towards a regional security community could conceivably complicate ASEAN's engagement strategy are questions of concern not only where the future of China–ASEAN relations is concerned, but the future peace and stability of Asia.

Strange bedfellows, 1980s

It bears remembering that ASEAN at its inception in 1967 was branded by China as an anti-Chinese, anti-communist alliance (Pollard 1970). The association's engagement of China began during the Cold War years (Sen 2002; Turley and Race 1980; Weatherbee et al. 2005). That Indonesia was one of the first countries to officially recognise the People's Republic in 1950 likely facilitated ties, despite Indonesia's troubles with communism in the mid 1960s (Sukma 1999). Despite the pervasive concern about the prospect of Beijing's ideological influence on internal communist subversion within South-East Asian societies—especially in Indonesia, Malaysia and Singapore—the Third Indochina War, which lasted throughout the 1980s, saw a cementing of the China–ASEAN political relationship as a consequence of China's need for ASEAN's diplomatic backing against China's main Cold War adversaries, Vietnam and the Soviet Union, and ASEAN's commensurate reliance on Chinese support in its diplomatic effort to prevent non-communist South-East Asia from falling into Vietnamese hands (Acharya 1996; Ba 2006:162). Crucial developments such as the Sino–Soviet split during the late 1960s and the Sino–American rapprochement of the early 1970s likely contributed, if only indirectly, to ameliorating concerns among ASEAN states regarding collaboration with China. [4]

In a rejoinder to Washington's rapprochement overture, Beijing apparently surprised the Americans—and probably ASEAN countries—by insisting it had always been Chinese policy 'to maintain friendly relations with all states, regardless of social system, on the basis of the Five Principles of Peaceful Coexistence' (Holdridge 1997:25). This proved a crucial gesture by the Chinese in signalling their intent for rapprochement and cooperation. In a manner of speaking, Beijing also signalled its 'acceptance' of Washington's policy of geopolitical triangulation and its readiness to play this game to enhance its and Washington's strategic interests at Moscow's expense (Biesner 2007). After the Vietnamese invasion of Cambodia on Christmas Day 1978, the Chinese signalled their willingness to cooperate with ASEAN, with the latter reciprocating in kind. Mutual reassurance arguably provided a basis for China–ASEAN cooperation against a perceived common aversion. Indeed, China actively sought, more than reassurance alone, ASEAN's involvement, as evidenced by repeated Vietnamese warnings against Chinese efforts at 'promoting confrontation' between the ASEAN states and Vietnam. In fact, Hanoi insisted that rather than pressuring

Vietnam, ASEAN should pressure China to find a solution to the Cambodian question (Chang 1985:141). In this respect, de facto China–ASEAN cooperation against Vietnam emerged as a function of mutual expedience. Nevertheless, that very basis for cooperation was removed after the termination of the Cold War and the settlement of the Cambodian conflict.

It has been argued, fairly or otherwise, that growing Chinese influence in post-Cold War Asia has arisen in relation to a concomitant diminution of American presence in or attention to Asia (Sutter 2005). This perception has led to a chorus of Asian voices, South-East Asian ones included, urging greater attention from Washington on the region (Kwa and Tan 2001). That said, it could be argued that the emergence of China–ASEAN ties during the 1980s, apart from the dynamics directly related to the Third Indochina War, was also partly attributable to regional perceptions regarding the draw down in American involvement in South-East Asia after the Vietnam War.

Decade of 'mundane accomplishments': 1990s

From as early as 1989, China, it could be said, morphed from strategic partner to strategic competitor for ASEAN, with the settlement of the Cambodian conflict and normalisation of ties between Beijing and various South-East Asian states, beginning with Indonesia. That said, China was less a competitor—if by this we mean a countervailing power—than a hegemonic presence for the considerably weaker ASEAN states, whose relations with China focused principally on managing their respective vulnerabilities and dependencies vis-à-vis the latter (Ba 2005). If anything, the sheer enormity of the Chinese presence in the region was something that could be neither ignored nor, for that matter, refused by China's considerably smaller and/or weaker regional counterparts. As Michael Mandelbaum once mused about America: 'If you are the 800-pound gorilla, you are bound to be concentrating on your bananas and everyone else is concentrating on you' (Sanger 1999). In the same way, no amount of protestations to the effect that China's rise in the post-Cold War period is inherently 'peaceful' will likely convince all South-East Asians to be completely reassured about Chinese intentions, not least when China's prodigious growth might (or, for some, has already) come at the ASEAN region's expense (Wu et al. 2002). [5]

Indeed, so acute was the perception of the threat that China apparently posed to ASEAN states in the immediate post-Cold War period that the prospect of China resorting to direct military coercion in support of its territorial claims in the South China Sea could not be discounted (Leifer 1991). In this respect, instances of China's territorial disputes with several ASEAN states—with the Philippines over Mischief Reef and Scarborough Shoal and with Vietnam over their land and sea borders in the 1990s—have since become, for the association, a stark reminder of unwarranted presumptions about China's goodwill. If anything, Chinese actions in the South China Sea, correctly or otherwise, gave credence to regional worries that the ultimate strategic objective of China would be, in the words of a Malaysian maritime specialist, to 'convert the entire South China Sea into a Chinese lake' (Acharya 1996:199). This thinking has clearly not gone away. For example, a recent study argues that Chinese strategic thinkers are predisposed to regard the South China Sea, through a Mahanian lens, 'as a preserve where commercial and political imperatives demand dominant [Chinese] naval power'; in short, China views the South China Sea as its own 'Caribbean' (Holmes and Yoshihara 2006:79). A difficulty complicating reassurance efforts has to do with China's lack of transparency concerning its security policy, which has hampered attempts by ASEAN security planners to form assessments of Chinese intentions and likely actions. More crucial than prospects for potential conflict, however, is that all sides have by and large sought to avoid tensions and promote an atmosphere of mutual respect and cooperation (Lee 1997:251). Elsewhere, it has been argued that the South China Sea has remained primarily a political rather than a military consideration due to China's desire to accommodate South-East Asian concerns and the limited naval capabilities of the various claimants (Emmers 2005).

Remarkably, it was against this backdrop of strategic asymmetry and pervasive regional circumspection regarding China's strategic intentions, and initial Chinese reservations about participating in ASEAN-centred regional arrangements, that marked improvement in China–ASEAN relations during the 1990s nevertheless occurred. It reflected the growing agreement on questions of regional peace, prosperity and security and the ways those questions were best approached. Such progress was, however, measured best not in terms of 'headline-making cooperative ventures' but by a process of gradualism or 'mundane accomplishments'—that is, various minor achievements in the minutiae of functional cooperation (Ba 2006:160; Khong 1997:291). A variety of parallel frameworks for dialogue emerged within the decade. Beginning in 1991, when Chinese Foreign Minister Qian Qichen was invited to attend the opening ceremony of the twenty-fourth ASEAN Foreign Ministers' Meeting, China became a consultative partner (the next year), joined the ARF as a founding member (in 1994) and 'graduated' to become official dialogue partner of ASEAN (in 1996). A year later, the first ever China–ASEAN summit was conducted in Malaysia, where President Jiang and his ASEAN counterparts issued a joint statement on the collective decision to establish a partnership of good neighbourliness and mutual trust between the two parties, thereby providing the groundwork for the so-called 'Joint Declaration of the PRC and ASEAN State Leaders: A strategic partnership for peace and prosperity', announced in 2003.

What conceivably led the Chinese to set aside their initial reservations about joining and participating in the myriad regional arrangements, particularly the ARF, could be partly attributed to the process-oriented ASEAN way, the holistic emphasis of which, on the common search for new areas of agreement rather than on contractually driven cooperation, likely persuaded Beijing that its interests would not be discounted. The very principles of the ASEAN way, the avoidance by ASEAN states of discourse that defines China as a threat, and so forth, have clearly resonated well with China. As Alice Ba (2006:160) argued, the association's pursuit of 'complex engagement'—'informal, non-confrontational, open-ended and mutual'—likely swayed China to reconsider its relations with ASEAN, to view ASEAN more positively and to be more responsive to ASEAN's concerns. The readiness to grant China a say was clearly apparent, for instance, when the ARF acceded to China's demand that the third phase of regional security cooperation as envisaged in the 1995 ARF Concept Paper—'conflict resolution'—be amended to 'the elaboration of approaches to conflict' (Tan et al. 2002:8). In all this, ASEAN 'second-track' diplomacy has arguably facilitated the building of mutual confidence and the dissemination/socialisation of regional conventions and norms (Katsumata 2003; Kraft 2000; Simon 2002; Tan 2007).

That China shares in the so-called illiberal values held by many if not most of the ASEAN countries has likely worked in the latter's favour (Kivimäki 2001). In this regard, it is possible that the controversial 'Asian values' debate of the 1990s, sparked by European criticisms of ASEAN and the rejoinders to that by some Asian elites—several from Singapore (Jones 1994)—aided ASEAN's engagement effort, not least by proving to China that ASEAN was no lackey of the West. In this respect, ASEAN involvement in that debate—which had quietly dissipated by 1997 thanks to the Asian financial crisis—arguably served as a costly signal of sorts from ASEAN to China regarding the association's 'credibility'. [6] For its part, China's growing involvement in and enthusiasm for ASEAN-based regionalism could also be viewed as a signal of its willingness to cooperate. More crucially, it could be seen as Chinese willingness to exercise strategic restraint (Ikenberry 2001).

In this regard, ASEAN's engagement of China, in the hope that the Chinese will embrace regionalism and thereby apply self-moderation in the regional interest, is not without precedent. Here, the experience of the association's own formation, and Indonesia's role in that, has vital significance. It has been argued, for example, that Indonesia's long-preferred formula of 'regional solutions to regional problems' has found little support among fellow ASEAN members, who view the Indonesian formula as a euphemism for Indonesian hegemony in South-East Asia and as such value access to external powers as sources of countervailing power (Leifer 1989:5–6, 2000:109). If anything, Malaysia's and Singapore's experience of confrontation with Indonesia in the mid 1960s rendered difficult any ready acceptance on their part of such a formula. Thus understood, ASEAN's formation in 1967 required not only Indonesia's agreement, but its readiness to forgo its hegemonic aspirations. In this respect, it has been argued that President Suharto of Indonesia understood the importance of restoring regional confidence and stability through locking Indonesia 'into a structure of multilateral partnership and constraint that would be seen as a rejection of hegemonic pretensions' (Leifer 1996:13). That Jakarta could be 'coaxed' into joining ASEAN indicated its willingness to cooperate with neighbouring states seeking to impose institutional constraints on it. More than anything else, Suharto realised the significance of reassuring his fellow ASEAN members by demonstrating good neighbourliness towards them (Narine 1998).

Crucially, to the extent that this example of 'political self-denial in the interest of regional order' on Indonesia's part can be 'emulated within the wider Asia-Pacific is central to any parallel between ASEAN and the ASEAN Regional Forum' (Leifer 1996:13). In other words, as an ASEAN-centred expression of pan-Asian security regionalism, the ARF is thereby an extension of ASEAN's model of regional security, not only because it relies on the ASEAN way in its deliberations, but because the Indonesian example of strategic restraint via regionalism has become the de facto model for integrating hegemonic China into the regional order. It was Indonesia's signal of its willingness to collaborate with its neighbours, at the expense of its own regional aspirations, that served as a key foundation for the success of ASEAN regionalism. In return, Indonesia received recognition from fellow ASEAN members of its *primus inter pares* status within the association. Has the Indonesian example proved a noteworthy precedent for China to emulate? According to one analyst, 'Beijing's move to involve itself in ASEAN activities since the early 1990s was part of the country's "good-neighbourliness" [*mulin zhengce*] policy that aimed at strengthening its ties with the neighbouring countries in the wake of the Tiananmen Incident in 1989', rather than a new orientation in the conduct of Chinese foreign policy (Kuik 2005:102). Whether the Indonesian precedent has influenced Chinese behaviour towards South-East Asia is uncertain. What seems clear enough, however, is ASEAN's apparent belief that the Chinese penchant for good neighbourliness and strategic restraint is something that deserves strong encouragement and reinforcement, with the promise of regional recognition of China's proper place as a regional leader, but one very much within an ASEAN-centred framework. It amounts to an invitation to China to assume its place in the regional order as a responsible stakeholder on ASEAN's terms.

Intensification of relations: 2000–08

The first decade of the twenty-first century has seen an intensification of China–ASEAN ties that builds on the developments of the previous decade. In 2002, Chinese goodwill led to the signing of the Joint Declaration of ASEAN and China on Cooperation in the Field of Non-traditional Security Issues and the Declaration on the Conduct (DOC) of Parties in the South China Sea. The DOC was not quite a real regional code of conduct, as some ASEAN countries had hoped for, but it constituted a step in the right direction (Buszynski 2003). Both sides agreed at their 2007 bilateral summit to expedite progress towards the establishment of a regional code of conduct. The other crucial development of 2002 was the agreement to establish the China–ASEAN Free Trade Area (CAFTA). The CAFTA deal clearly caught the Japanese off-guard, leading to Tokyo's attempt to catch up with the Chinese in 2005 by negotiating an ASEAN–Japan Free Trade Area, formally known as the Comprehensive Economic Partnership (Chirathivat 2002; Joint Declaration of the Leaders of ASEAN and Japan on the Comprehensive Economic Partnership, <http://www.aseansec.org/13190.htm>; Tongzon 2005; Wong and Chan 2003). As mentioned earlier, ASEAN and China inked their Strategic Partnership for Peace and Prosperity in 2003.

The evolution of Chinese diplomacy towards the ASEAN region from the 1990s to the present has been something to behold. From an initial distrust of multilateralism to becoming a sophisticated multilateralist, China has successfully transformed itself from past revolutionary pariah to present status-quo power. In the diplomatic–strategic arena, Beijing has advanced, with relative success, the idea that its rise to power is an essentially 'peaceful' development that does not threaten others. In the international economic arena, it has supported the World Trade Organisation (WTO) and promoted unilateral and multilateral liberalisation (Sally 2006). As Cornell historian Jian Chen (2008:148–9) has noted, 'China, in continuing its own course of development, found it necessary to establish an identity that would allow it to appear as an "insider" in the US/West-dominated international system while, at the same time, emphasising its unique contribution to the world's peace, stability and prosperity.' Indeed, so careful has China been in downplaying its ascendance that it assiduously avoids any fanfare for its soft-power policy for fear that it could be used by Western quarters as evidence to support the purported existence of a 'China threat' (Li 2008:23).

Arguably, to the extent that Chinese reassurance has succeeded in its aims, ASEAN countries today generally regard China 'as a good neighbour, a constructive partner, a careful listener, and a non-threatening regional power' (Shambaugh 2004–05:64). To be sure, Chinese circumspection over the inauguration of the East Asia Summit (EAS) in 2005 caused a division of sorts between those in support of the EAS and those who favoured ASEAN+3 as the appropriate regional vehicle to establish the proposed East Asian Community (Kawai and Wignaraja 2007; Malik 2005). There are, however, indications that beyond the rhetoric, Beijing is seriously prepared to countenance the EAS as a possible framework for regional economic integration, notwithstanding its express preference for ASEAN+3. [7]

That China has continued its policy of reassurance towards the ASEAN region despite the proclivity of South-East Asian countries to strategically hedge between China and the United States is a good indication of Chinese restraint and appreciation for South-East Asians' security conundrums and choices. China likewise needs ASEAN to ensure a peaceful environment in order to continue with her modernisation, as well as to 'prevent any possibility of encirclement to contain her in the future' (Wanandi 2004). It is unlikely that ASEAN will revise its overall regionalism strategy, whether in South-East Asia for managing intramural relations among ASEAN states, or in the wider Asian region for managing relations with major powers including China. At the intra-South-East Asian level, concerns about the rise of China and India have led ASEAN to take seriously regional institutionalism and community formation, as evidenced by the inauguration of the ASEAN Charter in November 2007 and, as the Vientiane Action Plan would have it, the establishment of the ASEAN Community (with distinct security, economic and socio-cultural facets) by 2020. Failure to render ASEAN more robust, so the logic goes, will incapacitate its ability to deal, competitively as well as cooperatively, with external powers.

Future ties: trouble ahead?

This chapter has argued that a mutual interest in seeking security has motivated ASEAN and China towards a strategy of reassurance and accommodation vis-à-vis each other. Ultimately, the continued success of ASEAN's brand of regionalism in ensuring that China's peaceful commitment to the regional status quo depends on whether problems that might arise in future China–ASEAN ties will be managed and resolved. As noted earlier, the ASEAN way is itself evolving—ironically, in response to new challenges confronting the region, not least the rise of China—which could complicate future China–ASEAN ties. The strength of extant China–ASEAN relations has largely been predicated on mutual adherence to and advocacy of the ASEAN way of consensus, consultation and non-interference. These very conventions, however, are ostensibly under review today as ASEAN acquires a legal identity and continues to evolve towards a regional security community. Whether this transformation will complicate the association's engagement strategy is an open question with implications not only for the future of China–ASEAN relations, but for the peace and stability of Asia. To be sure, the quality and extent of ASEAN's transformation remains debatable.

On the economic front, despite the optimism surrounding the CAFTA, nagging doubts remain about whether the paradoxes that accompany the pact can be resolved. Former Singapore Prime Minister Goh Chok Tong has argued that 'the more interlocked the economies of China and ASEAN are, the better it is for the long-term relationship between China and ASEAN, and to that extent the CAFTA is good news' ('ASEAN, China plan FTA', *The Straits Times*, 7 November 2001, p. 1). It has also been argued that given the evident sluggishness in negotiations within ASEAN+3, the potential significance of the CAFTA is thereby enhanced (Liang 2007:10). Given that the ASEAN Free Trade Area and ASEAN Economic Community are not expected to be implemented until 2015—indeed, some think it will be more than 20 years before the two are fully operational—there is, however, every possibility that the implementation of the CAFTA, anticipated by 2010, could prove detrimental for some of the economies of the ASEAN region, whose own free trade areas will not be ready for another five years. [8] Further, the CAFTA has been viewed by some as a political or diplomatic but not an economic pact, and to that extent it is uncertain whether the promised economic benefits will ever be realised (Cai 2003; Hund 2003; Sheng 2005).

China might have come in from the cold, but whether it will remain willingly within the fold of various ASEAN regionalisms—that is, as a committed supportive participant—is open to question.

References

Acharya, Amitav 1996, 'ASEAN and conditional engagement', in James Shinn (ed.), *Weaving the Net: Conditional engagement with China*, Council on Foreign Relations, New York, pp. 220–48.

Acharya, Amitav 1997, 'Ideas, identity, and institution-building: from the "ASEAN way" to the "Asia-Pacific way"', *The Pacific Review*, vol. 10, no. 3, pp. 319–46.

Acharya, Amitav 2003–04, 'Will Asia's past be its future?', *International Security*, vol. 28, no. 3, pp. 149–64.

Acharya, Amitav and Tan, See Seng 2006, 'Betwixt balance and community: America, ASEAN, and the security of Southeast Asia', *International Relations of the Asia-Pacific*, vol. 6, no. 1, pp. 37–59.

Adler, Emanuel 1997, 'Seizing the middle ground: constructivism in world politics', *European Journal of International Relations*, vol. 3, no. 3, pp. 319–63.

Antolik, Michael 1990, *ASEAN and the Diplomacy of Accommodation*, East Gate Books, New York.

Association of South-East Asian Nations (ASEAN) 2007, Chairman's statement of the 11th China–ASEAN Summit, 20 November, Singapore, <http://www.aseansec.org/21105.htm>

Ba, Alice D. 2003, 'China and ASEAN: re-navigating relations for a 21st century Asia', *Asian Survey*, vol. 43, no. 4, pp. 622–47.

Ba, Alice D. 2005, 'Southeast Asia and China', in Evelyn Goh (ed.), *Betwixt and Between: Southeast Asian strategic relations with the US and China*, Institute of Defence and Strategic Studies, Singapore, pp. 93–108.

Ba, Alice D. 2006, 'Who's socializing whom? Complex engagement in China–ASEAN relations', *The Pacific Review*, vol. 19, no. 2, pp. 157–79.

Batabyal, Anindya 2006, 'Balancing China in Asia: a realist assessment of India's look east strategy', *China Report*, vol. 42, no. 2, pp. 179–97.

Biesner, Robert L. 2007, 'History and Henry Kissinger', *Diplomatic History*, vol. 14, no. 4, pp. 511–28.

Buszynski, Leszek 2003, 'ASEAN, the Declaration of Conduct, and the South China Sea', *Contemporary Southeast Asia*, vol. 25, no. 3, pp. 343–62.

Caballero-Anthony, Mely 2005, *Regional Security in Southeast Asia: Beyond the ASEAN way*, Institute of Southeast Asian Studies, Singapore.

Cai, Kevin 2003, 'The China–ASEAN Free Trade Agreement and East Asian regional grouping', *Contemporary Southeast Asia*, vol. 25, no. 3, pp. 387–404.

Chang, Pao-Min 1985, *Kampuchea Between China and Vietnam*, National University of Singapore Press, Singapore.

Checkel, Jeffrey 2001, 'Why comply? Social learning and European identity change', *International Organization*, vol. 55, no. 3, pp. 553–88.

Chen, Jian 2008, 'China and the Bandung Conference', in See Seng Tan and Amitav Acharya (eds), *Bandung Revisited: The legacy of the 1955 Asian–African Conference for International Order*, National University of Singapore Press, Singapore, pp. 132–59.

Chirathivat, Suthiphand 2002, 'China–ASEAN Free Trade Area: background, implications and future development', *Journal of Asian Economics*, vol. 13, no. 5, pp. 671–86.

Curley, Melissa G. 2004, 'China and ASEAN: diplomacy during the Cold War and after', [Book review], *Journal of Southeast Asian Studies*, vol. 35, no. 2, pp. 355–6.

Deng, Yong and Wang, Fei-Ling (eds) 2005, *China Rising: Power and motivation in Chinese foreign policy*, Rowman and Littlefield, Lanham, Md.

Emmers, Ralf 2001, 'The influence of the balance of power factor within the ASEAN Regional Forum', *Contemporary Southeast Asia*, vol. 23, no. 2, pp. 275–91.

Emmers, Ralf 2003, *Cooperative Security and the Balance of Power in ASEAN and the ARF*, Routledge Curzon, London.

Emmers, Ralf 2005, *Maritime disputes in the South China Sea: strategic and diplomatic status quo*, Working Paper No. 87, Institute of Defence and Strategic Studies, Singapore.

Foot, Rosemary 2006, 'Chinese strategies in a US-hegemonic global order: accommodating and hedging', *International Affairs*, vol. 82, no. 1, pp. 77–94.

Garofano, John 2002, 'Power, institutions, and the ASEAN Regional Forum: a security community for Asia?', *Asian Survey*, vol. 42, no. 3, pp. 502–21.

Goh, Evelyn 2005, *Great powers and Southeast Asian regional security strategies: omni-enmeshment, balancing and hierarchical order*, Working Paper No. 84, Institute of Defence and Strategic Studies, Singapore.

Goh, Evelyn 2006, 'China and Southeast Asia', *FPIF Commentary*, 12 December, <http://www.fpif.org/fpiftxt/3780>

Goh, Evelyn 2007–08, 'Great powers and hierarchical order in Southeast Asia: analyzing regional security strategies', *International Security*, vol. 32, no. 3, pp. 113–57.

Goldstein, Avery 2005, *Rising to the Challenge: China's grand strategy and international security*, Stanford University Press, Stanford, Calif.

Haacke, Jürgen 2003, 'ASEAN's diplomatic and security culture: a constructivist assessment', *International Relations of the Asia-Pacific*, vol. 3, no. 1, pp. 57–87.

Holdridge, John H. 1997, *Crossing the Divide: An insider's account of normalization of US–China relations*, Rowman and Littlefield, Lanham, Md.

Holmes, James R. and Yoshihara, Toshi 2006, 'China's "Caribbean" in the South China Sea', *SAIS Review of International Affairs*, vol. 26, no. 1 pp. 79–92.

Holst, David R. and Weiss, John 2004, 'ASEAN and China: exports rivals or partners in regional growth?', *The World Economy*, vol. 27, no. 8, pp. 1255–74.

Hund, Markus 2003, 'ASEAN Plus Three: toward a new age of pan-East Asian regionalism? A skeptic's appraisal', *The Pacific Review*, vol. 16, no. 3, pp. 383–417.

Ikenberry, G. John 2001, *After Victory: Institutions, strategic restraint, and the rebuilding of order after major wars*, Princeton University Press, Princeton, NJ.

Indorf, Hans H. 1987, 'ASEAN in extra-regional perspective', *Contemporary Southeast Asia*, vol. 9, no. 2, pp. 86–105.

Johnston, Alastair Iain 2003, 'Is China a status quo power?', *International Security*, vol. 27, no. 4, pp. 5–56.

Johnston, Alastair Iain and Evans, Paul 1999, 'China's engagement with multilateral security institutions', in Alastair Iain Johnston and Robert Ross (eds), *Engaging China*, Routledge, London, pp. 235–72.

Jones, David Martin and Smith, Michael L. R. 2007, 'Making process, not progress: ASEAN and the evolving East Asian regional order', *International Security*, vol. 32, no. 1, pp. 148–84.

Jones, Eric 1994, 'Asia's fate', *The National Interest*, no. 35, pp. 18–28.

Kang, David C. 2003, 'Getting Asia wrong: the need for new analytical frameworks', *International Security*, vol. 27, no. 4, pp. 57–85.

Katsumata, Hiro 2003, 'The role of ASEAN institutes of strategic and international studies in developing security cooperation in the Asia-Pacific region', *Asian Journal of Political Science*, vol. 11, pp. 93–111.

Kawai, Masahiro and Wignaraja, Ganeshan 2007, *ASEAN+3 or ASEAN+6: which way forward?*, ADB Institute Discussion Paper No. 77, Asian Development Bank Institute, Tokyo.

Khong, Yuen Foong 1997, 'Review article: making bricks without straw in the Asia-Pacific?', *The Pacific Review*, vol. 10, no. 2, pp. 289–300.

Khong, Yuen Foong 2004, 'Coping with strategic uncertainty: the role of institutions and soft balancing in Southeast Asia's post-Cold War strategy', in J. Suh, Peter J. Katzenstein and Allen Carlson (eds), *Rethinking Security in East Asia: Identity, power, and efficiency*, Stanford University Press, Stanford, Calif., pp. 172–208.

Khoo, Nicholas and Smith, Michael L. R. 2005, 'Correspondence: China engages Asia? Caveat lector: a response to David Shambaugh', *International Security*, vol. 30, no. 1, pp. 196–205.

Kivimäki, Timo 2001, 'The long peace of ASEAN', *Journal of Peace Research*, vol. 38, no. 1, pp. 5–25.

Kraft, Herman J. S. 2000, *Unofficial diplomacy in Southeast Asia: the role of ASEAN–ISIS*, CANCAPS Paper No. 23, Canadian Consortium on Asia-Pacific Security, Toronto.

Kuik, Cheng-Chwee 2005, 'Multilateralism in China's ASEAN policy: its evolution, characteristics, and aspiration', *Contemporary Southeast Asia*, vol. 27, no. 1, pp. 102–22.

Kurlantzick, Joshua 2007, *Charm Offensive: How China's soft power is transforming the world*, Yale University Press, New Haven, Conn.

Kwa, Chong Guan and Tan, See Seng 2001, 'The keystone of world order', *The Washington Quarterly*, vol. 24, no. 3, pp. 95–103.

Kydd, Andrew 2005, *Trust and Mistrust in International Relations*, Princeton University Press, Princeton, NJ.

Lee, Lai To 1997, 'East Asian assessments of China's security policy', *International Affairs*, vol. 73, no. 2, April, pp. 251–62.

Leifer, Michael 1986, 'The balance of power and regional order', in Michael Leifer (ed.), *The Balance of Power in East Asia*, Macmillan, London.

Leifer, Michael 1989, *ASEAN and the Security of South-East Asia*, Routledge, London.

Leifer, Michael 1991, 'The maritime regime and regional security in East Asia', *The Pacific Review*, vol. 4, no. 2, pp. 126–36.

Leifer, Michael 1996, *The ASEAN Regional Forum: extending ASEAN's model of regional security*, Adelphi Paper No. 302, Oxford University Press/International Institute for Strategic Studies, London.

Leifer, Michael 2000, 'Regional solutions to regional problems?', in Gerald Segal and David S. G. Goodman (eds), *Towards Recovery in Pacific Asia*, Routledge, London, pp. 108–18.

Li, Mingjiang 2008, *Soft power in Chinese discourse: popularity and prospect*, Working Paper No. 165, S. Rajaratnam School of International Studies, Singapore.

Li, Nan 2004, 'The evolving Chinese conception of security and security approaches', in See Seng Tan and Amitav Acharya (eds), *Asia-Pacific Security Cooperation: National interests and regional order*, M. E. Sharpe, Armonk, NY, pp. 53–70.

Liang, Ruobing 2007, The politics of China's economic presence in the region: ASEAN as a case, Paper presented at Living with China Conference organised by the S. Rajaratnam School of International Studies, 8–9 March, Singapore.

Lim, Robyn 1998, 'The ASEAN Regional Forum: building on sand', *Contemporary Southeast Asia*, vol. 20, no. 2, pp. 115–36.

Liow, Joseph Chinyong and Tan, See Seng 2008, 'Southeast Asia', in Edward A. Kolodziej and Roger E. Kanet (eds), *From Superpower to Besieged Global Power: Restoring world order after the failure of the Bush doctrine*, University of Georgia Press, Athens, Ga, and London, pp. 115–33.

Loo, Bernard 2007, 'Military modernization, power projection, and the rise of the PLA: strategic implications for Southeast Asia', in Evelyn Goh and Sheldon W. Simon (eds), *China, the United States, and South-East Asia: Contending perspectives on politics, security, and economics*, Routledge, Abingdon, pp. 185–201.

Malik, Mohan 2005, 'The East Asia Summit: more discord than accord', *YaleGlobal*, 20 December, <http://yaleglobal.yale.edu/display.article?id=6645>

Narine, Shaun 1998, 'ASEAN and the management of regional security', *Pacific Affairs*, vol. 71, no. 2, pp. 195–214.

Narine, Shaun 2002, *Explaining ASEAN: Regionalism in Southeast Asia*, Lynne Rienner, Boulder, Colo.

Narine, Shaun 2004, 'State sovereignty, political legitimacy, and regional institutionalism in the Asia Pacific', *The Pacific Review*, vol. 17, no. 3, pp. 423–50.

Niazi, Tarique 2005, 'China's march on South Asia', *China Brief*, vol. 5, no. 9, 26 April, The Jamestown Foundation, Washington, DC, <http://www.jamestown.org/publications_details.php?volume_id=408&issue_id=3311&article_id=2369717>

Nischalke, Tobias Ingo 2000, 'Insights from ASEAN's foreign policy cooperation: the "ASEAN way", a real spirit or a phantom', *Contemporary Southeast Asia*, vol. 22, no. 1, pp. 98–112.

Oye, Kenneth A. (ed.) 1986, *Cooperation Under Anarchy*, Princeton University Press, Princeton, NJ.

Pollard, Vincent K. 1970, 'ASA and ASEAN, 1961–1967: Southeast Asian regionalism', *Asian Survey*, vol. 10, no. 3, March, pp. 244–55.

Rajaratnam, S. 1992, *ASEAN: The way ahead*, 1 September, <http://www.aseansec.org/13991.htm>

Ravenhill, John 2006, 'Is China an economic threat to Southeast Asia?', *Asian Survey*, vol. 46, no. 5, pp. 653–74.

Risse, Thomas 2000, 'Let's argue! Communicative action in world politics', *International Organization*, vol. 54, no. 1, pp. 1–39.

Sally, Razeen 2006, 'Free trade agreements and the prospects for regional integration in East Asia', *Asian Economic Policy Review*, vol. 1, no. 2, pp. 306–21.

Sanger, David 1999, 'The US is a 800-pound gorilla', *International Herald Tribune*, 9 July.

Saw, Swee-Hock, Sheng, Lijun and Chin, Kin Wah 2005, 'An overview of China–ASEAN relations', in Swee-Hock Saw, Lijun Sheng and Kin Wah Chin (eds), *China–ASEAN Relations: Realities and prospects*, Institute of Southeast Asian Studies, Singapore, pp. 1–18.

Sen, Rabindra 2002, *China and ASEAN: Diplomacy during the Cold War and after*, Manuscript India, Howrah.

Shambaugh, David 2002, *Modernizing China's Military: Progress, problems, and prospects*, University of California Press, Berkeley, Calif.

Shambaugh, David 2004–05, 'China engages Asia: reshaping the regional order', *International Security*, vol. 29, no. 3, pp. 64–99.

Sheng, Lijun 2005, *China–ASEAN Free Trade Area: origins, developments and strategic motivations*, ISEAS Working Paper, International Politics and Security Issues Series, no. 1, Institute of Southeast Asian Studies, Singapore.

Simon, Sheldon W. 2002, 'Evaluating track II approaches to security diplomacy in the Asia-Pacific: the CSCAP experience', *The Pacific Review*, vol. 15, no. 2, pp. 167–200.

Sukma, Rizal 1999, *Indonesia and China: The politics of a troubled relationship*, Routledge, London.

Sukma, Rizal 2003, The future of ASEAN: towards a security community, Paper presented at a seminar on ASEAN Cooperation: Challenges and Prospects in the Current International Situation, 3 June, New York, <http://www.indonesiamission-ny.org/issuebaru/Mission/asean/paper_rizalsukma.PDF>

Sutter, Robert G. 2005, *China's rise in Asia—promises, prospects and implications for the United States*, Occasional Paper Series, Asia-Pacific Center for Security Studies, Honolulu, Hawai'i.

Swaine, Michael D. and Tellis, Ashley J. 2000, *Interpreting China's Grand Strategy: Past, present, and future*, RAND, Santa Monica, Calif.

Tan, See Seng 2007, *The Role of Knowledge Communities in Constructing Asia-Pacific Security: How thought and talk make war and peace*, Edwin Mellen, Lewiston, NY.

Tan, See Seng and Acharya, Amitav (eds) 2008, *Bandung Revisited: The legacy of the 1955 Asian–African Conference for International Order*, National University of Singapore Press, Singapore.

Tan, See Seng with Cossa, Ralph A. 2001, 'Rescuing realism from the realists: a theoretical note on East Asian security', in Sheldon W. Simon (ed.), *The Many Faces of Asian Security*, Rowman and Littlefield, Lanham, Md., pp. 15–34.

Tan, See Seng, Emmers, Ralf, Caballero-Anthony, Mely, Acharya, Amitav, Desker, Barry and Guan, Kwa Chong 2002, *A new agenda for the ASEAN Regional Forum*, Monograph No. 4, Institute of Defence and Strategic Studies, Singapore.

Tang, Shiping 2007, *From offensive realism to defensive realism: a social evolutionary interpretation of China's security strategy*, State of Security and International Studies No. 3, S. Rajaratnam School of International Studies, Singapore.

Tongzon, Jose L. 2005, 'China–ASEAN Free Trade Area: a bane or boon for ASEAN countries?', *The World Economy*, vol. 28, no. 2, pp. 191–210.

Turley, William S. and Race, Jeffrey 1980, 'The Third Indochina War', *Foreign Policy*, no. 38, Spring, pp. 92–116.

Wanandi, Jusuf 2004, 'The effects of leadership changes in East Asia', [Part 1 of 2], *The Jakarta Post*, 27 January, <http://www.csis.or.id/tool_print.asp?type=opinion&id=55&op_id=81>

Wang, Hongying 2000, 'Multilateralism in Chinese foreign policy: the limits of socialization', *Asian Survey*, vol. 40, no. 3, pp. 475–91.

Weatherbee, Donald E., Emmers, Ralf, Pangestu, Mari and Sebastian, Leonard C. 2005, 'The Third Indochina War', *International Relations in Southeast Asia: The struggle for autonomy*, Rowman and Littlefield, Lanham, Md, pp. 75–82.

Wong, John and Chan, Sarah 2003, 'China–ASEAN Free Trade Agreement: shaping future economic relations', *Asian Survey*, vol. 43, no. 3, pp. 507–26.

Wu, Friedrich, Siaw, Poa Tiong, Sia, Yeo Han and Keong, Puah Kok 2002, 'Foreign direct investments to China and Southeast Asia: has ASEAN been losing out?', *Economic Survey of Singapore*, Third Quarter, pp. 96–115.

ENDNOTES

[1] Not all constructivist analysts share this more or less optimistic interpretation—for example, Haacke (2003) and Narine (2004).

[2] It has been implied obliquely that China's international efforts to win hearts and minds might not have been as successful in South Asia, where Chinese investments have been relatively minimal (Niazi 2005).

[3] On America's resort to an institutional strategy of strategic restraint after the end of the Cold War, see Ikenberry (2001).

[4] S. Rajaratnam, Singapore's first foreign minister, hinted at this in his broad-ranging reflection on ASEAN's historical development and new challenges in the post-Cold War world (Rajaratnam 1992).

[5] For a contrarian view arguing that the ASEAN region's apparent loss of economic investment to China is grossly exaggerated, see Ravenhill (2006).

[6] Not all ASEAN member states likely agreed to the concept of Asian values, not least the Philippines.

[7] This author's personal communication with Professors Su Hao and Cai Penghong, leading Chinese security analysts, in Singapore in January 2008.

[8] This point was made by Richard Martin, Managing Director of IMA Asia, at the Southeast Asia: The Next Phase Conference, organised by the Lowy Institute for International Policy, 6 July 1997, Sydney. See also Holst and Weiss (2004).

Chapter 13

'Architectural alternatives or alternatives to architecture?'

Robert Ayson and Brendan Taylor

'Architecture' has emerged as the latest catchphrase in Asian security politics. Scholars and practitioners alike have overwhelmingly—and largely uncritically—embraced the architectural metaphor. In so doing, however, they often end up talking past one another, seriously devaluing the debate about Asia's emerging security order in the process, and at a time when the rise of China and the region's consequent geopolitical transition is placing a premium on clear strategic analysis. To illustrate the shortcomings of applying the architectural metaphor to Asian security politics, we begin this chapter by examining the sources and limits of one of the latest and most controversial of Asia's architectural blueprints: Australian Prime Minister Kevin Rudd's Asia-Pacific Community (APC) proposal. We argue that criticism of the APC has been focused too squarely on the specifics of the proposal, while insufficient attention has thus far been given to the larger problems associated with employing the notion of 'architecture' itself. We go on to make the case for abandoning the term 'architecture' altogether, particularly the heavy managerial connotations associated with it. In its place, and drawing inspiration from the work of the renowned Australian international relations scholar Hedley Bull, we advocate a more 'informal' approach to Asia's security order, which emphasises relationships over organisations.

The Asia-Pacific Community: a case study

Prime Minister Rudd's proposal to establish an APC was formally announced, somewhat unexpectedly, on 4 June 2008 at the annual dinner of the Asia Society AustralAsia Centre in Sydney (Rudd 2008a). Speaking before approximately 500 guests, Rudd called for the establishment of 'a regional institution which spans the entire Asia-Pacific region—including the United States, Japan, China, India, Indonesia and the other states of the region'. The scope of this institution should be broad-ranging, he suggested, and 'able to engage in the full spectrum of dialogue, cooperation and action on economic and political matters and future challenges related to security'. Rudd designated 2020 as the year by which this vision for an APC should be implemented. He appointed Richard Woolcott, a former secretary of the Australian Department of Foreign Affairs, as a high-level envoy charged with taking the proposal to the capitals of the wider region for further discussion.

At least four motivations appear to have underpinned Rudd's APC proposal. First, the plan needs to be viewed in the Australian domestic political context. Since his election in late 2007, Rudd has signalled a renewed focus on Asia as a major pillar of his government's foreign policy approach. Comparisons with his regionally focused Labor predecessors, Bob Hawke and Paul Keating, have, however, been almost inescapable. Given the role these leaders played in helping to establish the Asia-Pacific Economic Cooperation (APEC) process, the APEC Leaders' Meeting and arguably even the Association of South-East Asian Nations (ASEAN) Regional Forum (ARF), Rudd has big shoes to fill here, especially when the regional agenda is already so full. Even the Asia credentials of his immediate predecessor, John Howard, have been reviewed fairly favourably, with Howard and his Foreign Minister, Alexander Downer, given much credit for securing Australia a seat at the East Asia Summit (EAS), as well as executing a simultaneous strengthening of Australia's bilateral relations with the United States, China, Japan and Indonesia (see Wesley 2007). Having consistently criticised the predominantly bilateral orientation of his predecessor's approach to the Asian region, Rudd's imperative to be seen to be moving towards a more obvious multilateral perspective thus also constitutes part of the explanation for his APC initiative.

Second, the fact that Rudd's Asia Society speech was made immediately before visiting Japan and Indonesia is revealing. During his early months in office, Rudd had come under increasing criticism at home and abroad for what some commentators regarded as an unhealthy bias towards Beijing (Sheridan 2008a).
[1] The Prime Minister's fluency in Mandarin, his longstanding scholarly interest and professional experience in China, coupled with the fact that he visited China—but no other Asian nation—on his first major overseas trip outside of Australia's immediate neighbourhood all contributed to this perception. Commentators have tended to cast this preference in zero-sum terms, as if Rudd's interest in China comes at the expense of Australia's ties with Japan, India and South-East Asia. The Asia Society speech thus appears to have formed part of a larger effort to counter this mounting criticism. Much of the speech itself was devoted to discussing what Rudd explicitly termed Australia's 'critical bilateral relations' with Japan and Indonesia. The order of the wording that Rudd employed when sketching out his vision for an APC—listing Japan ahead of China—was also highly symbolic.

Despite the emphasis given to the symbolic purposes of the APC proposal, Rudd clearly intended it to be more than merely an expedient political gesture. In tandem with his Foreign Minister, Stephen Smith, Rudd has continued to revisit the proposal during high-profile speeches (see, for example, Smith 2008:19–22;

Rudd 2008b). This also reflects the third consideration motivating the APC proposal: a growing sense of trepidation that Asia's institutional landscape is evolving in ways that could be increasingly unsuitable for the implementation of any effective regional 'architecture' and the sense of regional consensus that must ultimately underpin it.

A large part of the problem here stems from the fact that Asia's great powers have shown an increasing tendency to use regional institutions not as sites for cooperation, but as instruments of competitive influence: Beijing through ASEAN+3 and the Shanghai Cooperation Organisation (SCO); Moscow through the SCO; Washington in APEC and through its own ad hoc mechanisms such as the Proliferation Security Initiative (PSI); and Tokyo through the ARF and, increasingly, through the EAS as it strives to check China's growing influence in the ASEAN+3 grouping. Taken together, this has created a situation in which, as Lowy Institute Director, Allan Gyngell (2007:1), recently observed, 'The Asia-Pacific region has too many regional organisations, yet they still cannot do all the things we require of them.' The APC proposal might thus also be read as a genuine attempt to remedy these 'design flaws' in the region's emerging 'architecture'.

The fourth factor motivating Rudd's initiative is related more directly to Australia's own national interest and place in the Asian region. For significant parts of its history after European settlement, Australia harboured a deep sense of insecurity towards its region. The former head of the Australian Department of Foreign Affairs Alan Renouf, for instance, once described Australia as a 'frightened country' that lived in fear of its own Asian neighbourhood and sought out a 'great and powerful friend' to compensate for those insecurities (Renouf 1979). Harvard Political Scientist Samuel Huntington (1993:42, 1995:151–4) later described Australia as a 'torn country'—a society divided over whether or not it belonged to Asia. While many Australians have a much more confident and comfortable view of Australia's regional situation, echoes of the old concerns remain, although these often take the form of worries about being overlooked rather than overrun. Canberra remains fearful that it could—whether because of its size, cultural composition or geographical location—potentially yet find itself excluded from the region's most influential institutional processes. The two most worrying potentialities from an Australian standpoint are an institutionalisation of the Six-Party Talks process into a formal and highly influential regional security mechanism without any expansion of its membership, or a deepening of cooperation between the members of the ASEAN+3 process leading to the formation of a genuine East Asian community that excludes Australia. By playing the role of entrepreneur in putting forward the idea of an APC, and by proposing this as the peak institution in the region, Canberra could thus be seen to be guarding against the possibility of its economic and political marginalisation from this part of the world.

Notwithstanding these apparently genuine motives, Rudd's APC proposal has not met with widespread regional and domestic acclaim. Perhaps the most direct attack was delivered by the influential Singaporean commentator Barry Desker, who, when speaking before a Canberra audience in July 2008, described the proposal as 'dead in the water' (Walters 2008). More generally, criticism has tended to focus on four main areas. First, the harried style in which the initiative was announced was seen to have severely damaged its prospects. In the days after the Asia Society speech, for instance, media reports surfaced that Woolcott heard of his mission as special envoy only hours before its announcement (Sheridan 2008c). There also appears to have been a complete absence of consultation with other interested parties throughout the region. Little thought appears to have gone into how the new body will relate to existing structures, such as APEC, the ARF and the EAS. The inevitable dilemmas surrounding membership of the new grouping have also been glossed over. What, for instance, would be the membership status of Taiwan? Would the small island states of the South Pacific be invited to join? The hastiness of this proposal's delivery and its consequent disregard for these obvious dilemmas not only damaged its prospects in the eyes of many, it could have affected Rudd's Asia policy credentials.

Washington's response to the proposal was among the more open-minded. While calling for further detail, for instance, US Deputy Secretary of State, John Negroponte, emphasised the need 'to be open to new ideas and suggestions' (Flitton 2008). That the proposal was announced in the shadow of a US presidential election, however, at a time when Washington still appeared distracted by developments in the Middle East, was equally seen as a factor inhibiting its prospects. This issue of timing relates also to China. With its economic and strategic weight in the Asian region still on the rise, one could argue that it might not be in Beijing's interest to set in concrete an institutional structure reflecting today's power realties, when those of tomorrow could be weighted even more heavily in its favour, thereby enhancing its capacity to shape that structure.

Third, the prospects for Rudd's proposal were seen to be further diminished by his alienation of other regional actors, including some of the leading ASEAN countries and Japan. As Desker's comments suggest, the APC idea has not been particularly well received in some parts of South-East Asia, especially since Indonesia was the only ASEAN country mentioned by Rudd in the original list of leading participants. Canberra's lack of consultation with its South-East Asian neighbours has added to this problem and has been read as a lack of gratitude, in particular, by those governments who were so influential in helping Australia to secure a seat at the EAS (Medcalf 2008). While it is possible that ASEAN might no longer occupy the driver's seat of regional diplomatic processes by 2020—as economic and strategic weight shifts increasingly in favour of Asia's great powers, and in particular in China's direction—ASEAN retains a significant role in most of the region's prominent multilateral processes. The blessing of the main members of ASEAN is therefore arguably critical to the success of Rudd's APC idea. Likewise, Japan remains a leading and influential supporter of the same open and inclusive vision of regional architecture advanced in Rudd's proposal—as opposed to the narrow, more exclusive approach championed at times by China and Malaysia (see, for example, Walters 2005). Tokyo's wounds, however, remained raw for some time over what it perceived as Rudd's bypassing of Japan on his first major international trip—so much so that Japanese Prime Minister, Yasuo Fukuda, made but one passing reference to Australia in his own major speech on the future of Asia-Pacific security (Sheridan 2008b).

A final criticism that has been levelled at Rudd's proposal is that it threatens to exacerbate some of the same design flaws in the emerging so-called regional 'architecture' that it aspires to alleviate. It is seen to have the potential, for instance, to further fuel the competitive approach to institutions that is becoming a feature of great power politics in the region. Rudd was sufficiently careful in his Asia Society speech to specify that his proposal 'does not in itself mean the diminution of any of the existing regional bodies'. Even Woolcott himself, however, was later forced to concede that comparisons were inevitable. In his terms:

> One of the issues that needs to be addressed is the link between the Prime Minister's concept of an Asia-Pacific community and the variety of existing organisations in the field. There will be arguments I suppose, is it better to tinker with or adjust existing institutions or is it better to have a new overarching body? (Cited in Kelly 2008)

The real risk in all of this, critics contend, is that Rudd's APC proposal will become yet one more fixture on an already overcrowded institutional landscape.

The problem with architecture

Amid the barrage of criticism that Rudd's new architectural blueprint has been subjected to, little if any has focused on potential flaws in the concept of 'architecture' itself and its application to the Asian region. In the past decade, this terminology has become so deeply entrenched in the lexicon and discourse of Asian security politics that its usage has been taken almost as a given. As this section goes on to demonstrate, however, the term 'architecture' is really quite a confused and confusing one when used by scholars of Asian security. Further, a strong case can be made that the Asian region is simply not conducive to the application of the architectural metaphor, and even that architecture in any genuine sense of the term is, for the foreseeable future, unlikely to emerge in this part of the world.

Among Asian analysts, the eminent Indonesian scholar Jusuf Wanandi (1994) pioneered usage of the architectural metaphor in a paper delivered to the eighth Asia-Pacific Roundtable in June 1994. As Nick Bisley (2007:342–3) observed, however, its rise to prominence in the lexicon and discourse of Asian security politics was inspired primarily by calls during the late 1990s to reform the international financial 'architecture'—described by Barry Eichengreen (1999:1) very simply as institutions, structures and policies—in the aftermath of the 1997–98 Asian financial crisis. As often occurs in Asian security politics, strategic thinkers borrowed directly from their economic counterparts.

The subsequent decade has seen a veritable plethora of books, edited volumes, refereed journal articles, policy briefs and academic conferences embrace the architectural metaphor. Despite the popularity of its usage, however, only rudimentary efforts have been expended amid this flurry of intellectual activity to define explicitly what the term 'architecture' really means, especially within an Asian regional context. As the following analysis demonstrates, when employing the architectural allegory, many leading scholars of Asian security tend not even to formally define the terminology or to consider whether their implicit understanding of 'architecture' is consistent with how others are using it. This is problematic in that there appears to exist within the broader scholarly debate at least several clusters of assumptions as to what the term connotes.

First, different pride of place is afforded to the economic and security dimensions of regional architecture. Some, for instance, refer to an overarching regional or institutional 'architecture', but do not clearly distinguish between its economic and security components (see, for example, Patel 2008). Others specify an overarching regional architecture, but see it as comprising two distinct economic and security 'pillars' or 'legs' (see, for example, Nanto 2006). Yet another perspective views trade and security arrangements as distinct components of a broader Asian institutional architecture, but also considers the 'strategic interaction' between them (Aggarwal and Koo 2008). Last, but not least, a number of analysts refer to the Asian security architecture as a separate and largely distinct construct (see, for example, Ball 2004:48; Desker 2008a).

Second, 'architecture' is often employed as one and the same term, but with reference to quite different 'layers' or 'levels' of collaborative security arrangements. As the preceding paragraph suggests, for instance, the term can be used in a broad sense to describe the overarching architecture across an entire region. The question of where such boundaries can and should be drawn geographically, however, remains unclear. Some refer, for instance, to an 'Asia-Pacific security architecture', some to an 'Asian security architecture', while others refer to an 'East Asian security architecture'. The Singapore-based scholar Mely Caballero-Anthony (2007:1–3, 8, 10) even uses the terms 'Asia' and 'East Asia' interchangeably when referring to one and the same 'regional security architecture'. In many regards, however, these trends can also be seen as reflecting the contested nature of the concept of 'Asia' itself (Katzenstein 2005:10).

Compounding this problem, some scholars assume the existence of 'architectures' within the overarching *regional* architecture. David Shambaugh, for instance, suggests that 'the US-led [bilateral alliance] security system remains the predominant regional architecture across Asia'. Shambaugh (2005:3, 11, 14), however, also goes on to refer to an emerging 'multilateral architecture that is based on a series of increasingly shared norms (about interstate relations and security)' and suggests that regional security architecture can be likened to a 'mosaic' comprising 'different layers that address different aspects of regional security'. Similarly, Desker (2008a:56–8, 62, 70) writes simultaneously of 'Asia's security architecture' and 'the Northeast Asian security architecture'. Adding to the confusion, scholars seem unable to agree about whether the architectural terminology should be employed in the plural or the singular sense. Highlighting this tension, Nick Bisley's (2007) recent contribution to the National Bureau of Asian Research's annual *Strategic Asia* series is entitled 'Asian security architectures', while he refers to 'Asian security architecture' in the singular throughout the piece.

Finally, and perhaps most problematically, 'architecture' is also often used interchangeably with other terms. Tsinghua University Professor Chu Shulong (2007:8–11), for instance, uses the term 'architecture' interchangeably with that of 'mechanism' and 'framework'. Hanns Maull (2005:69) exchanges the term with what he considers the more 'appropriate' descriptor, 'security arrangements'. Along similar lines, while referring to the US-led alliance 'system' as 'the predominant regional security architecture across Asia', Shambaugh (2005:2–3) depicts an Asia-Pacific security architecture that is embedded within an imprecisely defined Asian regional 'system'. In so doing, he would appear to have blurred the distinction between the terms 'architecture' and 'system' to the point where they become almost indistinguishable.

A large part of the problem here could stem from the fact that Asia is simply not conducive to the macro-analytical notion of 'architecture', which implies that an overarching *structure* can be fashioned and implemented to address the daunting array of security challenges currently facing the region. The sheer diversity—economic, cultural, geographic, historical and political—of 'the region' could simply make it unsuited to such processes of formalisation. As Gyngell (2007:8) observes, 'the multiplicity of visions of the region and the variety of functional needs that must be accommodated' are such that 'the Asia Pacific has never been headed towards the goal of a comprehensive European-like arrangement: its history and geography are of a very different order'.

Structure or strategic relationships?

Even if scholars and policymakers are able to observe a consistent and coherent usage of the architecture metaphor (and we think this is somewhat unlikely), the problems with using this terminology will continue. Architects design buildings in which families, workers and other social groups exist. They provide blueprints for the construction of walls that keep people in. They use formal structure to define the environment. Even landscape architects use the structure of formal plantings and inanimate objects to organise a garden; they choose what goes in and what stays out. This approach presents problems for our subject: Asia's future security order.

The architecture debate encourages a focus on processes and structures rather than relationships and outcomes. Some participants in the discussion favour an ASEAN-centred universe in which the 'architecture' is built on and around the existing multilateral processes championed by many of the 10 South-East Asian countries (see, for example, Goh 2007–08). Others suggest that the foundations of that architecture are provided by Washington's set of bilateral alliances (see Baker 1991/92). Those with more pluralistic and flexible tastes suggest that we need to weld these together so that we can mix the hope of multilateral progress with the insurance of alliance (see, for example, Tow and Acharya 2007). While this combination reflects the inclination towards hedging strategies to cope with the uncertainty of Asia's strategic future, it is a potentially unmixable set of ingredients.

The inclusion of US-led alliances in Asia as part of the regional architecture is problematic on theoretical and practical grounds. In theoretical terms, it suggests that these alliances contribute to regional order because of their nature as organisations (compared, for example, with what the ARF can offer as a different type of intergovernmental grouping). Alliances, however, contribute to regional order because of the promises (including promises of security assistance) that exist between their members. These promises condition the expectations of states inside and outside the alliance relationship. As Coral Bell (1991:46) argued some years ago in a short study of Australia's alliance relationship with the United States, 'International politics works, unfortunately, on nothing more substantial than a system of expectations.' As shapers of expectations, alliances make their major contributions to order. They do not do so as organisational alternatives or supplements to multilateral diplomatic forums.

The practical difficulty in including alliances becomes clear when we remember that a regional architecture can be a set of walls that defines the conditions of existence for those who live within them. As such, it very quickly becomes a basis for *containment* and *control*. If one of the leading requirements for Asia's future order is China's effective participation in strategic relationships with other great powers in the region, an overarching architectural vision that incorporates the US alliance system (alongside everything else) could fall well short of the mark. While promising to provide an overarching framework for the management of Asia's strategic challenges, such an architectural vision will do more to divide the region and raise suspicions. It would resemble a Western attempt to reassert control over Asia's political evolution.

Each one of the architectural options assumes that order is a product of the way we organise ourselves. Here, order tends to be viewed as a function of external structure and not of strategic interaction, although somehow the latter is supposed to be inspired by the former. As an alternative to this organisational view of order, a relationship view focuses directly on the quality of the strategic interaction between the powers, rather than on the external structures within which their relationships are meant to develop. This means that the true building blocks of an Asian regional community are not a set of overlapping groups (from ANZUS and the Five Power Defence Arrangements through to ASEAN, the ARF and the EAS) and that the job of regional community building is not to work out which of these survive and how they might relate to one another. This is the nearly impossible task that Rudd and his colleagues have set for the APC on the basis that Asia's existing attempts at regional organisations don't yet add up to what we need (Rudd 2008a). In response to some of the criticisms within the region that have been levelled at the APC proposal, Rudd and his colleagues have also demonstrated the continuing appeal of the additive approach by pouring praise on the achievements of ASEAN, which they have retrospectively claimed the community can build on (see Smith 2008).

This mistakes the pots (which are simply containers) for the plants (where the true life exists). The real building blocks are the relationships between the powers highlighted in their strategic interaction. Here, the most important *institutions* of regional politics are not the formal organisations that hold regular summits, but the rules and patterns of behaviour that operate between the major actors on a daily basis. Such an informal approach would suggest that the basis of Asia's strategic future, including China's role, is not a regional architecture—which seeks to organise and perhaps even control the actors—but a set of regional bargains that nourish and support their most important strategic relationships. [2] One of these bargains is an effective but informal compact between the United States and China that they will recognise each other's leading role in regional affairs.

It is entirely possible that formal constructs could develop from these bargains: for example, a set of bargains between Asia's great powers might then be reflected in an Asian security mechanism of some sort involving China, the United States, Japan and India. There is, however, no reason to suggest that the relationship will work in reverse. One might establish such a forum only to find that the powers that have agreed to attend do not regard one of the others as a legitimate participant. Similarly, in domestic politics, the formal trappings of statehood rely on an informal bargain that is the basis of a social contract. (Bull [1977:59] saw pre-modern African societies that were stateless as a 'spectacle of "ordered anarchy"'.) Similarly, we need to insure ourselves against believing that the cooperative relations between Europe's former great powers since World War II have been due to the formal institutional relations between them and not to their political determination to limit the possibilities for dangerous competition between them, which allowed these regional organisations to develop. Likewise, for ASEAN to exist in the first place, its original founders needed an informal but robust bargain between them that represented their mutual interests in unmolested sovereign independence. That original and informal bargain is infinitely more powerful and important than ASEAN's more recent and more formal charter, which has attracted a mix of admirers and sceptics (see Desker 2008b).

A similar logic can be applied to the argument that the best answer for Asia's evolving power equation is a concert in which power is as much shared as contested. There is much to be said for this approach (see, for example, White 2007), at the heart of which is an informal agreement between the great powers to collaborate in the management of the relations between them. Indeed, Bull (1977:74) nominated the 'managerial system of the great powers'—which could take the form of a concert or a condominium—as one of the *institutions* of international order, by which he did not mean formal parts of an architecture within which the great powers were housed as essential pieces of the furniture. Instead, the institutional aspect relates to the patterns of behaviour among the great powers. The institutions here are more about practice and relationships than about formal structure. Bull (1977:74) explains that '[b]y an institution we do not necessarily imply an organisation or administrative machinery' (which is so commonplace in the contemporary discussion of Asia's 'architecture'), 'but rather a set of habits and practices shaped towards the realisation of common goals'.

Instead of thinking about which gatherings, arrangements, forums and processes can combine to produce Asia's future order, we are better to focus on what habits and practices the great powers need to adopt—and how smaller and medium powers in the rest of the region (such as Australia) can encourage that adoption. At the heart of the European concert of the early nineteenth century was not an ornate edifice of formal diplomacy (the trappings of Vienna) but a common realisation by the great powers that what Napoleon had been allowed to do to the regional balance could not be allowed to repeat itself. [3] Similarly, while Washington's diplomatic recognition of Beijing marked part of China's *formal* entry into the family of nations in the 1970s, the real work was done in the earlier bargain engineered by Henry Kissinger (a disciple of Metternich) and

Zhou En-Lai, which gave informal but very powerful recognition to the triangularity of Asia's strategic relationships (see Isaacson 2005:333–54).

The arrival of a genuine concert in Asia is no easy matter (Acharya 1999). For a number of the reasons outlined above, to stand any sort of chance it would probably need to begin in an informal fashion—as a series of mutually supportive great-power bargains—before the architects gained the opportunity to formalise (and often to de-energise) the cooperation. In today's climate, if one or more of the great powers made a serious proposal for a concert, it would most likely be treated as yet another architectural option. We would immediately shift to a discussion of when (and more importantly where) the first such annual gathering should be held, what its agenda should be and who should be invited (and left off the list).

Despite sporadic and very painful progress (and sometimes no progress at all), the Six-Party Talks that Beijing has hosted to address North Korea's nuclear weapons program offer a very subtle, almost undetectable, hint of great-power concert. Three of the major players—China, the United States and Japan—are on board, and signs of convergence between the positions of Beijing and Washington (if not shared by Tokyo) have perhaps been the main benefit of this process. Again, the value of the Six-Party Talks lies not in another architectural option for Asia's future order, but in the quality of the relationships between the great powers. An architect might propose that these talks are the building block or the scaffolding for an eventual East Asian security mechanism. The notion of a '6–1+3' approach (North Korea out and India, Australia and New Zealand in) presents, however, an architectural illusion that needs to be resisted (see, for example, Kessler 2006). Instead, the magic, such that it exists, lies in the very small and pale embryo of concerted behaviour—a pattern that might just be utilised further afield. Policymakers should aim to protect the relationship and not the organisation.

Conclusion

The fascination with Asia's *architectural* options is quite understandable. While Asian analysts have been quick to reject unkind comparisons with European regionalism, they have nonetheless been sensitive to claims of an Asian institutional deficit. At the same time, the proliferation of Asian regional organisations has provided many options from which to choose—in fact, rather too many overlapping options that necessitate some organisational spring-cleaning. The rise of China, and the general change in Asia's geopolitics, provides the obvious testing ground for this process of organisational selection.

Rudd's APC represents one attempt to put this organisational shop in order for the challenges to come as global power is increasingly decided in Asia. It is, however, proving difficult for the APC proposal to shake itself free of the vested and competing interests that are attached to existing approaches to Asian regionalism. Similarly, any grand notions of an overarching Asian architecture are hamstrung by a cacophony of competing perspectives on what that architecture comprises (differing views of its component parts) and how it is defined (differing views of its crucial features). Additional confusion is provided by the simultaneous existence of multiple 'architectures' and of multiple subregions to which these can apply.

At one level, the architecture debate naturally lends itself to some academically intriguing taxonomical puzzles. At another level, however, it can lead to a policy dead end, by exaggerating the importance of structure and by suggesting that order is a question of good organisation. An informal approach, which argues that order rests on strategic relationships, focuses our gaze on the bargains we need from Asia's great powers. As Australia and other regional countries grapple with the geopolitical changes that are already well under way in Asia, driven above all by China's rise, they need not be worried about building the best regional house that a good architect can design. Instead, they need simply to concentrate on the residents and whether or not they are able to live together. To do that, more walls and buildings might need to be torn down than erected, and we might need to employ more relationship specialists and fewer architects.

References

Acharya, Amitav 1999, 'A concert of Asia?', *Survival*, vol. 41, no. 3, Autumn, pp. 84–101.

Aggarwal, Vinod K. and Koo, Min Gyo 2008 (eds), *Asia's New Institutional Architecture: Evolving structures for managing trade, financial, and security relations*, Springer, Berlin.

Baker, 'America in Asia: Emerging Architecture for a Pacific Community', *Foreign Affairs*, 70 (1991/1992), pp. 1–18.

Ball, Desmond 2004, 'Security cooperation in Asia Pacific: official and unofficial responses', in Annelies Heijmans et al., *Searching for Peace in Asia Pacific: An overview of conflict prevention and peacebuilding activities*, Lynne Rienner Publishers, Boulder and London.

Bell, Coral 1991, *Australia's Alliance Options: Prospect and retrospect in a world of change*, The Australian National University, Canberra.

Bisley, Nick 2007, 'Asian security architectures', in Ashley Tellis and Michael Wills (eds), *Strategic Asia 2007–2008: Domestic political change and grand strategy*, National Bureau of Asian Research, Seattle and Washington, DC, pp. 341–69.

Bull, Hedley 1977, *The Anarchical Society: A study in world order*, Macmillan, Basingstoke.

Caballero-Anthony, Mely 2007, *Nontraditional security and multilateralism in Asia: reshaping the contours of regional security architecture?*, Policy Analysis Brief, The Stanley Foundation, June 2007.

Desker, Barry 2008a, 'New security dimensions in the Asia-Pacific', *Asia-Pacific Review*, vol. 15, issue 1, May, pp. 56–75.

Desker, Barry 2008b, 'Where the ASEAN Charter comes up short', *The Straits Times*, 18 July 2008.

Eichengreen, Barry J. 1999, *Toward a New International Financial Architecture: A practical post-Asia agenda*, Institute for International Economics, Washington, DC.

Flitton, Daniel 2008, 'US diplomat wary of Rudd's big idea', *The Age*, 30 June 2008.

Goh, Evelyn 2007–08, 'Great powers and hierarchical order in Southeast Asia: analyzing regional security strategies', *International Security*, vol. 32, no. 3, Winter 2007–08, pp. 113–57.

Gyngell, Allan 2007, *Design faults: the Asia-Pacific's regional architecture*, Policy Brief, Lowy Institute for International Policy, July 2007.

Huntington, Samuel P. 1993, 'The clash of civilizations?', *Foreign Affairs*, vol. 72, no. 3, Summer.

Huntington, Samuel P. 1995, *The Clash of Civilizations and the Remaking of World Order*, Simon and Schuster, New York.

Isaacson, Walter 2005, *Kissinger: A biography*, Simon and Schuster, New York.

Katzenstein, Peter 2005, *A World of Regions: Asia and Europe in the American imperium*, Cornell University Press, Ithaca and London.

Kelly, Paul 2008, 'Time may not be ripe', *The Australian*, 9 July 2008.

Kessler, Glenn 2006, 'With N. Korea talks stalled, US tries new approach', *Washington Post*, 22 September 2006.

Maull, Hanns W. 2005, 'Security cooperation in Europe and Pacific Asia: a comparative analysis', *The Journal of East Asian Affairs*, vol. XIX, no. 2, Fall–Winter.

Medcalf, Rory 2008, 'Rudd's Asian aria sounds familiar', *Australian Financial Review*, 10 June 2008.

Nanto, Dick K. 2006, *East Asian regional architecture: new economic and security arrangements and US policy*, CRS Report for Congress, Congressional Research Service, The Library of Congress, 18 September 2006.

Patel, Nirav 2008, *Value cooperation, not antagonism: the case for functional-based cooperation*, Policy Dialogue Brief, The Stanley Foundation, August 2008.

Renouf, Alan 1979, *The Frightened Country*, Macmillan, Melbourne.

Rudd, Kevin 2008a, It's time to build an Asia-Pacific Community, Address to the Asia Society AustralAsia Centre, 4 June 2008, Sydney.

Rudd, Kevin 2008b, Towards an Asia-Pacific century, Speech to the Kokoda Foundation, Australia–US Trilogy Seminar, 20 November 2008.

Schelling, Thomas C. 1960, *The Strategy of Conflict*, Harvard University Press, Cambridge, Mass.

Shambaugh, David 2005, The evolving Asian system: implications for the regional security architecture, Paper prepared for the Eighth Waldbroel Meeting on the European and Euro–Atlantic Coordination of Security Policies vis-à-vis the Asia Pacific, 14–15 December 2005, Berlin.

Sheridan, Greg 2008a, 'Region notices bias for Beijing', *The Australian*, 3 May 2008.

Sheridan, Greg 2008b, 'Rudd can fix Japan shambles', *The Australian*, 7 June 2008.

Sheridan, Greg 2008c, 'The new Mad Hatter', *The Australian*, 12 June 2008.

Shulong, Chu 2007, 'Beyond crisis management: prospects for a Northeast Asian regional security architecture', in Council for Security Cooperation in the Asia-Pacific (CSCAP), *Security Through Cooperation: Furthering Asia Pacific multilateral engagement*, CSCAP Regional Security Outlook 2007.

Smith, Stephen 2008, Australia, ASEAN and the Asia-Pacific, Speech to the Lowy Institute for International Policy, 18 July 2008.

Tow, William T. and Acharya, Amitav 2007, *Obstinate or obsolete? The US alliance structure in the Asia-Pacific*, Working Paper 2007/4, December, Department of International Relations, Research School of Pacific and Asian Studies, The Australian National University, Canberra.

Walters, Patrick 2005, 'Beijing plays spoiler on Asia summit', *The Australian*, 6 April 2005.

Walters, Patrick 2008, 'Rudd Asia plan "dead in water"', *The Australian*, 4 July 2008.

Wanandi, Jusuf 1994, The Future of ARF and CSCAP in the regional security architecture, Paper prepared for the Eighth Asia-Pacific Roundtable, 5–8 June 1994, Kuala Lumpur.

Wesley, Michael 2007, *The Howard Paradox*, ABC Books, Sydney, New South Wales.

White, Hugh 2007, 'Great power gambits to secure Asia's peace', *Far Eastern Economic Review*, January–February 2007, pp. 7–11.

Zamoyski, Adam 2008, *Rites of Peace: The fall of Napoleon and the Congress of Vienna*, Harper Perennial, London.

ENDNOTES

[1] Rudd and Howard have therefore suffered from the same criticism but in reverse order: Rudd was suspected of being too close to Beijing but has ended up emphasising the US relationship with some rigour; Howard was accused of favouring the United States over Asia but, at least in terms of Australia's China relationship, stands not guilty as charged.

[2] On strategic bargaining, see Schelling (1960).

[3] For a recent and approachable study, see Zamoyski (2008).

www.ingramcontent.com/pod-product-compliance
Lightning Source LLC
Chambersburg PA
CBHW040247290326
41929CB00054B/3448